For the Love of Learning

For the Love of Learning

Innovations from Outstanding University Teachers

Edited By Tim Bilham

palgrave
macmillan

First published 2013 by
PALGRAVE MACMILLAN

Palgrave Macmillan in the UK is an imprint of Macmillan Publishers Limited,
registered in England, company number 785998, of Houndmills, Basingstoke,
Hampshire RG21 6XS.

Palgrave Macmillan in the US is a division of St Martin's Press LLC,
175 Fifth Avenue, New York, NY 10010.

Palgrave Macmillan is the global academic imprint of the above companies
and has companies and representatives throughout the world.

Palgrave® and Macmillan® are registered trademarks in the United States,
the United Kingdom, Europe and other countries

ISBN: 978–1–137–33429–9 paperback

This book is printed on paper suitable for recycling and made from fully
managed and sustained forest sources. Logging, pulping and manufacturing
processes are expected to conform to the environmental regulations of the
country of origin.

A catalogue record for this book is available from the British Library.

A catalog record for this book is available from the Library of Congress.

Printed in Great Britain by TJ International, Padstow, Cornwall

Contents

List of figures and tables ix
Acknowledgements xii
How to use this book xiii
List of abbreviations xv
Foreword xvii
Series editor's preface xix

Introduction: Inspiration, innovation and excellence 1
Tim Bilham

Part 1 Crossing boundaries

Crossing boundaries: disciplines
1 The liquidity of knowledge: learning across disciplinary divides 11
Heather Barnett
2 Mixed cultures: microbiology, art and literature 21
Joanna Verran
3 Blending approaches to teaching in art and design:
case studies from glass and ceramics 29
Kevin Petrie
4 New learning ecosystems: blurring boundaries, changing
minds 36
Helen Keegan

Crossing boundaries: transitions
5 Learning to love learning 43
Peter Ovens
6 Crossing the boundaries of academic writing 49
James Elander and Lin Norton
7 Beyond competence: enabling and inspiring healthcare
students 54
Faith Hill
8 'Disability matters': the role of personal tutors for Inclusive
teaching and learning 60
Suanne Gibson

Part 2   Learning differently

Learning differently: approaches to teaching
9   Designs on learning: the role of cross-university collaborative
     undergraduate research symposia   69
     Kirsten Hardie in association with Annie Grove-White
10   Innovative approaches to learning design: harnessing new
     technologies for learning   76
     Gráinne Conole
11   Scaffolding problem-based learning   84
     Derek Raine
12   Developing subject-specific knowledge, digital creativity and
     soft skills: a games-based approach to teaching and learning   89
     Rachel McCrindle

Learning differently: teaching difficult topics
13   Teaching with assessment, feedback and feed-forward:
     using 'preflights' to assist student achievement   97
     Brian Whalley
14   Ongoing challenges in cross-disciplinary teaching: a case
     study from statistics   103
     Paul Hewson
15   Demystifying statistics: bring your imprimatur … to the
     laughter   109
     Andy Field
16   Performing critical thinking?   114
     Stella Jones-Devitt

Learning differently: assessment
17   Best practice in assessment and feedback: neglected issues   120
     Peter Hartley
18   Assessment strategies for developmental and experiential
     learning: successes and challenges   127
     Anita Peleg
19   Developing and assessing professional competence: using
     technology in learning design   135
     Luke Dawson in association with Ben Mason

Learning differently: international issues
20   Building curriculum internationalisation from the bottom up   142
     David Killick

21   New horizons and old challenges for distance learning:
      bridging the access gap in African universities   149
      Basiro Davey
22   Kinds of international: internationalisation through
      engagement with one another   156
      Jane Spiro

Part 3   Engaging students

Engaging students: in the process of learning and discovery

23   Doing, being and becoming: an occupational perspective on
      enabling learning   167
      Rayya Ghul
24   Learning together through student-lecturer collaborative
      enquiry   174
      Will Curtis
25   Creating space for student autonomy and engagement
      through partnership and letting go   180
      Colin Bryson
26   The student-professional   185
      Laura Ritchie

Engaging students: its wider influence

27   Wanted! Agents of change: enabling students to make change
      happen in their professional world   191
      Duncan Reavey
28   Authentic partnerships: inspiring professional identity and
      ownership in students   198
      Ruth Matheson
29   Learning from the real   204
      *Mary Hartog and Philip Frame in association with Chris Rigby
      and Doirean Wilson*
30   Looking at the mirror in the suitcase: encouraging students to
      reflect on their professional learning journey   212
      Anna Lise Gordon

Part 4   Employability: moving on

31   SOARing to success: employability development from the
      inside-out   221
      Arti Kumar

32   Telling tales: the use of story to enhance employability   228
     Beverly Leeds
33   Authentic assessment and employability: a synergy?   234
     Jane Thomas
34   Getting ready for action: student engagement in an
     employability project   240
     *Jamie Thompson in association with Laura Bullerwell, Catherine
     Foster, Russell Jackson and Nichola Larkin (students)*
35   English language learning for international employability   247
     Angela Goddard in association with Alastair Henry
36   Engaging with and owning the enterprise agenda   254
     Pauline Kneale

Conclusion: Sustaining excellence   262
Tim Bilham

References   264
Endnotes   284
Index   289

List of figures and tables

▶ **Figures**

1.1 Informal learning and sharing of expertise – a Life Sciences student of explains what is being viewed down the microscope (in this case, a histology slide of healthy and unhealthy liver tissue) 12

1.2 A Photographic Arts student instructs a scientist how to use a large-format plate camera in the photography studio 13

1.3 A Life Sciences student leading a blood-grouping exercise with staff from different disciplines 14

1.4 An Illustration student leading a group drawing exercise, following verbal descriptions and observing the range of interpretations 15

1.5 A student explaining work to visitors to a Broad Vision exhibition at London Gallery West 16

2.1 'Hands' demonstrating the presence of microorganisms on the hands – wanted: natural flora (henna) and unwanted: contaminants (paint) 23

2.2 Jewellery inspired by the artist Alphonse Mucha: a necklace representing malaria (mosquitoes and an infected blood cell) 24

3.1 MA Glass and Ceramics students working on a 10m-long collaborative drawing on a beach, as part of an introductory project at the start of their studies 33

3.2 The Crimson Jug on display in 'What's Your Story? Discovering Family History', an exhibition held at the Sunderland Museum and Winter Gardens, 23 June–27 August 2012 34

4.1 Students and staff from the UK, New Zealand and France collaborating on the production of a film on the topic of sustainability (via Google Hangout) 38

5.1 Organisation of the IIL Patchwork Texts Curriculum 46

9.1 The nature of undergraduate research and inquiry (Healey and Jenkins, 2009: 7) 70

10.1	The 7Cs of Learning Design framework	78
10.2	The principles associated with the learning intervention	79
10.3	Guidance and support	80
10.4	An example of a completed pedagogy profile	80
10.5	Three words used to describe the workshop	81
11.1	Average Year 2 marks for PBL modules plotted against Year 1 marks for the 2010–11 cohort	87
12. 1	Examples of games developed to teach software engineering to other students	92
12.2	Examples of posters promoting the games and demonstrating creative flair	93
12.3	Waiting for the names of the SEBA winners to be announced	93
12.4	A SEBA	93
16.1	The Snakes and Ladders critical thinking game	117
17.1	Varieties of Programme-Focused Assessment	122
17.2	The impact of Programme-Focused Assessment	123
19.1	The final technology-supported learning design	138
23.1	An occupational ontology of the person	169
23.2	An example of student theories of pain	170
23.3	Contexts of Participation (Ghul and Marsh, 2013)	171
29.1	The Learning Solution leading to the Postgraduate Certificate in Leadership and Management Practice	206
31.1	Driving behavioural competencies towards personal and interpersonal effectiveness, based upon a concept of reciprocal causal relations between self-evaluation, self-monitoring and achievement	224
34.1	Contingencies	242

▶ Tables

2.1	Books discussed in book-club format as part of the 'Infection and Immunity' module, Year 2, Healthcare Science degree	25
8.1	Factors contributing to the continued exclusion of students with disabilities in higher education	62
10.1	Using the 'course features' view	79
13.1	Examples of preflight activities used in a second-year geomorphology module	101
18.1	Experiential learning and formative assessment activity for Market Research and Public Relations Modules	129

19.1   Examples of qualitative feedback from student evaluation of
       the learning design   139
19.2   Data from staff evaluation of the learning design (n = 25) 140
20.1   How learning outcomes can be modified to reflect
       internationalism in the curriculum   146
22.1   Poems crossing cultures   160
28.1   Themes arising from student perceptions of the Health and
       Social Care programme   200

Acknowledgements

I must thank first all the authors who contributed to this volume and who have endured my suggestions, critiques, requests for change and always unreasonable deadlines with never a complaint and always with equanimity and enthusiasm. I thank them for their outstanding ideas and inspiration.

Grateful thanks are also due to NTF colleagues Charles Buckley, Kirsten Hardie, Alan Hayes, Arti Kumar, Martin Luck, Julia Pointon and Ian Scott, who reviewed drafts of the contributions and supported the project with such enthusiasm and unfailing goodwill, and again to Martin Luck who produced the index and List of abbreviations. Other NTFs contributed to the initial review of abstracts and further thanks are also due to them: Sally Brown, Annette Cashmore, Julie Baldry Currens, Lesley-Jane Eales-Reynolds, Mary Hartog, Pauline Kneale, Gordon Ramsay, Caroline Reid, Mark Schofield, Heather Skinner and Gweno Williams.

I would like to acknowledge the confidence and support of Jennifer Schmidt, Della Oliver and Juanita Bullough at Palgrave Macmillan in bringing this book to its audience and Sally Brown, Series Editor of the Palgrave Teaching and Learning Series, for her mentoring and invaluable advice.

I also thank all the other National Teaching Fellows who made the life of the Editor so difficult by submitting such an excellent range of abstracts, exhibiting such wonderful ideas, but for whom this volume was just too short.

Love and thanks to Tina, James and Emily for giving me the time and space to complete this project and for allowing me to monopolise the computer!

And finally I thank all the many thousands of students and alumni of our UK universities who currently and previously have provided the inspiration for the contributors to this book.

Editing it has been a privilege and always enjoyable. I have learnt a lot.

Tim Bilham
July 2013

How to use this book

For the Love of Learning consists of a collection of essays around broad themes of student and disciplinary transitions, technology, assessment, different teaching methods, student engagement and employability. Although grouped under these broad headings, many essays of course cover multiple themes. This table provides a guide to some of the sub-themes that emerge across essays.

If you are interested in a particular area you may find this table useful in identifying essays of interest. We are also sure that you will draw out your own sub-themes and make your own connections as you engage with the text.

Topics and sub-themes	Essays
academic literacy	6, 17
action learning/ action research	5, 27, 29
assessment	5, 6, 13, 17, 18, 19, 24, 27, 33
creativity, creative writing	12, 18, 22, 27, 30, 34
critical thinking	16, 23
employability	4, 24, 27, 31, 32, 33, 34, 35, 36
feedback	1, 13, 17, 18, 24
field studies	13, 27
games	12, 16
humour in teaching	15, 35
inclusion	12, 22
interdisciplinary learning	1, 2, 3, 4, 9, 11, 14
internationalisation/international teaching	3, 20, 21, 22, 27, 35, 36
learning design	1, 10, 19, 29

Topics and sub-themes	Essays
online learning, distance learning	4, 10, 21, 32, 35
problem-based learning/assessment	11, 27
professional development, lifelong learning	3, 7, 17, 19, 23, 26, 27, 28, 29, 30
public engagement, outreach	2, 3
reflection	23, 26, 29, 30, 32, 34
self-esteem, self-efficacy, self-concept, resilience	8, 17, 26, 30, 31, 34
storytelling for learning	22, 32
student-centred learning	21, 22, 29
student engagement	4, 5, 14, 18, 22, 23, 24, 25, 28, 29, 34
student experience	7, 8, 12
students as researchers	9, 14, 24
technology for learning	4, 10, 13, 19
threshold concepts, troublesome knowledge	13, 14, 16, 23, 31
transformation	14, 20, 22, 23, 30, 31, 33, 34
transition	6, 7, 22, 25
work-based learning, experiential learning	7, 18, 19, 29, 33

List of abbreviations

A&D	Art and Design
AHRC	Arts and Humanities Research Council
AMREF	African Medical and Research Foundation
ANTF	Association of National Teaching Fellows
ASEL	Audio Supported Enhanced Learning
ASILITE	Australian Society for Computers in Learning in Tertiary Education
CAUSE	Consortium for the Advancement of Undergraduate Statistics Education
CETL	Centre for Excellence in Teaching and Learning
CH	Combined Honours
COP	community of practice
CPD	Continuing Professional Development
DfEE	Department for Education and Employment
DfES	Department for Education and Skills
DL	distance learning
DLHE	Destination of Leavers of Higher Education
DRC	Disability Rights Commission
EAL	English as an additional language
ELF	English as a lingua franca
ELLIE	English Language Learning for Employability project
FMOH	Federal Ministry of Health (Ethiopia)
GDC	General Dental Council
HE	higher education
HEA	Higher Education Academy
HEFCE	Higher Education Funding Council for England
IE	inclusive education
IIL	Inquiry into Learning
IOC	Internationalisation of the Curriculum
IRS	Impact Review Sheet
ITE	initial teacher education
IV/T	Instrument/Vocal Teaching
JISC	Joint Information Systems Committee (for Higher Education)
KTP	Knowledge Transfer project

MCQ	multiple-choice questions (or questionnaire)
MOOC	Massive Open Online Course
MR	market research
NGC	National Glass Centre
NGO	non-governmental organisation
NHS	National Health Service
NSS	National Student Survey
NTF	National Teaching Fellow
NTFS	National Teaching Fellowship Scheme
NUS	National Union of Students
OSCE	Objective Structured Clinical Examination
OU	Open University
PBL	problem-based learning
PFA	Programme-Focused Assessment
PGCE	Postgraduate Certificate of Education
PLE	Personal Learning Environment
PLN	Personal Learning Network
PoE	e-Portfolio of Evidence
PR	public relations
QAA	Quality Assurance Agency
QWC	Quality of Written Communication
RAISE	Researching, Advancing and Inspiring Student Engagement
REAP	Re-Engineering Assessment Practices
SE	student engagement
SEBA	Software Engineering Brilliance Awards
SOAR	Self, Opportunity, Aspirations, Results
SPEED	Sharing Practice for Embedding E-design and Delivery (JISC project)
SSC	Staff–Student Committee
STEM	Science, Technology, Engineering and Mathematics
TESTA	Transforming the Experience of Students through Assessment
UNICEF	United Nations International Children's Emergency Fund
VLE	Virtual Learning Environment

Foreword

Great teaching is at the heart of an uplifting student learning experience. The Higher Education Academy (HEA) assists the higher education sector in ensuring it is well equipped to offer such experiences. The National Teaching Fellowship Scheme (NTFS) is a globally recognised means of recognising and rewarding excellent teaching.

In the UK the HEA manages the NTFS on behalf of the HEFCE, the HEFCW (the Higher Education Funding Councils for England and Wales, respectively) and DELNI (Department for Employment and Learning), and it has awarded nearly 600 national teaching fellowships to date. The NTFS alumni body, the Association of National Teaching Fellows (ANTF), was set up to ensure that this body of exceptional higher education staff were able to cross-fertilise ideas, and disseminate their innovative approaches for the wider benefit of the higher education teaching profession. Tracking national teaching fellows over the years provides an interesting story of 'going viral', as many approaches they have originated have now become common practice. Within the text which follows, the reader will recognise some earlier approaches that have been uplifted and further developed, and become embedded, taking notions of student engagement to a new level.

Attending the ANTF Symposium in 2013 allowed me to witness the huge talent, enthusiasm and passion of a group of what can only be termed as one of UKHE's great success stories. The buzz around the room was palpable as an update was provided on the forthcoming publication (which has now materialised and is in your hand!) of 36 'case-studies' outlining their outstanding contributions. The complete text is a great tribute to the hard work and dedication of a group committed to ensuring that they shared their insights for the benefit of others. Being invited to write the foreword for this book has been, indeed, a great privilege.

Those of you who know my work know that I have always advocated that to inspire learners, teachers needed to consider drawing on not only the cognitive domain, but also the affective. Teachers who are 'human' and authentic, energised, and able to make a genuine connection and provide deep engagement with their students are the ones who, evidence suggests, are repeatedly able to stimulate and encourage students to perform at significantly higher levels. Initiatives such as the co-creation of knowledge, 'real-life' enterprise activity, and the drawing on creative and performance approaches to a range of curriculum initiatives are all explored in this text. Key issues that higher education providers are grappling with globally such as transitions, employability, assessment, technology and internationalisation are all covered here also.

I encourage you to dip in and feel the passion with which this book has been written!

Professor Stephanie Marshall PFHEA
Chief Executive
Higher Education Academy

Series editor's preface

▶ Palgrave Teaching and Learning

This new series of books with Palgrave for all who care about teaching and learning in higher education is launched with the express aim of providing useful, relevant, current and helpful guidance on key issues in learning and teaching in the tertiary/post-compulsory education sector. This is an area of current very rapid and unpredictable change, with universities and colleges reviewing and often implementing radical alterations in the ways they design, deliver and assess the curriculum, taking into account not just innovations in how content is being delivered and supported, particularly through technological means, but also the changing relationships between academics and their students. The role of the teacher in higher education needs to be reconsidered when students can freely access content worldwide and seek accreditation and recognition of learning by local, national or international providers (and may indeed prefer to do so). Students internationally are becoming progressively more liable for the payment of fees, as higher education becomes seen as less of a public good and more of a private one, and this, too, changes the nature of the transaction.

Texts in this series will address these and other emergent imperatives. Among topics covered will be volumes exploring student-centred approaches at undergraduate and postgraduate levels, including doctoral work; the necessity to work in an internationalised and transnational, tertiary education context; the challenges of staff–student interactions where engagements are as likely to be through new technologies as face-to-face in the classroom; and issues about the levels of student engagement, especially where study is in competition with other demands on their time, including employment and caring responsibilities.

This new book is one I am particularly proud to see included in the series, growing as it did from a UK group of university teachers recognised by the nation as being outstanding proponents of their profession. The range of expertise included in this volume offers a diversity of perspectives across disciplines and types of higher education institutions, but what unites them all is a love of learning, indeed a passion for fostering and enhancing the student experience, together with a commitment to excellence that characterises National Teaching Fellows. Congratulations to Tim Bilham, the editor, and all the sub-editors and authors for producing such a thoughtful, scholarly and inspiring text, which is certain to support the work of other academic teachers aiming to put student learning at the heart of everything we do.

Sally Brown
July 2013

Introduction: inspiration, innovation and excellence

Tim Bilham (NTF 2007)

Tim Bilham is Director of Studies for postgraduate medical and healthcare programmes at the University of Bath and Honorary Associate Postgraduate Dean in the Severn Deanery School of Primary Care. A practitioner in distance and e-learning, having graduated in mathematics and engineering, he has worked across disciplines including technology, management, science and social science. He directed major international development projects that established two Colleges of Open and Distance Learning in Africa. Tim is a Higher Education Academy National Teaching Fellow reviewer and UK Professional Standards Framework consultant. Currently he is taking an MSc in Sustainable Development and experiencing at first hand how it feels to be a part-time, distance, mature student.

I was a first-year student of mathematics attending one of my first university lectures. I was keen to learn, committed to the subject and I think reasonably bright. The lecture was on mathematical analysis, a subject I enjoyed. At that time mathematics lecturers were prone to saying, 'and it follows trivially …' in the middle of proving some theorem. At this point the professor stopped in mid-sentence (he was writing on a blackboard, of course) and left the room. Ten minutes later he reappeared, continuing writing exactly where he left off, with the comment, 'Yes, it follows trivially that …'. It was far from trivially obvious to me and probably to many of my peers. I believe I learnt nothing.

Another student memory was a Saturday morning series of lectures (how times have changed!); the professor asked us to read his book before attending. I was impressed, as I had not met anyone before who had written a book. Perhaps unusually, I did read it – after all, it was quite short – and I understood it relatively well. So I attended the first lecture expecting great supplementary insights only to experience the professor reading his book verbatim. At one point he turned to an overhead projector slide, and I imagined something new, only to find that the image was a reproduction of a page of data from his book. Very few students attended the remainder of the lecture series.

I remember thinking at the time that there must be a better way of teaching and learning. I occasionally reflect whether those wretched learning experiences, and others, were responsible for me losing my enthusiasm for my first discipline and shaping my subsequent career.

Many years later, in May 2012, an idea was born.

It was the Annual Symposium of the Association of National Teaching Fellows (ANTF) and we had just experienced a series of extraordinary *Pecha Kucha*[1] sessions from colleague National Teaching Fellows (NTFs)[2] who were presenting an aspect of their teaching practice. It was an inspirational session. The symposium programme was abandoned, and by the end of the day the title and broad framework of 'For the Love of Learning' had emerged.

By the time we gathered a year later for the 2013 symposium the book was substantially complete; a call for contributions had resulted in well over one hundred submissions from NTFs, including written forms of some of those original *Pecha Kuchas*. There were many sparkling pieces; it is regretful that we cannot present them all. We eventually settled upon 36 intriguing essays, from this much larger and wonderfully diverse set of contributions, all written by NTFs drawn from across 13 years of the Higher Education Academy's NTF scheme.

The authors come from many disciplines: the visual arts, science, music, statistics, computer science, English, health and social care, social work, psychology, occupational therapy, marketing, technology and education including adventure education, medical and dental education, lifelong learning and professional development. They work in many different roles within, and outside, higher education, but their contributions come from their work as teachers in our universities. And what connects these narratives is an unswerving focus upon the student and on their learning. Indeed the 'student voice' has been explicitly drawn out in most essays, and in some cases students have also contributed to the final piece. The book is characterised by the way authors have transcended their own discipline and seen opportunities in others. That ability is a fundamental aim of the book – to inspire others to do the same.

The book addresses many of the important current issues in higher education: student engagement, transition, employability, assessment, technology, internationalisation, the student experience, curriculum development, interdisciplinary learning and teaching practices. It does so by highlighting teachers who have brought innovative, creative and novel approaches to these key issues that will inspire others to explore and experiment. Many authors advocate risk-taking and these examples demonstrate, we believe, what makes the work of NTFs excellent and intriguing.

▶ Nomenclature

We have called these contributions essays – a term that seems appropriate. Aldous Huxley (1960) describes the essay as existing in three forms: the personal and reflective, the objective and particular, and the abstract and universal. *For the Love of Learning* comprises essays covering all of these categories and many combine all three approaches. In doing so they provide insights into the personal drivers that inspire good university teachers, specific interventions that have introduced change and improvement in student learning at different scale, and observations on institutional, national and international contexts for higher education.

As befits the form, these essays are designed to be brief, personal and informal, often conversational in tone and expository in terms of their aims and content, presenting actual occurrences and inviting you, as the reader, to join them in the making of meaning for you (see Dillon, 1981). In many cases authors have provided suggestions and generalisations of their approaches that might be applied in different contexts and disciplines, but they speak from their specific experience; thus it is for you to apply it to your situations.

In this way it is not dissimilar to the learning design that promotes the social construction of knowledge (Wenger, 1998a) and student engagement (Bryson, 2013) that is a recurring theme throughout the book. And of course it is common for us to use the essay form in our own teaching and assessment of students.

▶ Who is this book for?

The book will be valuable to university teachers and learning support staff, course and programme leaders, staff developers, quality assurance staff, change agents, leaders and senior managers in the UK and internationally. It will also be relevant to staff in further education institutions where higher education is taught and students are training to be teachers in other contexts. This will include early career staff on initial training courses for higher-education teaching as well as experienced staff responding to change and seeking new ideas and methodologies.

▶ How is the book structured?

Many of the essays overlap and interlink, and the book is structured around some intersecting themes that emerged from the essays, in four parts, namely:

▶ *Crossing boundaries*: transitions to and from university, crossing disciplines
▶ *Learning differently*: novel approaches to teaching, assessment, the use of technology and challenges of teaching difficult topics
▶ *Engaging students:* in learning and discovery and their wider influences
▶ *Employability*: preparing for careers, enterprise and professional learning

There is innovation here and creativity. There is novelty and challenge. There may even be the odd polemic. We can accept that because we recognise the passion for learning and teaching that drives this community. But there is also the rigour that would be expected of leading academic teachers.

Of course our universities are full of creative, innovative, committed teachers who are recognised in numerous ways; what distinguishes NTFs is that their claim to excellence has been evidenced by student commendations, teaching evaluations, peer review, institutional nomination and a national selection process. And also that, of all the roles within academia, they are primarily focused upon learning and teaching.

We hope that there is something here for everyone. There are stories and experiences, theoretical models, evaluative studies, challenges to orthodoxy, calls for risk taking, experiential and experimental approaches and practical proposals.

Part 1 focuses on the work of NTFs that has challenged, or is challenging, what have been perceived as traditional boundaries in higher education, exploring how staff involved in educational support and delivery may seek to apply transdisciplinary or different epistemological and pedagogical structures to their teaching.

To begin with we explore cross-disciplinary teaching: Heather Barnett (essay 1) illustrates an institution-wide project in which students move across boundaries, becoming teachers, researchers and producers in disciplines from the life sciences and photographic arts. Joanna Verran uses art and literature, though involvement in a book club, in her teaching of microbiology, and involved her students in community engagement projects (2). Try Jo's quiz! Several authors demonstrate the use of literature and poems in their teaching. Kevin Petrie (3) engages his Glass and Ceramics students as knowledge producers through the blending of teaching and research and uses alternative teaching locations – on the beach! This introductory group of examples is rounded off by Helen Keegan (4), who describes how technologies are transforming our notions of teaching, and in doing so draws together many of the themes that the book goes on to explore: cross-disciplinary teaching, student transitions, emergent teaching approaches, student engagement and employability.

The importance of student transitions in moving into and out of higher education and the difficulties they encounter in learning are explored in several ways. We look at developing skills as a learner (Peter Ovens, 5) through the use of action inquiry, three projects – *Assessment Plus*, *Ready for University* and *Flying Start* – that help students improve their abilities in academic writing (James Elander and Lin Norton, 6) and the challenges of the transition to professional learning in the workplace (Faith Hill, 7). In concluding Part 1 Suanne Gibson (8) calls for greater engagement with our learners to promote inclusivity and provides a series of practical recommendations for action.

Part 2 looks at novel, innovative and challenging forms of teaching and learning. Kirsten Hardie (9) describes the use of research symposia for undergraduates, and Derek Raine (11) a study into the effectiveness of problem-based learning (PBL) techniques in interdisciplinary science teaching. Gráinne Conole (10) offers a framework for designing learning that uses technologies effectively and for the development of digital literacy skills in teachers. Rachel McCrindle (12) takes a games-based approach, which engages students in their own learning through PBL and projects that enhance their team-working and communication skills. Teaching of difficult, or less than popular, topics often creates challenges for teachers. Stella Jones-Devitt (16) promotes ways to develop critical thinking skills through performance and games. Paul Hewson (14) challenges our orthodox approaches in the teaching of statistics across disciplines, and this is juxtaposed with one possible solution of using humour (Andy Field, 15). Assessment features strongly in many essays. Peter Hartley (17) reflects upon some neglected issues, while others explore different techniques such as 'preflights' (Brian Whalley, 13). Luke Dawson (19) reports the findings of a development that uses technology to link assessments with professional competences, and Anita Peleg (18) on the way students can be engaged through experiential learning and formative assessment and feedback. Part 2 concludes with three essays on international dimensions. David Killick (20) demonstrates how internationalisation can be embedded within curricula, and the impact across the institution, and Basiro Davey (21) illustrates the way universities are increasing their contribution to educational capacity-building in developing countries. Finally, Jane Spiro (22) describes how four projects, including one that used poems, can help bridge the 'divide' between home and international students. These examples of student engagement provide a bridge to the next part of the book.

Involving students directly in their own learning has great rewards and many challenges. The first four essays in Part 3 illustrate several successful approaches that have involved deploying concepts of enabling learning and reflective practice (Rayya Ghul, 23), collaborative enquiry (Will Curtis, 24), student engagement (Colin Bryson, 25) and the development of professional and performance skills (Laura Ritchie, 26). The second half considers the wider influence of student engagement. Duncan Reavey (27) contrasts two approaches in South Africa and the UK and provides a set of 'golden rules' for those who wish to emulate them. Authenticity in teaching is a recurring theme; Ruth Matheson (28) looks at the need for authenticity in the establishment of professional identities and Mary Hartog and Philip Frame (29) describe a specific project in response to an external client. Anna Lise Gordon (30) concludes this part by looking at the way students can be engaged in reflecting upon their learning as they embark on their professional roles, a theme explored further in the final part.

Part 4 focuses upon employability. It considers a framework that exposes the lifelong and portable skills needed by our graduates (Arti Kumar, 31), the use of storytelling in 'sense-making' of work-based experiences (Beverly Leeds, 32) and the development of enterprise skills (Pauline Kneale, 36). International employability, and the importance of English as a common language, is the theme of Angela Goddard's essay (35), and the need for authenticity in assessment reappears in relation to providing real contexts for learning (Jane Thomas, 33). Preparing students for rewarding and effective lives is the focus of Jamie Thompson (34), who promotes the engagement of students in that learning process and demonstrates it through including students as co-authors to this essay.

▶ In conclusion

In *Rethinking University Teaching* Diana Laurillard begins her book with the premise that 'university teachers must take the main responsibility for what and how their students learn' (Laurillard, 1993). In other words, university teachers create the choices.

Much has changed in the twenty years since Laurillard's book and from my own early student experiences. We now have learning outcomes and professional frameworks, we have student engagement and an increasingly international campus, we have a focus on employability and core skills, we are concerned about student transitions and widening access, we have formative assessment and strive to provide more effective feedback to students. And we have technology.

But a fundamental truth remains, when it comes down to it ... university teachers create the choices for student learning. As university teachers we have a profound responsibility: we receive undergraduates many at their most formative stage, we have postgraduates for whom we can open up new possibilities and part-time returners and mature students who thought that such opportunities had been denied to them. For all of them we help shape their lives.

We hope that these essays will inspire you in exploring new opportunities for the learning of your students.

PART 1
Crossing boundaries

Disciplines   11

Transitions   43

1 The liquidity of knowledge: learning across disciplinary divides

Heather Barnett (NTF 2012)

Keywords: art/science collaboration, staff/student partnership, knowledge exchange, community of practice, emergent learning, complexity theory, interdisciplinary learning

Heather Barnett is a visual artist, researcher and educator working with biological systems and scientific processes. With interests ranging across medicine, psychology, perception and visualisation, her projects have included microbial portraiture, cellular wallpapers, performing cuttlefish and self-organising installations. She is Senior Lecturer in Photographic Arts at the University of Westminster, London, where she leads the Broad Vision project.

Broad Vision is an art/science research and learning project, which brings together undergraduate students and academic staff from diverse disciplines to engage in collaborative exchange and experimentation. Through interdisciplinary exploration students become teachers, researchers and producers as they engage with questions relating to biology and psychology, technology and creativity, art and science.

Drawing on my observations as Broad Vision project lead and the experiences of collaborating students and staff, this essay will frame the project in relation to interdisciplinary learning, academic hierarchies and emergent curricula – all of which are fluid and mutable.

▶ Learning design

The Broad Vision project is an educational research project 'in action', supported by an interdisciplinary pedagogic research fund at the University

Figure 1.1 Informal learning and sharing of expertise – a Life Sciences student explains what is being viewed down the microscope (in this case, a histology slide of healthy and unhealthy liver tissue) © *Chiara Ceolin*

of Westminster, London. Since 2010, it has developed learning opportunities across the arts and sciences, with students taking a central role in the design and delivery of an emergent curriculum. Its initial aims were to explore student (and staff) exchange across the disciplines, encourage cross-fertilisation of knowledge and observe outcomes. Motivated by my own experience as an interdisciplinary artist and the desire of colleagues to build relationships within the institution, it is our aim that students 'realise the value of their pre-existing knowledge; gain valuable insights from others; and develop an understanding of the value of interdisciplinary practice'.[1] In the project's lifetime, a phased interdisciplinary educational model has been developed, tested and refined; numerous public outputs have been produced in the form of exhibitions, publications and conference presentations; and an art/science collaboration module accredited, taking the project from an extracurricular programme to an assessed part of the curriculum.[2] To date, three generations of students and staff have participated in the project, many continuing their involvement in subsequent years, some even after graduation.

The overarching theme of the project has centred on vision and perception: examining how we see, capture and interpret the world around us.

Figure 1.2 A Photographic Arts student instructs a scientist how to use a large-format plate camera in the photography studio © *Chiara Ceolin*

Each year a set of images or a body of knowledge has provided a catalyst for student inquiry. For example, in the first year microscopy was employed to explore worlds beyond human vision, in the second a collection of contemporary scientific images prompted discussion,[3] and in the third, the theme of 'data, truth and beauty' provided stimulus for collaborative projects.

For each cycle, a group of students volunteer to participate in the project, recruited from courses in psychology, life sciences, imaging science, photographic arts, illustration and contemporary media practice. Interests vary, from scientists in need of a creative output, to artists inspired by scientific subjects and materials: all are curious to step out of their disciplinary comfort zone and experience new subjects and approaches. Whilst motives may differ between the sciences and the arts, both are deeply concerned with inquiry, exploration and the communication of concepts. Through a clearly defined structure of inter/disciplinary learning students are encouraged to 'differentiate', between their values, methods and mental processes: and to 'connect', identifying possibilities for collaborative working. The ultimate aim is that students should be able to move from mono-disciplinary thinking to the cognitive processes of a more complex interdisciplinary mind.

▶ Supporting structure

The Broad Vision project structure is formed of three distinct phases:

▶ 'disciplinary exchange', where students share an aspect of their growing expertise through a series of workshops, devised and delivered by students;
▶ 'interdisciplinary research', where projects are developed through creative discussions and collaborative research; and
▶ 'audience engagement', where students are encouraged to share their work through a range of public outputs.

Through these phases, students take on the multiple roles of teacher, researcher and producer, as they engage in research, exchange and dissemination. Whilst detailed descriptions can be found in the two Broad Vision publications (Barnett and Smith, 2011; Barnett, 2012), learning activities are broadly designed to shift the roles of students (and tutors) between the positions of expert and novice. The short taster sessions delivered by students in the early phase of the project introduce some aspect of each discipline to the whole group. Moving from laboratory to studio, from classroom to dark-

Figure 1.3 A Life Sciences student leading a blood-grouping exercise with staff from different disciplines © *Chiara Ceolin*

Figure 1.4 An Illustration student leading a group drawing exercise, following verbal descriptions and observing the range of interpretations © *Chiara Ceolin*

room, activities range from blood-grouping exercises to collective drawing, from photographic portraiture to observing tissue samples down a microscope (Figures 1.1–1.4). The movement between familiar and novel learning environments, combined with the varied roles undertaken and the focus on experiential learning, encourages multiple encounters between participants, where the individual can expand their possibilities through numerous interactions within the collective, turning a 'private solid state into a liquid network' (Johnson, 2010: 62). Materials and methods vary, as do intentions and approaches, creating a constant flow of knowledge, experience and interpretation.

The philosophy of the project places students at the forefront of curriculum design. Borrowing from theories of social constructivism (Vygotsky, 1978), the focus is on 'the processes by which learners build their own mental structures when interacting with an environment [through] self-directed activities orientated towards design and discovery' (Wenger, 1998a: 279). Through staff/student partnership the learning design creates 'a holding environment in which both staff and students can safely grow and develop, while challenging each other along the way' (Little, 2011: 9). Starting with a central theme or a set of images, ideas emerge and curriculum content responds to students' interest and questions.

Figure 1.5 A student explaining work to visitors to a Broad Vision exhibition at London Gallery West © *Chiara Ceolin*

All partners, lecturers and students alike, are involved in structuring knowledge within a 'community of practice' (Wenger, 1998a), and are able to contribute expertise. This framework, where 'emphasis is placed on the relationship between elements, rather than the elements themselves' (Mason, 2008: 21), relates to complexity theory, where 'what emerges will depend upon what interacts, which is at least partly determined by chance encounters and changes in environments' (*ibid.*: 9). In Broad Vision, the emergent projects often lead to outcomes reaching far beyond predictable or predefined intentions, for example; artworks are produced using scientific tools, psychology experiments are run in a gallery, science communication is performed, diagnostic images are presented as art (Figure 1.5).

Here, students become 'agents' within a system, operating as individuals within a collective 'learning super-organism'. All emergent systems – ant colonies, cities and internet networks alike – operate on a basis of random local interactions, a process of constant feedback, a capacity for pattern recognition, and, above all, they operate without direct control (Johnson, 2001). The principles of emergence at play within the Broad Vision structure encourage a fluid exchange of knowledge across the domains and provide continuous feedback, leading to the recognition of patterns (similarities and differences) through a non-hierarchical structure of control. All outcomes from the project emerge from chance encounters and unforeseen points of connection between collaborating individuals, showing that 'Relationships in these systems are mutual, you influence your neighbours, and your neighbours influence you. All emergent systems are built out of this kind of feedback, the two-way connections that foster high-level learning' (*ibid.*: 120). It is this equation, of low-level rules leading to higher-level learning, that the project has aimed to achieve.

▶ Responsive feedback

As the project has evolved, through three generations of students and staff, data have been captured via written observations, focus discussion groups and exit questionnaires. For myself as project lead, and for our embedded educational researcher, Dr Silke Lange, the material gathered offers insight into how students and staff experience the complexity of this emergent project, and helps us to understand the perceived benefits and challenges related to interdisciplinary learning. In the anonymous exit questionnaires, students identified strongly with the early phase of disciplinary exchange, commenting:

'It opened up my mind to the different subjects and how they work and think about things.'

Others recognised significance in the role of teacher undertaken, stating:

'It's really valuable to have the opportunity to try and teach others what you've been taught, helps to condense and revise.'

'One of the most important parts of the project for me was the ability to show people what I do in my course and how differently I think about them.'

When it came to self-organising research groups and developing collaborative projects, students expressed a range of experiences. In a staff–student co-authored paper one of the students states:

'The strength of the generative curriculum within this interdisciplinary research project was that it encouraged 'wandering', resulting in random encounters and interactions with concepts, materials and approaches to research from all participating discipline.'

(quoted in Lange and Dinsmore, 2012)

However, this student also acknowledged that the open-ended nature of the project was challenging for some who had to cope with 'being lost', itself a skill to be learnt. This was particularly true of the science students, whose project briefs tend to be more prescriptive. For students unaccustomed to self-directed project work, this phase could prove difficult, particularly as an extracurricular activity, competing for time and space with course deadlines and other commitments.

▶ Learning shared

The final phase of the project, Audience Engagement, provided a range of opportunities for students to build professional experience and enhance their 'graduate attributes', through the public sharing of work produced in exhibitions, publications and presentations. Acknowledging that students are motivated by extrinsic factors (public demonstration and reward of achievement), as well as those of an intrinsic nature (personal, social and intellectual development), the tangible outputs created considerable impact for some, one student commenting:

> 'I've never been part of an exhibition before, or had something commercially printed, or spoken at a symposium, or been included in a book. Not to be melodramatic, but that's life-changing.'

The sense of personal achievement combined with public recognition expressed through this statement highlights the value of real-world learning experiences, which may also give graduates a competitive edge in an increasingly uncertain job market. In the co-authored book from the 2012 project, one student described his experience of performing a public anatomical dissection at the exhibition opening:

> 'I had to take leadership of the procedure, liaise with others, but also work on my own – developing skills that, up to that moment, I was not aware I had. This made me realise that the lines that divide my student life and my professional life had started to disappear. I was no longer a student sat in a classroom listening passively to what my lecturers had to say. That moment I felt the pleasure of playing a more active role as a student. I was applying the knowledge gained during the past years of my studies and I was helping to build knowledge.'

(quoted in Barnett, 2012: 124)

The Broad Vision project encourages individualised outputs that contribute to both personal and professional development in a reciprocal manner; one art student noting:

> 'My involvement in shaping the Broad Vision project has stemmed from the Broad Vision project shaping me as an artist.'
>
> (quoted in Barnett and Lange, 2013)

Academic staff also engaged in the reciprocal processes of the project. Staff were curious to work within an interdisciplinary team, and were open to the outcomes. In a focus-group discussion, held at the end of a project cycle, the perceived benefits of observing different approaches to teaching were noted in areas such as group work, workshop facilitation and experiential learning. Tutors also enjoyed having a different relationship with students; for those with large cohorts and a largely lecture-based teaching programme, working with students as partners provided a refreshing change. Some tutors, particularly those working in the sciences, granted more freedom to students than would usually be permitted within laboratory protocols and noted changes in students' attitude and level of engagement. One lecturer commented at the end of the 2011 project:

> 'I've learnt a huge number of new skills that I hadn't anticipated, an opportunity to get involved with primary research and to carry out experiments in an art-gallery setting, which was a huge thrill … I really enjoyed working much more closely with students than I ever had before … and to be taught by students. In short, it's been the single most brilliant thing I've done professionally.'

The project thereby has provided a platform to experiment and explore uncharted territory for staff as well as students and many embrace the opportunity to push their own research and teaching in new directions.

▶ Institutional perspectives

Within the university, the Broad Vision project has generally been well supported, both in terms of project funding and in its continued dissemination. However, working across disciplinary divides and disparate faculties is not without its difficulties – this kind of endeavour takes considerable energy and perseverance for all involved – but the challenges have been chiefly logistic (concerned with timetables and resources) or bureaucratic (concerned with tightly guarded departmental budgets). Within the University of Westminster, the project has been recognised as an innovative and viable alternative to existing educational structures and is providing a model for interdisciplinary development in other areas of the institution. Universities more widely are now recognising the potential benefits of inter-disciplinary working, in their capacity to develop students with curious and flexible minds as well as specialist bodies of knowledge, to provide both breadth and depth of study.

As education systems become increasingly driven by market forces, and as student attitudes and expectations are affected by the growing financial burden of obtaining a degree, higher-education institutions will need to adapt in order to survive. I propose that a more mutable approach to collab-oration within and across disciplinarily and departmental divides may enable students, staff and the institutions in which they exist to co-evolve, which 'requires connection, cooperation and competition: competition to force development, and cooperation for mutual survival' (Mason, 2008: 17). Broad Vision itself must also evolve in order to build a sustainable future for itself, able to function within institutional frameworks. As part of this goal, an optional module has been accredited, completing its first run in 2013. The module design focuses on process rather than product and rewards risk, creativity and experimentation, as opposed to assessing predetermined outputs. I hope that the pedagogic philosophy of the project can be main-tained beyond an extracurricular framework and that the principles of curios-ity and complexity will continue to engage and excite the growing community of discovery through the unexpected and unpredictable learning yet to come.

The author acknowledges support from the University of Westminster, Interdisciplinary Pedagogic Research Fund, 2010–13, and wishes to thank the Broad Vision community of students and staff who have contributed to the devel-opment of the project.

2 Mixed cultures: microbiology, art and literature

Joanna Verran (NTF 2011)

Keywords: microbiology, sci-art, creativity, cross-discipline

> Joanna Verran is Professor of Microbiology at Manchester Metropolitan University. Her research, which focuses on the interactions between microorganisms and surfaces, is interdisciplinary, and she also uses other disciplines in her teaching to communicate important principles of microbiology to a wide range of audiences, including the general public.

▶ Microbiology

Students should be enthusiastic and informed ambassadors for their chosen subject, able to communicate at a level appropriate to a given audience. In science, I believe that such engagement can be achieved by utilising other disciplines perceived to be more accessible. So, throughout my career as a university microbiology educator, I have introduced innovative exercises to the undergraduate curriculum with the aim of helping students connect their microbiology studies with the world outside the university.

I want to encourage my students to reflect on how science can be communicated and to use their personal talents to enhance this communication. I want them to see themselves as cultural emissaries – making science understandable, exciting and essential to our audiences.

And I want them to learn about, and love, microbiology.

Initially, I introduced project group work where students were given a brief from an external client to design a form of public information – a leaflet, video or poster (Verran, 1992a, 1992b, 1993). The pitches, and the work, were peer assessed, client assessed and tutor assessed, and on occasion used by the clients: for example, a leaflet on toxoplasmosis produced for Manchester Environmental Health Department; a leaflet on cytomegalovirus produced for a charity; posters on immunisation for travellers displayed in a travel clinic and assessed by patients, with a prize awarded by a major pharmaceutical company.

▶ Microbiology and art

As my career progressed and my confidence grew, I learnt about different communication practices across disciplines. My research is innately cross-disciplinary, but my collaborators are scientists and engineers. We study the interactions occurring between microorganisms and inert surfaces, with a view to controlling the consequences – for example infection control, oral hygiene, cleaning and disinfection. But it was discussion with artists, initiated by an 'arts for health' project at the university, which gave new vision to my practice. I was fascinated by the way artists looked at the world, and the challenging questions they asked, such as:

▶ 'Why do the bacterial colonies look like that?'
▶ 'So, when classification systems change, the bacteria lose their names and identity? That's genocide!'
▶ 'Can I track the movement of a bacterium around the world through the climate cycle?'

I began to feel that my students could be constrained by the requirements of scientific writing style, and limited by the type of assessment provided. I wanted to offer a taste of freedom, and an opportunity for them to explore their talents and interests, by introducing a 'microbiology and art' exercise for first-year undergraduates (Verran, 2010).

I give an annual overview lecture to up to 250 students on the links between microbiology and art – which are more numerous than might be imagined: biodeterioration and conservation of cultural heritage; the beauty of images of microorganisms; the role of disease in history and art, and contemporary sci-art collaborations. Students can opt to do an assignment on the topic (they select one assignment from six choices: the other five are more traditional leaflet/poster/website evaluation tasks), involving the development of a creative output that links microbiology and art, preceded by negotiation of assessment criteria with me, as tutor. The microbiology underpinning the product must be presented, for example as a sketchbook, notebook, poster or PowerPoint presentation, along with information on the intended use of the product. Over the years, hundreds of outputs have revealed quite staggering creativity and enthusiasm – from jewellery and

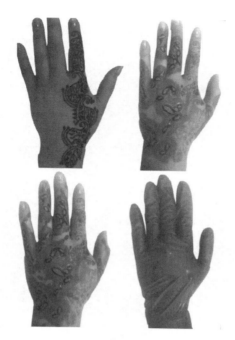

Figure 2.1 'Hands' demonstrating the presence of microorganisms on the hands – wanted: natural flora (henna) and unwanted: contaminants (paint)

fashion inspired by microorganisms, models of viruses, teaching aids, artwork, film, squares for the AIDS quilt, scientific posters, to songs posted on YouTube, photography and baking.[4] Some images have been reproduced in calendars, others have been used in publications and all works are displayed at an annual exhibition in the university. I also curated an exhibition at a local gallery during the 2011 Manchester Science Festival.

I reviewed 'hard' evidence for evaluation of the activity. In monitoring and evaluation documentation, that recorded student comments for three consecutive years, the 'art project' was the only assignment that students mentioned by name (always positively). In addition, there was no relationship between marks awarded for the 'art project' and overall year or degree performance – perhaps reflecting the diverse academic and creative nature of the students who selected the art assignment. However, as one assignment choice from six available the marks awarded are almost peripheral to the learning achieved, the work cannot be deemed a distraction or dilution of 'the science'. Indeed, the time taken by some of the students to produce their art was well in excess of that for parallel assignments. There were never any complaints about this. The NUS briefing paper on 'assessment: purposes

Figure 2.2 Jewellery inspired by the artist Alphonse Mucha: a necklace representing malaria (mosquitoes and an infected blood cell)

and practices' referenced the exercise as exemplary (National Union of Students, 2009).

I have been really impressed, enthused, inspired and moved by the creativity of my science undergraduates, and I feel that this work has truly benefited both my, and their, experiences of innovation, exploration, problem-solving and communication across subject boundaries. Students really enjoy the activity, and get great benefit from participation:

'it's the project I enjoyed the most.'

'She really gets the new students' attention by showing how microbiology is accessible to anyone, even how it is used in art'

'I'm sure you're being bombarded with emails today and everything, you should have seen people [rush] to the sign-up sheet.'

These experiences also enhance the students' skills portfolio and in subsequent years, many of these budding communicators become involved with outreach events and public engagement activities, and some explore their work further via their final-year research project.

Thinking about using art to communicate science, I started to wonder whether I could also use popular fiction ...

▶ Microbiology and literature

In 2009, I set up the 'Bad Bugs Book Club', which comprises a group of scientists (including undergraduates) and non-scientists (Verran, 2013a). We meet around six times a year to discuss novels where infectious disease is central to the plot – enabling us to read across a wide range of genres. It is quite surprising how many novels are available to us! I also plan meetings to coincide with special occasions in the science calendar. All meeting notes and reading guides are posted on my 'badbugsbookclub' website[5] and we also make suggestions for student extension work. Indeed, in science education, book

Table 2.1 Books discussed in book-club format as part of the 'Infection and Immunity' module, Year 2, Healthcare Science degree (up to 20 students per session)

Book/author/year	Reason for inclusion	Outcome of session
The Immortal life of Henrietta Lacks Rebecca Skloots, 2010	Factual, easy to read, issues of ethics, race, finance, progress of science addressed	Wide-ranging discussions, particularly on ethics and funding of research
Nemesis Philip Roth, 2010	Fiction, easy to read, renowned author, disease transmission, impact of immunisation apparent	Impact of polio prior to immunisation, importance of knowledge of transmission as key points
I am Legend Richard Matheson, 1954	Science fiction, easy to read, investigating aetiology of disease, enabling critical comment	Enthusiastic contributions from zombie/vampire enthusiasts with interesting transferability to infectious disease
Microbe Hunters Paul du Kruif, 1926	Semi-factual *Reader's Digest*-style stories of key discoveries, importance of controls and experimental design, ethics apparent	Too many short stories made it difficult for all students to complete the reading. Will select key scientists/chapters in future

clubs have been used by others to encourage science literacy and critical reading skills in medical students (Calman et al., 1988), and have been successfully employed as assessed components of undergraduate microbiology courses (Aaronson, 2008). Ashamedly, I have to confess that I have not yet used the huge potential for wider dissemination and participation via social networks.

Currently the book club is rather more of a public engagement activity than one used to enhance the student learning experience, but student involvement is increasing. I have introduced four novels with accompanying discussion sessions into a second-year medical microbiology module (see Table 2.1). Some students have selected novels and hosted their own book clubs (Verran, 2013b).

▶ Microbiology and monsters!

Students who have been interested by these outward-facing activities have worked with me throughout their degrees in developing public engagement events as project work, for example focusing on children as participants in 'mini-bugs book clubs'.

At the Manchester Children's Book Festivals[6] we have captured current fascination with 'the undead' by using vampire and zombie teen novels as a focus for discussion about the spread of infectious disease. One workshop comprised a biology lab set up to re-create a scene from the 'Twilight' novel (Stephenie Meyer, 2006), where we examined microscope slides showing the cell cycle (as did Bella and Edward, the main characters in the story) and used selected readings as hooks for discussion to link events in the novel with principles of infection control and epidemiology (answers at the end!):

1 What was Edward dying of before he became a vampire?
2 How is that disease transmitted?
3 How is vampirism transmitted?
4 You have come up with three routes for transmission of disease. What is the other one?
5 How do you prevent yourself from getting infected?
6 Is there any cure?

Bedecked with vampire-bite tattoos, and equipped with information sheets on hand hygiene, the young audiences left happy and more knowledgeable about disease transmission – evidenced by the 'Post-it' notes they attached to our Edward silhouette!

But what about zombies? Potentially more attractive to boys than girls, zombie novels are multiplying fast, providing an opportunity to engage new audiences with the marvels of microbiology. Building on our cross-disciplinary work, the 'Microbiology, Maths and Monsters' group was conceived. A postgraduate maths student developed mathematical simulations (Crossley and Amos, 2011)[7] to illustrate how diseases spread. Two thousand dots (individuals) moved around a specified area, and infected dots were programmed with specific parameters for transmission of infection, identified by participants. Parameters for zombies (slow moving, active all the time), vampires (fast moving, active only at night) and werewolves (fast moving, active once a month) create different types of disease outbreaks, enabling discussion about spread of disease, control and prevention. Zombie novels tend to focus on coping strategies, either via isolation of zombies (quarantine), or isolation of uninfected humans (a parallel with the protection gained by vaccination), again enabling principles of epidemiology to be uncovered through discussion. For zombies we developed two workshops, one an epidemiology lab where participants were required to identify prevention strategies from scenarios identified in different novels, and another as a 'what to do in a zombie attack' boot camp. We also used the skills of our local further education college media make-up students to create zombies – which obviously increased in number during the day! (For images, see the Endnotes.[8])

These public engagement activities encourage learning and enhance student communication skills – and they are really good fun to devise and deliver. However, there is plenty of scope for development – we need to tell more people about what we have done, devise more critical ways to evaluate the work, and describe the projects for publication in appropriate journals, and we need some more cross-disciplinary input to enhance our experience of the relevant qualitative and sociological literature.

I believe that our students should be emissaries to the wider world, enhancing our awareness of science, and saying something about its importance in our past, present and future lives. We should be infecting them with our passion, and letting them spread it about! I like to think that these activities go some way to enabling this to happen.

Thanks are due to the Society for General Microbiology and the Society for Applied Microbiology for financial support for some of the events described. Many thanks to all participating students, particularly Matthew Crossley (zombie mathematician), Naomi Jacobs (project management support) and James Redfern (versatile microbiology communicator!).

QUIZ ANSWERS

1 Influenza
2 Inhalation, contact
3 Puncture
4 Ingestion
5 Garlic, religious symbols (prevention – immunisation), don't invite them in! (modify behaviour)
6 No cure other than stake to the heart and beheading (no antibiotics!)

3 Blending approaches to teaching in art and design: case studies from glass and ceramics

Kevin Petrie (NTF 2010)

Keywords: art, design, glass, blending, research, outreach

Kevin Petrie is Professor and Head of Glass and Ceramics at the University of Sunderland. He studied Illustration at the University of Westminster, Ceramics and Glass at the Royal College of Art and gained a PhD from the University of the West of England. Kevin has lectured around the world.

The subjects of glass and ceramics are a strand of art and design training and often form part of applied arts or 3-D Design departments. At the University of Sunderland, glass and ceramics is a standalone subject area within the National Glass Centre (NGC). The centre is a public visitor attraction with an exhibitions programme, shop, education studios and production facility. Alongside this public-facing role we teach around 100 BA, MA and PhD students in glass and ceramics. This essay focuses on aspects of my approach to teaching, which I see as symbiotically linked and integrated to research and professional practice. I have attempted to extend the boundaries of my subject through what might be termed a 'blending' approach, referring to the blending of teaching and research so that the two are intimately connected but also to blending other subject areas with glass and ceramics.

▶ Blending subjects

The inspiration for the idea of 'blending' came early in my career when I started to see the creative potential of blending methods from two distinct strands of art and design, glass/ceramics and printmaking, which drew upon teaching and research to provide step-by-step guidance on methods, enhance technical understanding, illuminate aesthetic qualities and potential, and disseminate the latest practice and research (Petrie, 2006, 2011a). In my discipline teaching is often through workshop-based classes in which techniques are taught largely by demonstration and after which students learn the process through doing and by producing their own designs. By research, I mean studio-based research where methods are developed through testing and making artworks. In art and design, this approach has been termed 'practice-based' research (Gray and Malins, 2004). Research also includes the development of the history of creative processes and the drawing together of case studies of contemporary practice.

The idea of the Venn diagram is a useful model for considering 'blending' in research (Petrie, 2007), which is equally applied to teaching and the personal development of students. In this context, the term 'developing' is used to indicate a number of ways in which the subject area might be changed, grown or refreshed and consequently become more innovative, original and creative. In turn, we might then expect the discipline to be considered more impressive and successful to others, enhancing the potential for further development. In the model each circle represents a sector or subject area. Both fields comprise specific approaches, techniques, histories, assumptions and methodologies that influence professional practice. If teaching and learning strategies can be developed to initiate overlaps between the sectors, then new areas for development frequently emerge. These evolve from individual creative needs or interest, specific research projects, or the demands of a commissioned brief. The development focus is always the interface between the areas. The work of Yrjö Engeström (2006) on activity theory and expansive design provides a detailed theoretical perspective and visual model for this kind of development.

I see little distinction between teaching, research or publication; all are connected, all inform each other and together they make for an integrated or blended approach. As one example, my own publications are a vehicle to extend my 'teaching' beyond the university, imparting information and insights gained both from research but also importantly from experience of teaching. The common questions, mistakes, misunderstandings and areas of student interest, which arise from teaching, inform these publications, which in some cases can be 'text and image' versions of practical classes. After students have engaged with various approaches, it is always a delight to observe how they develop and adapt what they have learnt. The learning is mutual and students' methods are frequently published alongside mine. So together, we are contributing to and creating established literature and developing a 'community of practice' (Wenger, 1998a).

▶ National and international postgraduates

This community of practice is a worldwide interest group focused around my discipline in which we meet and exchange approaches through conferences. Art and design conferences often have demonstration strands where practical methods are taught and where 'master-class' teaching is another common and effective approach. As Programme Leader for MA Ceramics and MA Glass programmes I encouraged the participation of students from different backgrounds such as fine art, jewellery, textiles, printmaking and even engineering. Bringing together diverse disciplines is hugely rewarding but also creates challenges. In our case some students joined with no glass experience and as a teaching team we needed to modify our teaching approaches and thus help students recognise how they might adapt their existing skills to working with glass. These courses regularly achieved 100 per cent retention and pass rates and the opportunity to allow students to consider 'blending' their knowledge of one field with glass or ceramics has helped increase research student numbers in glass and ceramics from zero to a current figure of 30. Much of the MPhil and PhD research in our department blends subjects to create a focus for the development of new knowledge (Petrie, 2007, 2011b). For example, an MPhil student blended ceramics and travel/tourism in a project about how ceramics have been used to express aspects of tourism and which led to publication in tourism literature (Thompson, Hannam and Petrie, 2012).

As our research student numbers in glass and ceramics grew, we established a 'glass and ceramics research student forum' complementing existing faculty and university training for research students, building communities designed to reduce student isolation and facilitate the sharing of ideas. For example, a 'creative methodologies peer discussion' day brought students together to discuss creative work. This was replicated at a national level through the 'Parallels and Connections' research student conferences.[9] Most recently student teams designed research posters, coordinated tours and prepared a research exhibition of artworks. This project was significant, perhaps unique, in that it offered a specific student-focused view of research taking place nationally (and into Europe) in ceramics and glass and 'life after the PhD'.

▶ The 'Book Project'

Successful art students need to extend their 'horizons' and draw upon diverse cultural influences to keep their work fresh. Indeed, at Masters level the Quality Assurance Agency for Higher Education (QAA) expects 'originality in the application of knowledge' to be a criterion for holders of the award. As a teacher I try to create contexts for students to experience new and unexpected influences. Many art students find academic writing difficult and we provide extensive support for postgraduates in this area. Reflecting upon my own experience as a student, I believe that I advanced my writing skills through curiosity and reading 'good' books. For the 'Book Project', developed with a colleague Dr Jeffrey Sarmiento, we buy students a 'classic' novel and ask them to identify some relationship to glass or ceramics in an imaginative and broad sense. We ask them to think about symbolism, metaphor, simile and allegory – all-important terms for artists to consider – and then write a short piece uploaded to on the online learning environment. Students read what their peers have written and in a linked seminar discuss their ideas emanating from their book. Collectively we identify links between books, themes and potential applications to glass and ceramics (Petrie and Sarmiento, 2010).

Student feedback is positive:

'The "book project" is one of the best projects I have ever been assigned. It started with a "present", a gift from the university. What a great way to start! Every student was given a different book of classic literature. The project asked us to critically analyse the text, to find references to glass and/or ceramics and then discuss our thoughts on the student website before discussing in a more formal group situation.

The project was a brilliant and sensitive way to introduce me to more British literature and to broaden my understanding (as an overseas student) of British culture in a wider context. I loved this project, as it was not involved directly with glass making but more with the conceptual perceptions and essence of glass in a different medium.'

KF, MA Glass student

Recently we blended this project with a drawing workshop and asked students to represent visually the ideas emerging from their reading; student groups produced large-scale cardboard and paint sculptures. This served a number of purposes. It 'kick-started' a new stage of learning on the programme, helped students to develop new and unexpected ideas, encouraged them to link their ideas with other creative genres and finally offered an experience of working creatively in teams.

Figure 3.1 MA Glass and Ceramics students working on a 10m-long collaborative drawing on a beach, as part of an introductory project at the start of their studies. They later used this and other drawings to develop works in glass and ceramics. Could this be a good icebreaker for non-arts courses?

It is important to say that the pieces made in this project were not beautifully crafted but 'rough and ready' visualisations of ideas, and so this approach could be adapted for 'non-art' subjects. For example, might psychology students make 'sculptures' to express aspects of the mind as catalyst to better articulate concepts? Could English students be encouraged to talk about artworks and link them to texts they are reading in order to broaden understanding of how themes might be expressed in different media?

▶ Connecting communities

I often tell my students that I am not interested in the inanimate materials of glass and ceramics but rather in how they can be manipulated into artworks that allow communication between people. An Arts and Humanities Research Council (AHRC) 'Collaborative Doctoral Award' funds a PhD student to work with a 'non-academic partner'. The 'Community in Clay' project is with Sunderland Museum and Winter Gardens, which has an outstanding collection of nineteenth-century Sunderland lustreware pottery. These jugs, mugs, plates and plaques often bear a printed image of the 1791 Wearmouth Bridge, which was the longest single-span cast-iron bridge in the world at the time. They commemorate important events and people, and reflect local life, such as images and verses relating to sailors or military endeavour. This collection offers

Figure 3.2 The Crinson Jug on display in 'What's Your Story? Discovering Family History', an exhibition held at the Sunderland Museum and Winter Gardens, 23 June–27 August 2012. Ceramic artist Christopher McHugh[10] collaborated with Howard Forster, descendant of Sunderland potter William Crinson (d. 1836), to create a commemorative porcelain jug exploring his family history. At the bottom right can partially be seen Rifleman Hiles's IED brush, a ceramic rendering of the real paintbrush used by Hiles to excavate roadside bombs on his tour of Afghanistan with the 3rd Battalion The Rifles. Photograph: Colin Davison, 2012. Courtesy and © Sunderland Museum and Winter Gardens

a unique 'portrait' in ceramics of the town of Sunderland in the nineteenth century. 'Community in Clay' develops an outreach project exploring how an artist might use such a collection to engage with, and express aspects of, the local community. The student, Christopher McHugh, had a background in archaeology before becoming an artist, and is himself an example of 'blending' approaches. Community projects arising included working with soldiers who served in Afghanistan and translating their stories into ceramics objects and working with a local writers' group to create ceramics featuring their contemporary verse. A project with young offenders led to designs for mugs and tea towels to be sold in the museum shop.

▶ Real-world experience and opportunity-rich environments

I believe strongly in the benefits of 'real-world' challenges for students so they can build professional skills and a track record before graduation, including student exhibitions at one of the UK's largest commercial galleries, the 'Biscuit Factory' in Newcastle-upon-Tyne.[11]

Providing an opportunity-rich environment adds huge value to staff and students alike. A good example of this is our Ceramics Technical Demonstrator, Robert Winter, who is working with a fairtrade company and various potteries around the world (including India, Peru and Vietnam) as a technical and design consultant to help them to develop their products for a western market. He has started to take students with him on these trips to help in the design process, giving our students invaluable 'real-world' experiences of working in their industry. Following a recent trip to Peru, where she was asked to design ranges of work for potters to produce, one student commented:

> 'It was amazing and the most hard work I've done in my life! I learnt so much – managing people, working to a deadline, multi-tasking and communicating through drawing. Given the language barriers – it really made me see why our tutors insist on drawing as a key professional skill.'

As universities face increasing financial pressures, I believe that we must seek to preserve the potential for all staff and students to undertake opportunities like this that enable them to engage with and develop themselves in their subjects. More engagement is likely to lead to more inspiring teachers and more inspired students. I hope that this essay offers an insight into how one academic has attempted to foster innovation through an integrated approach to learning and teaching, research and outreach that those in other disciplines might adapt.

4 New learning ecosystems: blurring boundaries, changing minds

Helen Keegan (NTF 2012)

Keywords: participatory culture, social media, technology, open education, social networking, new media literacies, digital identity

> Helen Keegan is a Senior Lecturer and Researcher in Interactive Media at the University of Salford. Her expertise lies in curriculum innovation and the development of new pedagogies through social and participatory media, with a particular focus on creativity and interdisciplinarity. She works across the sciences and media arts, developing partnerships and creative approaches to learning and collaboration.

As an educator who focuses on using emerging technologies to blur traditional boundaries and foster new media literacies across disciplines, I feel as though we are living through a time which is both exhilarating and challenging: a transformation in education which has the *potential* for reimagining learning, leading to more open, participative pedagogies where learners are able to use web-based technologies (e.g. blogs, wikis, MOOCs) to forge connections beyond the classroom and take ownership of their learning in previously unanticipated ways. In this essay, I draw together many of the themes of this book (learning across disciplines, crossing boundaries, transitions, engagement, employability) through describing the use of social and mobile technologies to connect learners with peers and industry experts across the world.

► Changing landscapes

Since the beginning of the twenty-first century, the growth in the adoption of free and open platforms for teaching and learning (often termed as 'disruptive technologies', as they are not owned or controlled by institutions of higher education) has led to the rise of new learning ecosystems where learners and educators are able to develop personal learning networks and communities of interest beyond the walls of the institution, thus disrupting established practices. Traditional boundaries are blurring as new pedagogies emerge; open and networked approaches to learning and teaching that challenge the roles of educators, learners and institutions themselves (Brown, 2000; Davidson, 2011). Social technologies and networked publics have not only blurred the boundaries between personal and professional, formal and informal, but are leading to a fundamental rethink of: the ownership of knowledge in a participatory culture; the roles of learners and educators; the relationships between education and industry; and the boundaries between disciplines as networked technologies increase conceptual and personal connections between previously siloed fields.

Since 2006, I have been working with students from a diverse range of disciplines and cultures using social technologies to develop their digital identities, online networks and collaborative skills. These new media litera-cies, involving meaningful participation through collaboration and network-ing, are defined by Jenkins et al. (2006) as 'a set of cultural competencies and social skills that young people need in the new media landscape'. I am constantly energised by the creativity of our learners and the serendipitous opportunities that arise for them when they master these new online spaces.

Openness is the key driver here: opening up educational resources and practices, and opening up ourselves as lifelong learners who engage in collaborative enquiry together with our students. I offer a brief description of the notion of blurring boundaries through new learning cultures.

▶ Students as producers of knowledge and resources

Traditionally, educators and institutions were seen as the providers of educa-tional resources. The production of those resources was largely in the hands of these traditional gatekeepers, both in education and in industry. Nowadays, our learners are able to produce content themselves, often using the devices in their pockets; smartphones are becoming one-stop production and knowledge-sharing tools. Learners can consume, produce and curate content any place, any time. Remix culture and the rise of alternative forms of licensing are giving learners the opportunity to reimagine and reappropri-ate content in new ways, developing new media literacies in the process. Furthermore, the use of web-enabled personal devices and the proliferation of platforms and apps have made the Personal Learning Environment (PLE) a reality.

For several years now, our learners have been producing short films using their mobile phones (Keegan and Bell, 2011). Having started as an exercise in transmedia production (their films were published on YouTube, while they used personal blogs for reflective commentary, wikis for project management and group reporting, and Flickr for 'making-of'-style photo-diaries), the mobile film project has become a global collaboration. They are now working in international teams with learners around the world, producing films on topics of global concern such as sustainability. Learners are connecting across time and space, using mobile devices to meet synchronously (via Google hangouts), and cloud-based platforms to collaborate asynchronously.

'It's really hard at first, getting used to working like this. Time zones are a challenge – and working with people you've never actually met. But once you get into it it's great! I feel like I've learnt loads about new ways of working.'

BSc Professional Sound and Video Technology student

'It's been brilliant. Really enjoyed being part of this!! An honour to have been involved and loved working using G+ hangouts, that was real fun! I'd definitely do it again!'

BSc Professional Sound and Video Technology student[12]

Figure 4.1 Students and staff from the UK, New Zealand and France collaborating on the production of a film on the topic of sustainability (via Google Hangout)

As well as producing the films themselves, learners produce video blogs, reflecting on the role internationally that collaborative, mobile filmmaking might play in effecting cultural change, along with their experiences of working with both local and global teams. The resources they produce become open educational resources for others, particularly for future students to learn from what has gone before. As tutors in this project, we model openness and networking practices through collaborating on the development of the project through open, online platforms and inviting learners along to our online meetings. Our learners begin to adopt these practices, becoming dynamic agents in constructing their own learning through active involvement, and through the production of educational content that in turn can be reused and remixed by others. The learners benefit from one another's cultural perspectives while developing new skills in remote collaboration through meaningful participation in a networked society. While the content produced might not always be as polished as 'traditional' content, their contributions are nevertheless valuable to future cohorts as examples upon which future work can be developed.

▶ Student engagement through online networks

Social networking tools have the potential to strengthen relationships between learners and educators due to their capacity to enhance social presence in an online environment and increased student–tutor interaction (Anderson, 2005; Kamel Boulos and Wheeler, 2007). While there has been much debate on the complexities of 'friending' in online social spaces (boyd, 2009), learners who have a solid understanding of digital citizenship and networked cultures can benefit hugely from the blurring of traditional boundaries (personal/professional; formal/informal). Currently, one of the most popular platforms in this respect is Twitter. When we begin to connect with our students on Twitter, we are able to set up course hashtags which allow us to share and co-curate subject specific resources. Hashtags and tweets are then found by others who join us as mentors on our learning journey; we have an increasing number of past students who now ask 'what's this year's hashtag?' They connect with current students, offering peer support and sharing their expertise, as they've made the transition from networked learners to industry professionals. Through hashtags, learners are constantly amazed by the personal, social and professional connections that are made:

'How often do you get the attention of industry experts or CEOs!'
                                                    ex-student, MSc Audio Production

'Guess what – somebody found out about my Stereoscopic research project after I tweeted about it using the hashtags #3D #stereoscopic. It's going to be published!'

MSc student

Learners are able to easily follow and engage with their peers, tutors and external experts. As tutors, we are making our own learning visible, sharing resources and ideas with others around the world, our own PLNs.

▶ Employability and developing links between education/industry

Through guided development of their social identities in cyberspace (digital identities) across multiple platforms, learners are negotiating the complexities of a networked society and learning to operate in new spaces that open them up to invisible audiences and potentially clashing contexts (boyd, 2010). By taking control of their online presence, and publishing their work openly (a living CV/work showcase), learners develop their professional identities. Their educational outputs are no longer confined to the institution: through personal blogs and other social platforms their work can be discovered by experts in their chosen field. What starts out as a personal learning blog (essentially an ePortfolio) becomes their professional website. In recent years I have seen numerous students approached by industry on the basis of their professionalised online presence, often leading to job opportunities while they are still in formal education.

'I started following the Executive Producer of ATV on twitter and requested him to be one of my connections on LinkedIn so that I could understand what really goes on at ATV. They invited me to their offices, and I'm now working as their online community manager, also developing content for broadcast.'

MSc student, 2012

'People always talk about how they make contact through Twitter with industries, leading to work or contacts to work, never did I think this would come to me but it did. Uk360 is a community channel, which is shown on Sky, Freeview and the internet. They contacted me through Twitter to produce some animations for their rebranding. This is an amazing opportunity for me to get some broadcasting credits and as well as give some industry experience.'

MSc student, 2013

'I've been invited to speak at Mobile Monday Manchester after they heard about my work – bit scared, I'll be the only student on a panel with academics and people from the BBC!'

Second-year undergraduate

Through demonstrating their passion and expertise in their discipline, and participating in online networks, our learners are connecting with experts and peers around the world, leading to increased self-efficacy and deep engagement. They feel valued as future professionals, which is hugely motivating for them and helps ease the transition from formal education to their chosen career.

▶ Disciplines

Traditional disciplinary boundaries are also blurring through the use of multiple means of communication, which Wellman (2001) terms hyper-connectivity, along with the emergence of open practices and the convergence of multiple viewpoints in networked spaces (Burnett, 2011) such as Twitter. Networked technologies and digital cultures allow communications between diverse groups and unprecedented access to huge amounts of data. An obvious example of disciplinary convergence would be the growth of Digital Humanities (the intersection of humanities and computing), but with regards to the *learner* experience, we are able to connect learners with others, sharing diverse ways of seeing. In another example of interdisciplinary global collaboration, we are involved in an ongoing project where learners from different disciplines and cultures produce transmedia reports for one another on 'social media, in my industry and my city'. In this project, learners from the UK, Spain, Germany and New Zealand, from levels ranging from second-year undergraduate to Masters, and disciplines spanning architecture, web sciences, education, audio angineering and public relations, learn together and from one another. Rather than study technology *per se*, they are treating technology itself as a post-disciplinary topic (Balsamo, 2011) while gaining deeper insights into knowledge generation and cultures across the globe.

Nevertheless, when exploring the blurring of boundaries in higher education as a result of widespread technological disruption, it must be acknowledged that these new ways of connecting and participating are not uncontroversial (Keen, 2008; Carr, 2010). The role of social technologies in networked publics is under constant scrutiny, often polarised between techno-utopian and moral panic, and subject to endless debate between radical progressives and educational traditionalists.[13] Furthermore, while many educators celebrate the affordances and pedagogic potential of social technologies, their adoption is by no means universal. Learners themselves may be adept at everyday social networking practices, but participation in spaces that open them up to multiple viewpoints, invisible audiences and possibly even public critique demands careful thinking about appropriate online behaviours (Rheingold and Weeks, 2012). The digital divide is no longer defined *purely* by access, but by opportunities for meaningful participation in networked publics. By providing learners with opportunities for collaboration and co-creation across time and space, and supporting them in the development of their digital identities and personal networks, we see our learners developing new media literacies *through* meaningful participation in networked publics.

▶ **Conclusion**

Gradually, our conceptions of learning are becoming more inclusive as technologies facilitate pedagogies that are increasingly flexible, social and personal. The read–write web has created a participatory culture that can support social, lifelong learning (Brown, 2000). We are seeing the actualisation of Illich's Learning Webs (Illich, 1971), and approaches to learning that have been described as 'emergent', as they are self-organised through communities of practice (Williams, Karousou and Mackness, 2011); *rhizomatic* in the sense of multiple and interconnected (Cormier, 2008); and *connectivist*, linking work experience, learning and knowledge and shifting control from the tutor to an increasingly autonomous learner (Seimens, 2005; Kop and Hill, 2008).

As an educator I embrace the blurring of traditional boundaries between knowledge and production, education and industry, and disciplines themselves. Through using social technologies to reimagine the learner experience, we've been able to engage with learners in new ways and support their professional identity development as they negotiate the digital terrain. Most importantly, through moving towards a more negotiated curriculum across networked spaces, we are able to engage learners through their participation in knowledge production in new learning ecosystems; spaces that encourage autonomy, serendipity and ease the transition from education into employment.

5 Learning to love learning

Peter Ovens (NTF 2005)

Keywords: action research, autonomy, learning to learn, person-centred, patchwork texts, formative, peer assessment

Peter Ovens is an Honorary Research Fellow at the University of Cumbria and previously Principal Lecturer in Professional and Curriculum Development at Nottingham Trent University, where he worked on *Inquiry Into Learning*. He has used action research approaches in personal, professional and curriculum development projects in early years and primary school settings and Patchwork Texts in curriculum development and assessment contexts in higher education.

Working together, colleagues and I have evolved an innovative approach to help undergraduate students 'learn how to learn'. Seeing learning as a *moral practice,* rather than a skillset to be trained in decontextualised ways, we enable students to improve their learning, and themselves as learners, through collaborative action inquiry. They undertake a series of action inquiry cycles, each developing an aspect of learning practice in the context of its use within their studies. Tutors provide safe but challenging contexts for inquiry, resources for data gathering, reporting and evaluating and for the testing of action steps for improvement. We create multiple group settings for critical discussion of each other's development, using process criteria for peer and self-evaluation of both formative and summative kinds. Most students using this approach, called *Inquiry into Learning* (IIL), overcome fears, gain confidence, develop insights into difficulties, refine their skills and deepen their understanding of themselves as learners.

They learn to love learning well.

My beliefs about *autonomous learning* are consolidated when I'm surprised or intrigued by students' spontaneous insights and probing questions, which seem to be free from internal and external compulsions that inhibit learning. It satisfies their 'internal locus of evaluation' (Holt, 1982; Rogers, 1994) so as to 'please themselves' (Ovens et al., 2011: 18) as well as others. Learning is valued intrinsically, as well as for its instrumental value. *How* they learn seems intuitively as important as *what* they learn. Qualities of learning like curiosity and imagination, plus capacities like resilience, resourcefulness, reciprocity and reflection (Claxton, 2002), are as important as learning outcomes. As well as becoming scholars of an academic subject and/or professional practitioners of a vocation, I want students to be reflective and reflexive towards themselves, each other and their learning; apprentices in thinking (Rogoff, 1990), becoming 'critical persons' (Barnett, 1997) in a 'community of practice' (Wenger, 1998a). For instance, genetics students' love of learning might show itself in ethical as well as theoretical questioning about DNA databases and debate about their use, not just remembering facts about the helical structure. Crucially, I believe learning how to learn should be an integral part of degree learning, not by artificial, bolt-on, decontextualised training.

However, students increasingly expect to learn in narrow, arid, passive ways without independent, inquiring, knowledgeable thinking. Finding it difficult to construct personal understanding through dialogue with public knowledge, many students are acutely aware of having been 'over-directed and spoon-fed' by schoolteachers' detailed directions, to achieve prescribed outcomes, externally motivated by relentless testing. In UK schools, learning seems perpetually in deficit to National Curriculum outcomes. The domination of rationalistic market values of competition, compliance with authoritarian control, certainty, value-neutrality and uniformity seems like 'wilful blindness' (Hefferman, 2011) to evidence of the damage to learning. Poisoned by managerialist school inspection, school ranking and the tyranny of pupil testing (Mansell, 2007), learning is not loved. It is 'something you just get on and do', to 'get a pass grade'. Laden with inner and external compulsions, many students speak and write about their negative attitudes to tasks like reading academic texts, lacking inner motivation, a paralysing fear of failure and poor self-organisation and time-management abilities. Learning is uncomprehendingly, but accurately, reproducing public knowledge without understanding, interpreting or evaluating it for oneself. Many students have been trained rather than educated (Stenhouse, 1975; Ovens, 2000). Intolerant to ambiguity, uncertainty or doubt, they hate debate which questions, explores or problematises knowledge. They want teaching which unambiguously *delivers* a cerebral commodity, unrelated knowledge-bites, to 'buy' a pass grade, uncomplicated by thoughts, feelings or personal and social concerns. This is, I believe, a growing crisis in autonomy avoidance!

▶ Inquiry Into Learning

The IIL approach complies creatively with institutional demands (outcomes evidence, bureaucratic accountability, marketisation, kitemarks and charters) while sustaining a vision for learning how to learn. During ten years of tutors' collaborative action research (Elliott, 2006), the team I led met weekly to evaluate evidence of our own and students' experiences. Progressively, we integrated our practice with deepening theorisation about our vision, each improving the other, and best understood interdependently. Evidence was obtained from students' action inquiry reports and blog writing, our records of talk in tutor–student discussion and peer discussion, and from question-naires and instance-interviews. For example, we radically revised our under-standing and practice relating to *structure*. Realising the strength of students' expectations for authoritarian task setting, the format of IIL handouts reverted to a more directive appearance, while the tasks increasingly elicited students' personal reflection and independent decision-making. In tutor–student and peer communication, we fostered a blend of uncondi-tional positive regard for, and empathy with, students' perspectives, with honest, critical feedback. Rejecting the rationalist separation of values/aims from how to achieve them, which is poisoning education, our action research 'findings' are not generalised 'truths' for imposition on other contexts, but hypothetical principles, embedded in our practices, for testing by colleagues' own action research to improve realisation of their values for students in their situation.

The IIL approach starts with students taking an evidence-based look at their perceived strengths and difficulties as learners, in the context of an aspect of current learning practice within their programme: taking lecture notes; understanding set texts; managing distractions to concentration; making contributions to seminars; etc. Working individually and with *Learning Partners*, their first 'Learning Inquiry' monitors thoughts, feelings and actions as they learn, discussing this evidence with critical friends, to understand more deeply what the difficulty might be. Possible action steps (hypothetical improvements in learning behaviour) are explored and each one is evaluated in a fresh episode of practice, creating contexts to apply practical tips, learning skills and theories of learning as meaningful resources for improvement. The credibility of a student's claim that Inquiry improved an aspect of their learning is recognisable by its authenticity and evidence base.

More Learning Inquiries follow, fresh evidence of improved practice alter-nating with evaluative review. Development is sustained by individual reflec-tion, small-group discussion in a mutually accepting, tolerant and

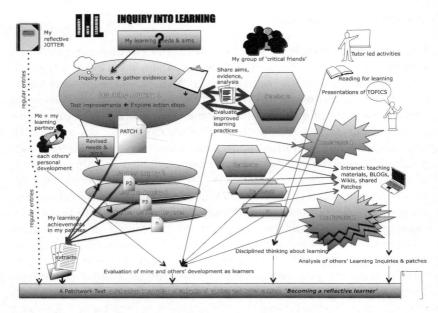

Figure 5.1 Organisation of the IIL Patchwork Texts Curriculum

encouraging ethos exchanging honest feedback, whilst celebrating diversity and difference. Personal reflections are routinely recorded in *Jotters* or *Blogs*. Relevant learning communities discuss each Inquiry, shared electronically in reports ('patches'), contributing to regular, year-group *Conferences* about learning achievements. The evaluation of these *Conferences*, combined with lectures providing theoretical resources for students' understanding of learning, are used to stimulate inquiry topics for the next cycle.

Three qualities of students' work emerging from the Learning Inquiry – *Involvement; Awareness of personal development* and *Credible practical knowing* – are used as formative criteria for informal, small-group peer and self-assessment of inquiry work throughout, as well as in the formal assessment of the assignment, which is a *Patchwork Text* (Ovens, 2003) made from edited 'patches', 'stitched together' with an integrating, critical, reflective review which draws upon the *Jotter*. The Patchwork Text gives a progressive *repertoire of cases* (Schön, 1987) of *becoming a reflective learner*.

At any point, improvement may depend on developing one, or a combination of, many ideas, skills or attitudes related to learning. A fundamental hypothesis of IIL is that, with preparation and support, it is the student her/himself who is the best person to consider all these personal and contextual factors (including values, beliefs and interests) in choosing the next step, as a potential improvement in their learning. This is education for autonomy!

Awarded in 2005, my National Teaching Fellowship enabled development of the IIL approach, which is presented in *Developing Inquiry for Learning* (Ovens et al., 2011) as a detailed, action research account of teaching, learning, assessment and curriculum development. It exemplifies the practical guidance given to students and their responses, providing extensive evidence of achievements and frustrations, plus the tutorial team's theoretical and philosophical reflections on our action steps to improve our practice.

▶ The student perspective

An illustrative example of one student's Learning Inquiry, that I summarise here, is about being 'too easily distracted from concentrated study'. Self-monitoring with brief personal notes at frequent intervals, across several situations, established how well she sustained focused thought during study. It revealed the main distractions, how and how well they were managed, feelings about the experience and assessments of what helped or hindered her learning. This evidence of current practice, discussed with Learning Partners in critical friendship discussion, was analysed to generate emergent action steps for testing in fresh learning episodes. Repeated cycles of action and reflection, interspersed with discussion and background reading, yielded progressive, personal improvements, a blend of changed practices; adjusted habits; revised assumptions; wiser choices; refined understanding of learning and insight into one's attitudes, dispositions and beliefs as a learner. Further progress strengthened her motivation for learning, and addressed an emerging concern to improve eating and sleeping patterns.

> 'This Inquiry greatly improved how I feel about my learning: I'd begun to feel like a poor student who did little work, but now I do see myself as able to be more studious.'

Learning Inquiry focuses commonly relate to:

- ▶ difficulties using learning resources (notably textbooks)
- ▶ organising and managing time or learning relationships
- ▶ threats to self-confidence
- ▶ balancing study with 'having a good time'!

Unexpected inquiries arise, such as 'Are my opinions relevant?' This student's previous schoolteacher had said not, so she explored their value to her internal and external dialogues between personal understanding and formal, public knowledge. Another sensitive inquiry into study habits probed deeply into maintaining a balance between autonomy as a 'need to take my own direction', and homonomy, a 'need to feel that I belong to my group'. Techniques such as *Intervision* (Wells, 2011) raise the cognitive challenge of peer reflection and promote students' voice, including those whose Learning Inquiries enabled *attribution retraining* (Dweck, 2000) of their unintentional collusion with a self-image of inadequacy.

Many students seem liberated by IIL, rapidly showing genuine engagement (Bryson and Hand, 2007) with university learning. Others develop significant features of autonomy more gradually. With increasingly realistic self-appraisals they show confidence in their learning strengths. Despite tutors' best efforts, a few retain dysfunctional practices and beliefs about knowledge and learning represented by early stages of Baxter Magolda's (1999) schema for students' intellectual development (adapted as a monitoring instrument). Their perfunctory Learning Inquiries lack credible practical 'knowing' because superficial or bland evidence of learning does not justify vague claims about improvement.

▶ Conclusion

Developing a love of learning requires changes of paradigmatic proportions for a growing minority of students. I offer you this approach as a proven stimulus to students developing a love of learning. Organised as a module or something less formal, you could enable students' progressive, collaborative action inquiry into the improvement of their practice as learners and their development as learners. I invite you to test the value of IIL principles, such as tutors' blending an acceptance of students' difficulties with challenging them to practise autonomous learning, in your own context.

6 Crossing the boundaries of academic writing

James Elander (NTF 2004) and Lin Norton (NTF 2007)

Keywords: transitions, academic writing, assessment

James Elander is Head of the Centre for Psychological Research at the University of Derby. With a longstanding interest in student learning, he has a special interest in the development of academic writing.

Lin Norton is Emeritus Professor of Pedagogical Research at Liverpool Hope University. She continues to actively research aspects of pedagogy with a specific focus on assessment. Lin is an associate editor for *Psychology Learning and Teaching* and is on the editorial board of *Innovations in Education and Teaching International*.

How can we help students to make a successful transition to the demands of academic writing at university, when their pre-university education may have given them hardly any experience of extended written composition?

In this essay we reflect on this question in the light of our efforts during a decade of working together in collaborative projects to help students improve their academic writing.

▶ Assessment Plus

Our efforts to improve student writing began with research on what university tutors and students believed was important when assignments were marked (Norton, 1990), and on students' misconceptions about what would improve their grades (Norton, Dickins and McLaughlin Cook, 1996). During that period, policy and good practice recommendations emphasised that students had a right to know how their work would be assessed, and that the assessment criteria should be as explicit as possible (QAA, 2000). Researchers increasingly focused on the assessment criteria in their efforts to help students improve their written assignments (Rust, Price and O'Donovan, 2003).

The *Assessment Plus* project,[14] which was psychology-based, took that approach by identifying a small number of 'core criteria' for academic writing, and then developing and evaluating workshops to help students understand the meanings of those criteria. The workshops covered addressing the question, structure, showing understanding, developing an argument, use of evidence and evaluation. The workshops were run for first- and third-year psychology students, and elements were incorporated into a generic academic skills programme designed for undergraduates from all disciplines and for postgraduates in business. The evaluations were encouraging (Norton et al., 2005; Harrington et al., 2006), as these student comments illustrate:

> 'Highly recommend, especially for getting a better understanding of how to structure and how to argue in essays.'
>
> Third-year Psychology student

> 'Helped me to start writing at Uni level.'
>
> First-year Psychology student

> 'Helped clear up my mind, as it was getting very confusing as every teacher had their own demands and I was not knowing how to respond exactly.'
>
> MBA postgraduate

Although this was encouraging, we began to think more critically about our general approach. One concern was that focusing on students already at university meant that we overlooked how academic writing develops over long periods alongside the development of approaches to learning and beliefs about knowledge. The psychology students we encountered at university who had most difficulty with academic writing were usually in their first year, so we wanted to work with students before they arrived at university. We wanted to develop proactive rather than reactive interventions, and also to address the broader policy context, which increasingly drew attention to ways that pre-university study and qualifications did not prepare students adequately for university (Lowe and Cook, 2003).

▶ Ready for University

The *Ready for University* project[15] employed the core criteria approach with pre-university students in further education, and the results surprised us. First, compared with university students, the pre-university students had greater confidence about their ability to meet the core criteria, despite having less sophisticated understandings of what is required in university assignments, so they appeared to overestimate their understanding and ability in relation to academic writing (Jessen and Elander, 2009). Those findings certainly help to explain the disorientation and confusion that students often report when undertaking their first written assignments at university, and they might be explained by pre-university learning that prioritises facts and information over analysis and evaluation of knowledge, but overestimating one's ability is probably not a good starting point for university study.

Second, when we delivered workshops about the meanings of the core criteria to the pre-university students, we found that they led to more sophisticated beliefs about what makes a good essay, but they also reduced students' confidence and self-rated ability to meet the criteria (*ibid.*: 2009). Reducing students' confidence is an unusual goal for a pedagogic intervention, but having a more realistic assessment of one's ability may be necessary for the development of academic writing, which is an important element of successful transition from pre-university to university study.

▶ Flying Start

Those findings made us consider the pre-university learning environment more carefully, and in the *Flying Start* project[16] we focused more systematically on the contrasting approaches to learning and teaching in the further and higher education sectors. We conducted a series of cross-sector action research projects that looked at transitions in specific subject areas, and found that the differing approaches to learning and teaching in each sector reflected the particular perspectives and priorities of the practitioners and students involved. For example, case studies in history and geography showed that school-based interventions to help students make the transition to university must take into account earlier transitions within the school environment, like those from Key Stages 3 and 4 to AS and A level, which involved reduced feedback and guidance and greater expectations of independent work (Norton et al., 2009a). In some subjects, students often have little experience of academic writing until they reach university. In Music, for example, Quality of Written Communication (QWC) is included in the A-level syllabi but not the BTEC qualifications, and Edexcel BTEC HND Music has 4 out of 8 units that contain no written work (Walters, 2010).

Another of our concerns was that focusing so much on assessment criteria would encourage students to adopt an overly strategic or assessment-focused approach to learning, attending to superficial aspects of the assessment task rather than engaging in meaningful learning. An analysis of the types of learning required to meet the core criteria suggested that meeting most of the criteria involved deep and/or complex learning (Elander et al., 2006), so one solution may be to reconceptualise assessment criteria as learning criteria (Norton, 2004). This is especially important on the university side of the transition, where institutions have been developing models of study support and learning development for students. In some cases these include writing centres like the *Write Now* Centre at London Metropolitan University,[17] but these are relatively rare in the UK compared with North America. An alternative is to integrate writing instruction and support more closely with subject teaching. As Lea and Street (1998) and Lillis (2001) have argued, many of the problems with student writing derive from confusion about the demands and epistemology of the subjects they are studying, so what is needed is an inclusive approach that views writing as the province of all teaching staff rather than just writing specialists. This means greater incorporation of writing into the academic curriculum (Clughen and Connell, 2012).

We also began to think about giving students a more prominent role in helping other students to understand what makes good academic writing, and the more we developed ways of allowing students' voices to be heard in the advice, information and guidance we produced, the more we appreciated what a powerful learning tool the student voice can be (Norton et al., 2009b):

'I used to not really look at the assessment criteria and wonder what the tutor was looking for, but as I have progressed through the years I have realised that if you don't follow what they ask, then you tend not to do very well. That's probably why I failed my first year.'

Third-year Psychology student

'Just because something's been taught in a lecture doesn't mean it's right, so it's about looking at it and saying whether you think you agree with it, rather than just writing it down. We are taught this model – well, what do I think of it? You need some differing opinions as well, those who criticise, and those who say, "no, it's good". Bumping opinions against each other.'

Second-year Psychology student (reflecting on being critical)

At the *Write Now* Centre, student peer mentoring was developed specifically in the context of student writing, and was shown to be an effective way to support students in developing and improving their academic writing (Bakhshi, Harrington and O'Neill, 2009; O'Neill, Harrington and Bakhshi, 2009). In the *Flying Start* project, we adapted the student peer writing mentor model for transitional writing development, which involved training university students to act as writing mentors for pre-university students in further education (Elander et al., 2011). This not only helped the mentees but the mentors also benefited from the process:

'I find it very enriching, personally, because it allows you to develop your own skills on both an intrapersonal and interpersonal level. You learn more about the inner workings of how certain things in academia work, you learn good ways – a little bit of it is networking as well because you get links inside the school.'

Student writing mentor

▶ Reflections

Reflecting on the outcomes of these projects, as well as on our own practitioner experiences, has led us to conclude that only by understanding students' own real experiences of academic writing at different levels can we appreciate the complexity of the transitions involved. Our work has focused at different levels, from individual students to learning contexts in different sectors, different disciplinary demands, and differing requirements of assessment within and across sectors. We do not pretend that the task is easy, but we do believe that in order to help students make transitions in academic writing, all of us must find ways to reach beyond the tightly bound parameters of higher education and see academic writing as a context-dependent and evolving ability. Our work has shown that greater awareness of experiences in different sectors is helpful and that disciplinary differences are critical. Most importantly, however, approaches like transition mentoring programmes and incorporating writing into the disciplinary curriculum can be practical ways of helping students make the necessary transitions in the development of their academic writing.

7 Beyond competence: enabling and inspiring healthcare students

Faith Hill (NTF 2009)

Keywords: transitions, healthcare placements, workplace learning, medical education, staff development, student engagement

Faith Hill is Head of the Academic Unit for Medical Education at the University of Southampton and holds the title of University Director of Education – the professorial equivalent for outstanding educators. An active and inspiring medical educator, she has developed a highly innovative programme of staff development for clinicians and academics throughout the Faculty of Medicine and the South Central NHS.

Healthcare students have to make a transition into higher education and into workplace learning. National Health Service (NHS) placements provide vital learning opportunities but the transition from university is far from easy. Students on placement must work with patients, relatives and colleagues and conform to professional standards – even at undergraduate level.

It is recognised that moving to workplace learning causes stress and uncertainty for many healthcare students. The literature confirms that early clinical placements are particularly difficult (Dolmans et al., 2008; Haglund et al., 2009; James and Chapman, 2009; Seabrook, 2003). Furthermore, new challenges are emerging in response to institutional and policy factors that are rapidly changing the NHS. For example, increasing student numbers and the changing profile of hospital patients mean that students are now competing for patient access. Privatisation of healthcare limits the availability of NHS placements. The reorganisation of junior doctor training, shift-work and the European Working Time Directive limit access to clinical teachers.

These changes are of great concern to me. My main role is to provide staff development for NHS clinicians who teach medical students. I need to understand the ways in which the student experience is changing in order to help clinical staff provide the best possible learning opportunities. The award of a National Teaching Fellowship for staff development at Southampton University enabled me to apply to the Higher Education Academy for funding to explore the issues in greater depth and to improve our understanding of students' experiences as they move into clinical learning environments.

Working with colleagues in Southampton and Leeds, the 'Beyond Competence Project' (2010–12) involved collaboration between the two Medical Schools and included research into the experience of medicine, nursing and audiology students. This essay describes key aspects of the study undertaken in Southampton as part of the overall project, with particular reference to medical students.

▷ Researching the student experience

My main priority was to increase our understanding of the student transition to *initial* clinical placement – what actually happens to students as they make the move away from classroom environments? For medical and audiology students, despite some early clinical experience, the main transition occurs in the third year; for nursing students it is after four months in university. For all students this is the time when they first encounter the challenges described and when the many NHS changes might be expected to impact on them the most.

Our research looked at this critical time for students through the use of semi-structured individual and focus group interviews with staff and students; self-reported student data; and a student survey. We conducted 38 student interviews; 17 staff interviews; and collected data from 25 self-reports. The survey response averaged 48 per cent across the three professions (362 completed online questionnaires).

The findings were complex and varied across professions, but a number of key messages emerged. The first of these relates to the preparation, structure and guidance given before and on placement. The students valued the advance briefing but some wanted more preparation for the practical and emotional realities of healthcare environments. Because healthcare environments differ considerably from one placement to the next and because placements can be quite short, students felt it was important to have guidance and structure at the start of each placement.

Students did not want to be 'spoon-fed', and many discussed the value of transitioning to independent learning as soon as possible. They differed in their understanding and expectations of how they should make this transition, and some wanted more time to shadow clinicians and observe clinical practices before undertaking any activities. There was general consensus that feeling 'part of the team' was important and that having a genuine role within the clinical environment facilitated learning. Most students described taking every opportunity to be part of the clinical team, but some reported finding this difficult, as in these two quotes:

'[L]ike, say, when I was in the anaesthetic room … I was just put on the monitoring and there's not a lot else I felt I could do, and I'd just sort of feel a bit of a spare part watching all the time.'

Nursing student

'You'll spend a lot of time not knowing what you're doing and being yelled at and getting in the way.'

Medical student

The students reported making a conscious effort to adjust to different teaching methods but voiced strong views about clinical teaching abilities. They identified criteria for 'good' teaching, including: enthusiasm; setting the scene; and acting as good role models. They also identified criteria for 'bad' teaching, including: not valuing student contributions; not directing their learning; and failing to acknowledge their presence. They disliked 'teaching by humiliation', preferring encouraging teachers and a 'mentoring' approach. They also valued feedback and were very critical if this was not forthcoming.

Students and staff reflected on changing realities within the NHS. For example, students expressed concern about making demands on ever-busy clinicians and sometimes reported feeling in the way of patient care. While strongly valuing the opportunity to learn from patients, students complained that there are not always enough patients per student. They also report that patients are usually, but not always, willing to be seen by them. These last two points were noted by staff, who commented on the changing patterns of healthcare where patients are in hospital for shorter times and are much sicker while there. As one said (comparing his experience as a student years ago when there was plenty of time to talk to patients who were not too ill and when there were hospital hairdressers), these days:

'[I]f you are well enough to have your hair cut, you are not going to be in a hospital.'

Hospital consultant

Students also reported on emotional challenges. The changing nature of 'teams' within the NHS may mean there is less emotional support for them than in the past. At the forefront of their concerns was witnessing suffering, death and dying while on placement. Some students were reluctant to engage with patients for fear of causing them more pain or suffering. Students also voiced surprise and confusion about the degree of prejudice, cynicism and poor role-modelling they believed they had seen.

However, most students valued the learning experiences and commented positively on the support from clinical staff. As one student reported:

'And she [the consultant] was really nice about it [dealing with bad news] and, you know, she just gave me that time off, and it was really good of her, and she just talked me through it, and it was really nice of her. I mean I'm a lot better equipped to deal with it now.'

Medical student

▶ Enhancing the student experience

My approach has always been to use research to inform education developments. In this project we used the findings to enhance the student experience in three main ways. The first was engaging students with the findings and working with them to produce online guidance for future students. The resources were piloted with a wider group of students and scrutinised by staff from each of the professions. They are freely available through a website entitled *new2placements*,[18] and student feedback is very positive:

'I just wished these [resources] would have been available when I was starting out on placement.'

Student evaluation comment

Building on the existing expertise of the Southampton e-learning team, we also produced a staff resource entitled *From Classroom to Clinical Learning*. Lively and interactive, this online resource disseminates findings from the project and encourages clinical teachers to review their teaching. The focus is on medical education and it is freely available.[19] These materials have also been well received:

'They are so creative and practical! It is a really good use of education research.'

National workshop participant

In addition to online resources, my main commitment is to face-to-face staff development. I really believe in the value of bringing clinicians together to discuss their teaching and in talking with people one-to-one. Our final strategy therefore was to organise a number of workshops with teachers and to talk personally with programme and module directors. This approach is influencing major revisions to the medical curriculum. For example, from 2014 we will be requiring students to work as healthcare assistants in their second year to increase familiarity with clinical environments prior to full-time placement.

▶ Discussion

This was an ambitious project. We were exploring the challenging transition healthcare students make from classroom to clinical learning. In the process, we crossed many boundaries:

- ▶ boundaries between healthcare professions and training
- ▶ boundaries between universities and the NHS
- ▶ boundaries between staff and students
- ▶ boundaries between research and development

Crossing these boundaries and working *with* staff and students from a range of settings, we were able to produce wide-ranging advice and guidance *for* staff and students.

Inevitably we encountered some challenges. For example, engaging students for interviews and resource production proved more challenging than we envisaged. On placement students experience significant additional travel or stay away from home and are working long hours. During other times other priorities resurface. For the researchers, this led to additional travel, switching from some face-to-face interviews to telephone interviewing and working late hours.

Despite these problems, involving students proved to be one of the main strengths of the project. Another major strength was our determination to ground developments in the literature and in rigorous pedagogic research. We now have a strong evidence base for the changes we are making and the resources we are developing. We were also very fortunate in having the support of 'key contacts' – senior professionals from each of the professions. They were invaluable in sharing details about programmes, commenting on research findings and reviewing resources.

Initial feedback from staff and students is very positive but it is too soon yet to say what impact our developments will have on the student experience. Our intention is for future medical students beginning full-time clinical placements to have an enhanced experience. We will closely monitor the revised medical curriculum at Southampton over the next five years to review this. We are also helping other healthcare professions make use of the findings and have been approached by a number of higher education institutions wishing to use the materials.

The Beyond Competence Project has increased our understanding of the transition healthcare students make into workplace learning, and the findings have influenced the development of our programmes and provided the basis for staff and student resources and workshops. We have disseminated the project nationally and internationally. As a National Teaching Fellow my ambition is to develop this work to help significantly transform the student experience. By building on the project outcomes we can truly enable and inspire the next generation of healthcare students.

The author would like to thank all the staff and students who took part in the project. In particular: the Project Manager, Dr Anja Timm; Southampton researchers, Dr Stuart Ekberg and Dr Regina Karousou; our partners in Leeds, Professor Trudie Roberts, Dr Alison Ledger and Sue Kilminster; the two universities and the financial support from the Higher Education Academy.

8 'Disability matters': the role of personal tutors for inclusive teaching and learning

Suanne Gibson (NTF 2012)

Keywords: *access, disability, inclusion, personal tutor, student experience*

Suanne Gibson's specialist areas of teaching and research are disability, special educational needs and critical pedagogy. She leads the BA Education Studies at Plymouth University, tutors and lectures undergraduate, Masters and PhD students and has published widely in the area of special education needs and teaching and learning in higher education. In 2013 she was awarded an International Scholarship with the Higher Education Academy for her work on 'inclusive pedagogy'. Her work currently focuses on questions of the nature, importance and complexities of 'relationship' in inclusive education.

Growing up in Northern Ireland during the Troubles, I had a rich experience and understanding of conflict and needless violence. It gave me the realisation that life can be short, unfair and disturbing; that for many people, born into poverty and/or disability in the midst of social turmoil, the world is not a pleasant place. It is one that prevents them from shining and having a significant kind of education which promotes human flourishing and success. My teaching experiences and related research address the field of education and disability; outputs have supported and encouraged education practitioners working with learners in need at various levels of education. I draw upon it in my work as an educationalist, encouraging my university students and others to grow, to be empowered by and through each other and make a positive impact upon their communities. My adage in life and learning is to embrace and enjoy the challenges it throws at us and do our best to find in them opportunities for growth and fulfilment. This essay presents insights from my work and experiences.

'At university it helped having a key contact on the course, a personal tutor you felt was approachable, someone you could share your concerns with, somebody you felt understood and accepted you.'

First-year student, BA Education Studies

This student statement highlights one of the most significant tools that supports students with disabilities, that of the personal tutor (Gibson and Kendall, 2010; HEA 2011a). Her story, like that of many other students, supports the view that tutors need to show greater understanding and awareness of the lived experiences of undergraduate students with disabilities and use this knowledge to facilitate inclusive teaching strategies.

▶ What are the issues for students with disabilities in higher education?

We have witnessed a significant increase in numbers of non-traditional students in higher education since the 1990s. This is linked to the widening participation and inclusive education (IE) drives (Dearing 1997; DfEE, 1999; DfES, 2001; DRC, 2006). However, students with disclosed disabilities continue to be underrepresented. The reasons are varied and complex; we may blame a dominant neoliberal ideology informing policy decisions, a lack of practitioner preparedness, regressive statements by political figures or the omission, in the original 1990s Inclusion policy debate, of the link between the politics of disability and special education (Armstrong, 2005). Whatever the reasons the challenges to the higher education sector remain:

▶ what are the issues for students with disabilities?
▶ what tools might be of use to enable the boundaries between tutor and student to be transgressed?
▶ how can a fuller account of the student as learner be arrived at and responded to by inclusive tutor practice?

Successful inclusion requires cultural changes to bring about sustainable practical changes.

Inclusive education is a transformatory process for all participants. Social justice, acceptance and promotion of diversity inform its practices. Political in nature and purpose, difference is acknowledged, critically explored and related outcomes or changes in practice regularly reviewed.

Table 8.1 Factors contributing to the continued exclusion of students with disabilities in higher education

Student decision to non-disclose, thus preventing access to support services	Gibson and Kendall, 2010
Lack of information before and during studies regarding the institution's responsibility and linked resources	Vickerman and Blundell, 2010
Lack of effective communication between university disability services and academic teams, resulting in gaps in provision	Mortimore and Crozier, 2006
The stigma of 'disability' and related disablist cultures, e.g. disablist assumptions by students and university staff	Mortimore, 2013
Inconsistent practices in academic personal tutor roles and knowledge of inclusive teaching and learning policy and provision	Jacklin and Robinson, 2007
Matters of learner identity and self-esteem impacting on academic attainment	Gibson and Kendall, 2010

Much of the research notes that whilst there are forms of provision for 'effective' learning experiences and academic outcomes, beyond the surface of institutional policy, the reality of university life for students with disabilities is one of continued exclusion and barriers to learning. This is well documented, and Table 8.1 draws on sources that highlight the factors contributing to the continued exclusion of students with disabilities from university.

Madriaga (2007) alludes to practices of disablism within education due to a culture steeped in modernist education practices and practitioner and student assumptions that 'difference' equals limitation. One of my students confirmed this when she reflected on her dyslexia:

'Although I call it a learning difficulty I am quite passionate that it's been created because of the educational system.'

First-year student, BA Education Studies

Many students with disability have experienced inclusion and segregation in their education. The impact this has had on them as learners, in particular their self-esteem, needs to be a crucial concern for university tutors. This is something I have taken on board in my practices with students, listening to and encouraging those who, for reasons connected to a disability, have struggled to achieve. The following citations stem from first-year students I have worked with; they highlight where and how they have experienced inclusion and exclusion.

'I didn't know what the term dyslexia was then, it didn't come to light until the end of secondary school, the last year of my A-levels. I used to cry quite a lot, I got frustrated no one would understand.'

'Tutors might not be aware of disabilities or individual student learning needs.'

'It helped having a contact on the course, a personal tutor you felt was approachable, someone that you could actually share your concerns with, somebody you felt understood and responded positively to your needs.'

'In the small groups at university there is this connectedness with other students and you get to know them as friends and feel more secure in sharing things.'

'The first university I went to was just horrific, from sorting out my student loans coming in the post, finding that really difficult. I was lucky as I was with my parents because I did get support through that, but I found the whole process really confusing, to moving up there, to just being given a bundle of paper in your halls, it was just so overwhelming.'

'It was freshers' week and everyone was out bonding and I was still trying to read my map and get myself around. I came home at Christmas I was working literally 6 in the morning until 10 o'clock at night on Christmas Day and I just remember getting really upset and I was like I can't and I don't want to go back and I withdrew.'

'I think some of the student reps we were introduced to on the first day, one of them had a disability, and she always said that if I had any problems I could come to her, that has really helped.'

The 'social' aspect of their lives as students is all-important (Gibson and Kendall, 2010; Gibson, 2012). In particular, positive social interaction with peers and tutors and finding themselves as learners within an institution where the culture does not stigmatise disability is integral to their abilities to achieve and enjoy university. The importance of friendship circles offering support for students with disabilities has been noted by other academics (Jacklin and Robinson, 2007). Other important aspects are working in small student groups, which encourages and enables confidence building, and meeting, and being supported by, student representatives from their programme at the early stages of their studies, ideally during induction week.

▶ Tools for inclusive practice

Listening to my students, working closely with our university's 'Disability Assist'[20] service and carrying out research on an Higher Education Academy Education Subject Centre project, 'Exploring transitions to Higher Education for students with identified disabilities' (HEA, 2011a), has enabled me to change my practices and also encourage change in those of others. When considering professional development for tutors in the area of supporting students with disabilities I recommend the work of Grenier (2010). She argues (p. 387):

> 'difference, like nature, calls forth possibilities for developing transformative relationships'.

▶ Recommendations for enabling inclusive education

Personal tutors, working with students who have disclosed disability, need to begin with the question, 'how has education as a learning experience been for you?' The open-endedness of the question allows for the student to draw on what has been most profound for them and to talk about the positive and negative in their education life. There is, I believe, a need for educationalists to develop fuller and more critical insights into the education stories of learners with disabilities, to consider linked student self-esteem issues and from this reflect on their teaching practices (Gibson and Kendall, 2010).

Recommendations for practices that engender inclusive teaching and learning, drawn from my experiences and from the voices of my students (Gibson and Kendall, 2010), are outlined below. Established as a fundamental part of a BA degree programme in Education, they aim to enable positive and effective education for all my students.

▶ The need for students to receive information about university policy on 'Disability and SEN' and related services in advance of induction week.
▶ The importance of students with disability having a named contact or personal tutor whom they trust and can turn to with questions or concerns as and when they arise.
▶ The need to ensure all lecturers and tutors are clear on the particular learning needs of students and that information is relayed in confidence and in advance of term.
▶ The benefit of 'Disability Assist' services having a high profile within the university's student services.

▶ The benefit of students meeting course representatives in induction week.

▶ The benefit of having a Virtual Learning Environment (VLE) where lecturers ensure that PowerPoints and additional reading material are made available.

▶ The role of personal tutor being understood as essential within student learning. *Plymouth University's Seven Steps to Effective Personal Tutoring* is an example of such practice.[21]

▶ Diverse approaches to assessment, with noted alternative arrangements in place where necessary.

▶ Regular staff continuing professional development on the matter of 'disability', to encourage and support understanding of the issues experienced by students, challenge negative social attitudes and enable a professional grasp of the complexities that exist in our learning spaces for those with disability.

▶ Conclusion

Factors such as peer relationships, tutor relationships and institutional practices and culture have a key hold on whether students with disabilities are enabled or disabled from academic progression (Gibson, 2012: 366):

> 'One does not exist in isolation, and learning requires more than the development and growth in understanding of subject knowledge ... the research highlights the positive impact of friendships, peer support networks, significant education contacts and studying in an environment where the culture promotes diverse learning.'

Through engaging with the voices of our learners and working to understand the various constraints they experience, a move forward emphasising the importance of the personal tutor role may encourage more meaningful inclusive education practices in university.

PART 2
Learning differently

Approaches to teaching	69
Teaching difficult topics	97
Assessment	120
International issues	142

9 Designs on learning: the role of cross-university collaborative undergraduate research symposia

Kirsten Hardie (NTF 2004) *in association with Annie Grove-White*

Keywords: *collaboration, research poster, undergraduate symposium, writing, dissertation, cross-discipline, theory/practice divide*

Kirsten Hardie, Associate Professor at the Arts University at Bournemouth, is a graphic design historian and cultural theorist, who works internationally across disciplines in research areas which include notions of taste and design (including a passion for the investigation of all things flocked); creative pedagogic practice, including role play; and teaching without talking. Her activities include External Examinerships, peer review and collaborative project work. She is the current Chair of the Committee of the Association of National Teaching Fellows.

This essay considers the value of an undergraduate research symposium as an annual cross-institutional collaborative initiative that aims to develop and celebrate students' dissertation work. In particular it considers the research poster as an important learning tool. It discusses the BA (Hons) Graphic Design symposia that make more meaningful and successful the dissertation's progress towards completion. It considers how problem-based learning and collaborative learning methodologies (Dillenbourg, 1999) create 'structured interactions' (Dillenbourg, 2002) where students work collaboratively as a community of practice (Wenger, 1998b). It provides a flexible model that can easily be applied to other disciplines, in a single or cross-disciplinary manner.

▶ Undergraduate research

The undergraduate dissertation has the potential to provide students with the highpoint of their research experience. In Art and Design Higher Education (A&DHE) the dissertation can inform a student's studio practice and can provide students with an opportunity to produce work of which they are rightly proud. For some, however, the experience may be very different, leading to frustration and disappointment.

Appreciating the value of research and critical thinking and the development of an ability to communicate and exchange ideas are central to a good university experience. Students should experience learning through, and about, research and ideally should be active stakeholders in a research community in which their appreciation of research mirrors that of their lecturers. However, students' participation in, and exposure to, a research culture varies across institutions. Healey and Jenkins (2009) identify the different ways that a student may participate in research activity and make distinct the extent to which an approach may be mainly staff-focused, with students regarded as the audience, or student-focused, where they are considered as participants (Figure 9.1).

Healey and Jenkins assert that currently too much learning and teaching exists and in which students do not consider themselves as active partici-

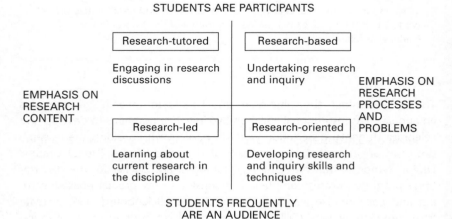

Figure 9.1 The nature of undergraduate research and inquiry (Healey and Jenkins, 2009)

pants in a research culture. They argue that programmes should address this issue by 'recasting their understanding of "student-centred" ... learning', actively bringing undergraduate students into the world of university research. Importantly for this study, they advocate building formative and summative research opportunities for undergraduates such that they 'retrace and register how academic staff develop and disseminate their own research or learning in their own discipline or professional area' (Healey and Jenkins, 2009: 28). This latter activity, they suggest, can take the form of undergraduate research journals, student research conferences and networks, broadcasts and exhibitions.

Dissemination of results is an integral part of the research process. Events such as symposia can enhance the dissertation experience and provide valuable opportunities for students to advance their research. In particular it offers 'a rare platform on which to test out ideas and celebrate hard-won findings with a receptive and empathetic audience' (Edge, 2009). As this essay explains, this approach encourages students to become stakeholders and co-owners of such events. In this way, we demonstrate that students are both participants and audience who are learning and extending their research content as well as developing their research processes and problems, with minimal staff direction.

The Undergraduate Research Symposium '*Designs on Research*'[1] is an annual collaborative project that involves Graphic Design staff and students from the Arts University Bournemouth (AUB), Cardiff School of Art and Design (CSAD) (2009–11) and Coventry University (2011). Students are invited to present short papers at themed sessions chaired by staff from both studio practice and theory (contextual studies) and to display a research poster at the symposium. Guidelines on how to present and produce posters are given in advance. In addition to this, a guest design professional is invited to participate. This establishes the symposium as a valid professional and academic event, and bestows a value and recognition of the student contributions beyond the confines of the university into the professional design world.

Building such dissemination opportunities into the curriculum at a mid-point in the dissertation's progress is shown by our research to provide a crucial opportunity for formative assessment to occur. It encourages students to clarify for themselves to what they are aspiring and to communicate that to their peers. Presentations and posters provide ideal formative opportunities for students to give peer feedback and exchange ideas that progress their work towards its final summative assessment.

▶ Writing in Art, Design and Media

We have developed the symposium in our attempt to ease the challenges students face with the dissertation. We believe that writing can be a dynamic and shared experience and we agree with Clarke's observation that writing should be taught 'not as static, nor as an isolated, individual activity, but as a social practice that is as malleable and contextual as artistic media' (Clarke, 2007: 8).

A&DHE has long recognised the writing tensions experienced by many students. Orr, Blythman and Mullin (2006) identified that students compared writing with 'being painfully constipated; pulling teeth; having brain surgery'. Writing-PAD (Writing Purposefully in Art and Design),[2] the network that aims 'to explore and develop the notion of thinking through writing as a parallel to visual discourse in art and design practice', encourages staff 'to collaborate in order to better understand the writing needs of their students'. It identified that some learners face specific challenges and commented:

> 'A surprising number of A&D students are dyslexic and often feel alienated by a writing culture that diverts or inhibits their practice-centred fluency of thought.'

Tension exists where students preferred learning that sits within a practice context – a practice preference. As Orr et al. (2006) noted, 'not surprisingly, students are more personally involved in the Art and Design side of their work than the writing side', and Cunliffe-Charlesworth (2008) observed: 'many art and design students who are highly articulate in verbal reasoning and visual thinking are frustrated in their attempts to transfer ideas into a written format that complies with the university academic requirements'.

Thus the dissertation is often viewed as an arduous task. Through the symposia we try to ease tensions and make research and writing more exciting and explicit through design.

▶ Posters

The research poster, central to our symposia, is used as an active, tangible vehicle to encourage students to communicate their ideas concisely and directly. The visual representation of research involves students' visual literacy skills to produce visual metaphors that summarise research. The poster operates as bridge to help students cross from one point in their learning to the next. We encourage students to communicate in a form that they find more pleasing and more comfortable. The poster's creation is advised jointly by studio and contextual staff to help bridge any perceived practice and theory divide and helps to reinforce the symbiotic relationship of all skills involved. Students share their work with staff teams, not just their individual supervisors. To add incentive and accolade to the posters' design, students judge the posters and prizes are awarded to the best three.

▶ Results

We have hosted a number of symposia reciprocally to create 'communities of common purpose' (Kilpatrick, Barrett and Jones, 2003). Students have evaluated the events (Arts University at Bournemouth and Cardiff School of Art and Design in 2009 and 2010) and the majority have identified that the symposium helps them to develop their work. For example students commented:

'Preparing ... a PowerPoint presentation helped with essay structure – I may continue to develop my essay through this media – individual concepts and links become clear.'

'Preparing for potential questions about my work helped me define and understand key themes of my dissertation. It was a challenge but a good one.'

Students have confirmed the value of the poster, for example:

'Breaking a whole dissertation down into such a small amount of text pushed me to seek out what was the most important, it was clarification.'

'[It was] hugely beneficial as it brought a focus and structure to my study ... allowed me to identify my topic more clearly and structure it better for easier routes of research.'

'I came up with my final title from doing my poster. It helped me simplify what I thought was a long-winded essay.'

'Working in a visual way helped, as [it] is a preferred way to work.'

whilst another commented that the poster was:

'Good for portfolio.'

Students' responses also confirmed that presentations were important, observing:

'It helped me understand how to focus lines of enquiry within my written work.'

'Good to present as you view it [dissertation] from a different perspective, and the descriptions helped with the words used in the essay.'

'It gave me confidence and experience presenting in front of an audience.'

The energetic response 'Absolutely brilliant actually, made me think that everyone would have benefited from doing a presentation' was particularly heartening.

Few students were critical, though one student responded:

'Interesting, not helpful for my dissertation – helpful in getting me to think about design.'

Student feedback has developed the event, for example the suggestions that the symposia should be longer and could 'Possibly [have a] pre-social event to help meet new people and network further' resulted in a two-day event with social activities. This facilitated immediate happy collaboration and subsequent enduring friendships. Our students recognise that their experiences and interests are shared and that a common ground offers opportunities beyond the focus of the dissertation. The student's recommendation that 'Next time maybe have group sessions in the afternoon whereby students with similar or linking topics can then discuss and debate their work. In turn you will have smaller, more focused groups and it will be less intimidating' subsequently enhanced the event.

The symposia model is now used across a number of courses. At the 2012 AUB symposium Graphic students and staff at from an institution in South East Asia joined in activities via Skype.

▶ Conclusion

This model, a powerful collaborative learning experience, can operate as a vital tool in staff research and scholarship as lecturers can work cross-institutionally to develop their understanding and provide greater support of student learning. The event has improved student grades and student confidence. It gives life to research that otherwise would be confined to the pages of a dissertation read by few. The presentation of work open to public scrutiny makes students more responsible for their study. The research poster draws both a curious and critical eye to student work in a way perhaps other conventional learning and teaching methods simply do not. The traditional approaches for students to present their research within a peer group or to a defined audience, such as the seminar, studio critique or presentation, offer tried and tested methods that usually require that the researcher speak. The poster, by comparison, must communicate its content in the absence of its author.

Whilst research events for postgraduate students are common, and help students disseminate and test their research amongst their peers, events for undergraduates are unusual. The British Conference of Undergraduate Research provides an important example and we believe that institutional symposia can provide powerful learning and teaching experiences where cross-discipline networks can flourish and student work is advanced.

Annie Grove-White, Teaching Fellow, University of Wales, is working with colleagues to establish an All-Wales Centre for Creative Pedagogy in Art and Design. Her research in learning and teaching in art and design includes the effectiveness and value of audio assessment, and how heuristic tasks can promote student creativity.

10 Innovative approaches to learning design: harnessing new technologies for learning

Gráinne Conole (NTF 2012)

Keywords: *learning design, e-learning, course features, course map, activity profile*

Gráinne Conole is Professor of Learning Innovation at the University of Leicester. Her research interests include the use, integration and evaluation of Information and Communication Technologies and e-learning and the impact of technologies on organisational change. She regularly blogs on www.e4innovation.com and has published or presented over 1000 conference proceedings, workshops and articles, including in the use and evaluation of learning technologies. Her latest book is entitled *Designing for Learning in an Open World*.

New technologies offer a plethora of ways in which learners can curate and manage content, and communicate and collaborate with peers. Social and participatory media enable learners to be part of a rich ecology of peer learners, potentially distributed worldwide. Mobile learning is now a reality through smartphones and tablets, meaning that learners can truly learn anywhere and at any time. Virtual worlds and serious games provide rich authentic environments that can foster approaches to learning such as role-play and problem-based learning.

Despite this, there is a gap between the potential and the reality. Teachers and learners lack the necessary digital literacy skills (Jenkins, 2009a) to be able to harness the affordances (Conole and Dyke, 2004) of new technologies. Based upon work developed as part of the OU Learning Design Initiative[3] and the University of Leicester's *Carpe Diem* model, this essay will describe a new learning design methodology,[4] which has been created to help teachers make more informed design decisions that are pedagogically grounded and make effective use of technologies to foster different pedagogical approaches. These include:

- a range of learning design representations, which:
  - guide the design process
  - make the design explicit and hence sharable with others
- harnessing social media to promote discussion and engagement with peers and in particular use of a specialised social networking site for sharing and discussing designs[5]
- a range of workshops created and evaluated as part of our 7Cs of learning design framework[6] (Armellini, 2012; Conole, 2012).

Learning design

Designing for learning is arguably the key challenge facing education today (Conole, 2013a). Education operates in a complex external environment, with increasing financial constraints and challenges to traditional institutions, for example, as a result of the emergence of free Massive Open Online Courses (MOOCs). Furthermore, with increasing tuition fees, learners are thinking more critically about their choice of institution and their expectations of a high-quality learning experience. Despite the potential technologies offer in supporting learning, they are not being used extensively in higher education, often because teachers lack the necessary digital literacy skills (Jenkins, 2006, 2009a).

The 7Cs of learning design framework

The 7Cs of learning design framework illustrate the key stages involved in the design process, from initial conceptualisation of a learning intervention through to trialling and evaluating it in a real learning context (Figure 10.1). The framework consists of the following stages:

1 **Conceptualise**: What is the vision for the learning intervention, who is it being designed for, what is the essence of the intervention, what pedagogical approaches are used?
2 **Capture**: What Open Educational Resources are being used and what other resources need to be developed?

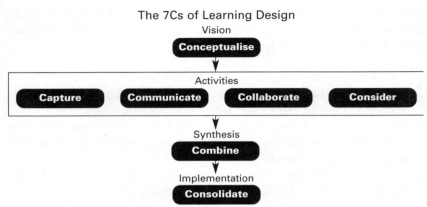

http://www2.le.ac.uk/projects/oer//oers/beyond-distance-research-alliance/7Cs-toolkit

Figure 10.1 The 7Cs of Learning Design framework

3 **Create**: What is the nature of the learning intervention the learners will engage with? What kinds of learning activities will the learners engage with?

4 **Communicate**: What types of communication will the learners be using?

5 **Collaborate**: What types of collaboration will be learners be doing?

6 **Consider**: What forms of reflection and demonstration of learning are included? Are the learning outcomes mapped to the activities and assessment elements of the learning intervention?

7 **Consolidate**: How effective is the design? Do the different elements of the design work together?

For each of the seven stages we have developed a series of conceptual designs, building on our work and that of others in the field. Three of these are described here: the 'course features' view, the 'course map' view and the 'pedagogy profile' view.

The first is the course features view, which is associated with the '*conceptualise*' element of the 7Cs framework. This enables teachers to think about the overall essence of the learning intervention and how it will be delivered and supported. Participants interact with a pack of cards around the elements shown in Table 10.1.

Once the course features view has been completed, teachers can fill in the course views map, which considers what '*Guidance and Support*' is provided, what '*Content and Activities*' the learners will engage with, what forms of '*Communication and Collaboration*' are included, and the types of '*Reflection and Demonstration*'. This includes details of which tools and resources are

Table 10.1 Using the 'course features' view

Principles	What is the essence of the course, what are the core principles? For example cultural or aesthetic aspects may be important, the intervention may have a practical focus or be about applying theory to practice, it may be based on a professional community of peers or it might be important that the intervention includes elements of serendipity (Figure 10.2).
Pedagogical approaches	What pedagogies are involved? For example is the intervention based on constructivist principles, is it problem or inquiry-based?
Guidance and support	What guidance and support are provided? For example in terms of a website or module handout, or access to study materials (Figure 10.3).
Content and activities	What kinds of activities are included and what content will the learners be using?
Reflection and demonstration	Are the learners actively encouraged to reflect at key points? How are they demonstrating their learning? What forms of diagnostic, formative and summative assessment are included?
Communication and collaboration	How are the learners interacting with each other and their tutors? Are there any elements of collaboration included?

associated with each of the elements and any notes such as details of pre-requisites required or description of the philosophy underpinning the learning intervention; for example it might be that peer interaction is deemed important or that learners are expected to generate their own materials.

The third example is the pedagogy or activity profile view. This enables teachers to map the types of activities the learners will engage with. There

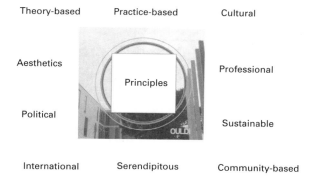

Figure 10.2 The principles associated with the learning intervention

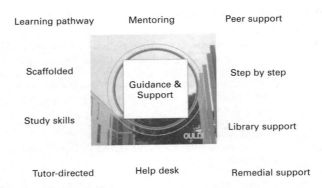

Figure 10.3 Guidance and support

are six types, as shown in Figure 10.4: assimilative activities (reading, view-ing, listening), information handling, communicative, productive, experien-tial (such as drill and practice exercises) and adaptive (such as modelling or simulation). The profile also indicates the amount of time spent on assess-ment activities. The profile is available as an online flash widget.[7]

Storyboarding is a well-established approach to visually representing a temporal sequence of activities. For example, it is used in the film industry to represent the key sequences involved in a plot. Storyboarding is used in our Learning Design work, as a means of representing the overall design. It

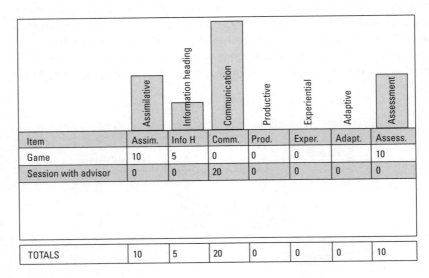

Item	Assim.	Info H	Comm.	Prod.	Exper.	Adapt.	Assess.
Game	10	5	0	0	0		10
Session with advisor	0	0	20	0	0	0	0
TOTALS	10	5	20	0	0	0	10

Figure 10.4 An example of a completed pedagogy profile

enables the teacher/designer to see how the different elements of the design process fit together. It consists of a timeline, with the activities included in the design along the middle. Learning outcomes are mapped to the assessment elements. Above the activities any inputs to the individual activities are included: for example reading materials or podcasts. Below the activities outputs are listed, for example contribution to a discussion forum or creation of a blog post.

▷ Evaluation

The framework is aimed at both teachers who want support and guidance to improve their design practice and those staff who provide institutional support to improve learning and teaching and promote more effective use of technologies (i.e. instructional designers, learning designers, educational developers and librarians). It has been trialled in a range of contexts.

The JISC-funded SPEED project[8] enabled a series of face-to-face workshops, and synchronous sessions to four UK institutions. In addition, workshops have been held at a number of international conferences. The evaluation consisted of observations of the workshops and gathering of data from participants around four main questions: which three words best describe the workshop, what did you like, how could the workshop be improved and what action plans would participants do as a result of participation? Overall the evaluation was positive, and participants found the workshops engaging, useful and even inspiring. They found that the learning design activities enabled them to think beyond content to learning activities and the learner experience. They enjoyed the mix of micro-level designs to create learning activities and the ability to think of the learning intervention at a holistic level.

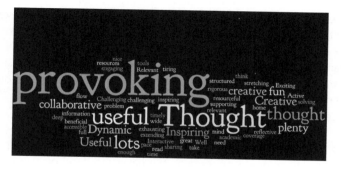

Figure 10.5 Three words used to describe the workshop

To give an indication of the evaluation comments, data from a workshop run with 25 participants at the ASCILITE 2012 conference are provided. Figure 10.5 shows a word cloud of participants' descriptions of the workshop.

Participants particularly liked:

▶ the wide coverage and the rich set of resources provided
▶ the fact that the workshop had a strong focus on pedagogy and being able to see the bigger picture in terms of course design
▶ the course features card set (this was particularly popular).

Interestingly, this group wanted more on the theoretical underpinnings to the ideas presented.

In terms of action plans, participants stated that they wanted to explore the conceptual views within their own courses and that they would like to share these with colleagues in their own institution.

A researcher at the Institute of Learning Innovation has undertaken an extensive evaluation of the use of the 7Cs framework as part of the JISC-funded SPEED projects, which involved running a series of Learning Design workshops with four UK institutions (Derby, Liverpool John Moores, London South Bank and Northampton universities). The following quotes, from this evaluation, demonstrate that the 7Cs model enables teachers to think differently about their design and to make more pedagogically informed choices:

'We made a big breakthrough. We have achieved the insight about the need to structure it as a course, an online course, and not just simply as a set of learning activities plus integrated resources.'

'The visual nature of the tools and the quick and easy way that one could use it without too much elaborative training ... help stimulate us to look at the course in a different way, in a natural and creative way even if we didn't see all the little links right upfront.'

'I wanted to have my thinking challenged with regard to course design and development and I definitely left reflecting and questioning our unit's current approach and have some good tools and approaches to pilot with course design teams.'

'It's a way of freeing your mind and putting all the ideas of all the people in the course team down somewhere, not having to be so prescriptive. It was just a much freer and [more] creative experience than getting the learning

outcomes and writing them as active verbs, and getting in at a granular
level. It was quite sort of a liberating thing to just have everybody move
components around and say, "Do you know I really like all these features.
I'd like to do some problem-based learning. I'd like to do peer-review".'

The evaluation indicates that the framework is welcomed and that the
conceptual designs enable teachers to rethink their design practice to create
more engaging learning interventions for their students. The conceptual
views can also be used with student learners, to give them an indication of
the nature of the courses they are undertaking. The activity profile is particularly useful as it enables learners to see the mix of different types of learning activities they will engage with. We aim to continue to refine the
elements of the framework. In particular more work is needed around the
'consider' and 'consolidate' elements, including rubrics for assessment and
evaluation of the effectiveness of the design.

▶ Conclusion

This essay has described a new learning design framework and illustrated
some of our conceptual learning designs. The 7Cs Learning Design framework provides a holistic framework, covering all the stages of design from the
initial conceptualisation and vision for the design through to implementation
and evaluation in a real learning context. The conceptual views associated
with each of the 7Cs help guide teachers' design practices and also enable
them to make the designs more explicit. This is important because it helps
teachers think beyond content to activities and the ultimate learning experience. The design representations can also be shared with learners.

11 Scaffolding problem-based learning

Derek Raine (NTF 2004)

Keywords: *problem-based learning, research-based learning, scaffolding, interdisciplinarity, natural sciences, teaching fellows*

> Derek Raine is Professor of Interdisciplinary Science and Director, the πCETL and the Centre for Interdisciplinary Science at the University of Leicester. His research has included astrophysics, quantum physics and complex systems. As Director of Teaching he introduced problem-based learning into physics and what is now called the 'flipped lecture'. He was awarded the Bragg Medal of the Institute of Physics and is an MBE for contributions to Science Education.

The leading journal *Science* regularly publishes articles extolling the virtues of problem-based learning (PBL) in colleges and universities.[9] The underlying message is that students learn science best by doing science; that is through engagement with the research process. Furthermore we are constantly reminded of the increasing importance of interdisciplinarity in scientific research[10] (O'Neill, 2011). Nevertheless, very little of either the research process or the cross-fertilisation between disciplines has found its way into undergraduate curricula in the UK. One of the aims of the Physics Innovations Centre for Excellence in Teaching and Learning (PCETL) at Leicester was to bring these two aspects together in a fully integrated PBL programme in natural sciences.[11] This essay charts the progress over eight years towards scaffolding this PBL programme.

PBL is 'a student-centred method of teaching in which students learn by investigating real-world problems and, working in groups, seek out the tools necessary to solve them' (Raine and Symons, 2012: 39). Because students find parallel PBL modules difficult to time-manage, our programme is delivered through five sequential core modules per year. The programme covers key topics in biological sciences, chemistry and physics, with some earth sciences. Each module is based around an interdisciplinary problem that integrates two or more of the disciplines. The content and delivery are entirely new and unique to the interdisciplinary science programme, not shared with other science courses.

The core content was decided by academic staff, choosing topics in contemporary research, which they felt it most important or inspiring for our students to encounter. Starting from a blank sheet proved enormously motivating for the academic staff. This process determined the prerequisites within each discipline that could be built into problems deployed in the earlier years. There are additional non-PBL support courses in computing, laboratory practicals and professional skills. Mathematics is taught by a version of the Keller plan (Keller, 1968; Kulik, Kulik and Carmichael, 1974), which requires that students demonstrate competency in each topic before progressing (Raine et al., 2010). The programme currently accepts around 20 students per year.

Meeting the challenges of PBL

Despite the enthusiasm of its proponents, PBL can present a challenge for some students (Wiznia et al., 2012). Particular issues we have found include surface learning, lack of pre-session preparation and an inappropriate division of learning within groups through excessive focus on the group assessment scheme for the problem.

Surface learning can arise for a number of reasons: we traced it to a lack of inquisitiveness on the part of students once they had found a web search term that yielded a paragraph or so vaguely relevant to the problem. Of course, this could be corrected in facilitation sessions, but not without the waste of a good deal of time between meetings. Increasing the number of facilitation sessions to one per day (O'Grady et al., 2012) did not alleviate the problem, because students often felt too rushed for detailed preparation. We have settled on two facilitation sessions per week, one of two hours and one lasting one hour, using the floating facilitator model (Duch, Allen and Groh, 2001) where a single facilitator moves between groups.

If groups divide the learning issues inappropriately, students end up covering only a subset of the learning objectives. For a 'pure' PBL programme this may be of no consequence: basically in these implementations there is no core syllabus. Although we encourage free investigation within modules, for us to remove the fairly extensive requirement for core learning would be a step too far. Instead, we now address this issue by setting assigned questions each week, which are marked and which form the basis of a weekly class tutorial. Thus, students contributing to the PBL group work from a common core of knowledge.

To address the lack of class preparation, and to guide students to the depth of knowledge they require, we set pre-session tasks in the form of questions for discussion, recommended reading and detailed learning objectives (running to around 60 pages for the programme as a whole). This may seem some way from a pure form of PBL, but we regard it as embodying the basic concept of PBL: the student as researcher, adapting the relationship between postgraduate student and supervisor to the undergraduate context.

The final aspect of our scaffolding, which was fully introduced at the start of the 2010–11 academic year, was the systematic use of dedicated teaching fellows as facilitators, based on the practice in the 'iSci' programme at McMaster University, Canada. We currently have one teaching fellow in each of the core disciplines, replacing ad-hoc arrangements of multiple postgraduate demonstrators for the different topics in the programme.

▶ Evaluation

In the course of its development we have twice had the programme externally evaluated.[12] We therefore have a range of qualitative data to evaluate the changes, although one must caution that all of our data are based on small numbers of students.

> [Action on feedback] has included changes to the facilitation arrangements, specifically the change from a broad group to a more limited set of continuing facilitators, partly at least in response to concerns about the variability of facilitation styles. The view [amongst students] was that the new approach will lead to ... a stronger sense of how to support [students] in the PBL process.
>
> Unpublished Report by the Centre for Recording Achievement
> (29 July 2010)

We also have quantitative data from students who entered the programme in 2009–10 who will have experienced the change in facilitation. This is shown in Figure 11.1: Year 2 marks are plotted against Year 1 marks for this cohort. Expected marks were determined from the average marks of cohorts prior to the introduction of scaffolding. Actual marks are those from students when scaffolding was introduced in Year 2.

There is a statistically significant increase in Year 2 marks compared to Year 1 for the target cohort relative to previous years. This suggests that the changes were effective.

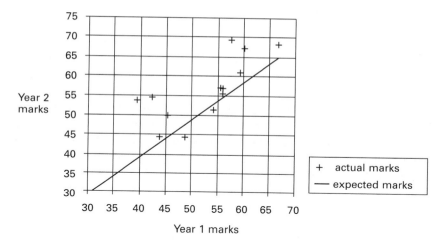

Figure 11.1 Average Year 2 marks for PBL modules plotted against Year 1 marks for the 2010–11 cohort. The straight line is the expected relationship based on the average relationship from previous years

In order to establish possible reasons for this we conducted two focus groups. For the arrangement of facilitation sessions:

'I prefer it, the way they worked it out is we have the two-hour session on the Tuesday so you've got the weekend and the Monday to do the reading for the longer session and then just the Wednesday you do the reading for the hour session; I think that works quite well.'

For the use of dedicated teaching fellows:

'There's been a change since the first year where the PhD students that were there were just there to make sure we'd do the work rather than assisting and facilitating, whereas now they'll prompt you towards an answer if you're not quite getting it.'

On the fear that recommended reading would constrain investigation, we found that students often deviated from the suggested reading and generally recognised that material is available from a wide range of sources. They also found the suggested discussion questions useful for focusing their reading and the intended learning outcomes helpful for their revision.

▶ Wider implications

PBL is often thought to be highly resource-intensive and therefore, in the UK, often thought of as a niche activity. However, for very small numbers of students PBL requires fewer staff resources than a conventionally lectured course, since lectures can be replaced by fewer facilitation sessions. For very large classes, it is equally obvious that lecture programmes are more efficient in the delivery of assessed material. If one is simply interested in costs, the argument is therefore about where the break-even point is. Accurate figures are difficult to obtain, but our data appear to show that our costs per student are no greater than those in a Physics class of around 100 students. There are issues, however, of quality and the effective division of labour amongst academic staff that, I believe, should in any case make our structure of wider interest for higher education.

First, there is the enthusiasm of the teaching fellows who are trained teachers in higher education and for whom teaching is a passion, not a diversion from their discipline research. The continuity provided by their engagement comes close to replicating the benefits of the Oxbridge tutorial system. Second, there is the enthusiasm of around 60 academic staff. Many do just a single session, which is often voluntary (in the sense that it is not included in their workload, although their departments are recompensed). Their session often provides them with the opportunity to engage students with their research without negatively impacting on it.

Finally, there is a focus on minimising recurrent resources in favour of 'capital' investment. Typical module documents run to over 100 pages. This is sustainable because they are deployed electronically (as pdfs and in Kindle versions) and can include links to multimedia resources (many developed for the programme) in addition to the text.

Not everything works well. In particular the structure does not articulate well with the working patterns of students who maximise their social activities during term and their studies during vacations (Edmunds, 2009).

Nevertheless, we leave the last word to a student:

> 'There's been a few job interviews that I've gone to and they've been really interested in what I've been doing; I-Science has been a unique selling point for me.'

The programme development has been supported through Higher Education Funding Council for England (HEFCE) grants, partly in conjunction with the Institute of Physics and through HE STEM. I am grateful to Dr Sarah Gretton who assisted in the preparation of this article.

12 Developing subject-specific knowledge, digital creativity and soft skills: a games-based approach to teaching and learning

Rachel McCrindle (NTF 2012)

Keywords: games-based learning, ludic engagement, software engineering, technical knowledge, soft skills, digital creativity, transferability, teamwork

Rachel McCrindle is Professor of Computer and Human Interaction and Director of Enterprise in the School of Systems Engineering, University of Reading. She has won a number of national awards for her Knowledge Transfer projects (KTP), as well as the KTP Academic Excellence Award (2010), the Higher Education Academy Engineering Teaching Award (2010) and a University of Reading Teaching Fellowship in 2012.

The aim of this essay is to describe and reflect upon a games-based assignment that engages students in the learning process such that they improve their technical knowledge, enhance their creative thinking and develop their soft skills in areas such as teamwork and communication. The assignment, which runs for 20 weeks, is undertaken as part of a compulsory 20-credit software engineering module taken by all students on degree programmes in the School of Systems Engineering at the University of Reading. Over 1200 students have participated in the activity over an eight-year period. Although this approach has been applied in the context of software engineering, the underlying pedagogy and the activities undertaken can be transferred to other disciplines.

▶ **Software engineering**

Software engineering is concerned with developing and maintaining soft-ware systems in order that they satisfy user requirements, behave reliably and efficiently, and are developed and maintained within allocated budgets and planned time scales. As such the subject covers not only the technical aspects of designing and developing software systems, but also associated management issues, such as planning, budgeting and quality assurance. During their degrees in computer science, information technology, cybernet-ics and electronic engineering-related disciplines and while on industrial placement, students programme their own software, integrate software components into larger systems, or develop mechanical or electronic systems within which software is a core component. It is therefore important that they all have knowledge of how to engineer software.

▶ **Rationale for using a games-based approach**

The declarative knowledge for the module is provided by a traditional lecture course of two lectures per week where the theoretical aspects of the subject are covered. The point at which to teach software engineering is a classic chicken-and-egg situation – it is important for the students to have knowl-edge of software engineering prior to their need to use it (in later parts of their degree work, while on their placement year, or when they graduate). However, until they have used it, they often do not fully appreciate the importance and relevance of its procedures and practices. Additionally, until they experience it for themselves in real-world situations, despite best efforts at making lectures interesting through incorporation of case studies, cartoons, videos, real-world examples and industrial speakers, etc., many first-year students find it quite a 'dry' subject and potential engagement issues arise. I therefore wanted to introduce an assignment that would grab the attention of the students, stimulate their creative thinking and make the learning of software engineering more fun and engaging, whilst simultane-ously raising their proficiency in the subject from the declarative knowledge of the lectures to deeper levels of learning encompassing comprehension, application, analysis, synthesis and evaluation (Bloom, 1956).

The students work in teams (of 4–6 members) to develop a board game that will teach novice software engineers or first-year students 'software engi-neering'. The assignment combines the ludic[13] enjoyment of games with more serious design issues and innovative ways of incorporating software engineering concepts into their games. Within an educational context, ludic engagement has been shown to blur the traditionally separate academic theories of learning and theories of play into creative, immersive and engaging environments for learning (Selander, 2008) such that participants are motivated by curiosity, exploration and reflection rather than the externally defined tasks (Gaver et al., 2004).

There has been considerable interest and success in the use of serious games and game-based learning in recent years (McClarty et al., 2012), however these tend to centre on virtual worlds and electronic games (de Freitas, 2006; Connolly, 2011). The focus of this assessment is a board game rather than a programmed game as the physical nature of the game makes the product more tangible, the process stages more defined, and progress against the specification more visible. It also ensures that ambition is not restricted by the programming ability of the students, nor the time restrictions imposed by a single learning module. This approach also promotes transferability across disciplines, as no specialist programming knowledge is needed to develop the game.

Although software is not being produced, all the nuances of programming and the technical problems that might arise during the coding process can still be incorporated into the game play. Whilst it could be argued that a programmed game would be more realistic, it would be impossible in practice for the students to produce the level of design complexity of their physical games in software at this stage of their course. However, some students do elect to develop digital versions of their games as final-year projects.

▶ The activities undertaken

A key goal of the work is to convey to the students that software engineering is a multi-skilled real-world process and hence, in addition to learning life-cycle stages/activities and management principles/practices, they also develop their range of 'softer' key skills (teamwork, communication, time management, etc.). These 'softer' skills are examined in combination with their software engineering knowledge and digital creativity in a series of ten group deliverables that are both formative and summative; and a final individual critique of their work and the effectiveness of the assignment as a pedagogic activity.

The team deliverables encompass:

▶ Written reports for assessment of skills, project management, risk analysis, resource planning, games design and description of how they have incorporated software engineering into their games.

▶ Physical implementation of the board game and its associated playing pieces and cards.

▶ A digitally created board design, game manual, poster and self-running presentation/video/animation explaining how software engineering has been embedded in their game.

The assignment promotes learning on two levels: (1) the students experience the engineering process themselves and (2) they review their lecture notes and textbooks in order to embed the software engineering principles into their game. This helps promote an ethos of independent learning, encourages students to take responsibility for expanding their own learning and enables them to critically examine new facts and ideas.

Throughout the process students need to understand and communicate their work to others both within and outside their teams. The teams may base their games on existing concepts, mash-ups of concepts, or offer entirely original game play. The game-based approach gives students the opportunity to be innovative and creative with their game designs, its theme, and the choice of software engineering concepts that they incorporate into their game. Designs may be linked to a subject discipline (e.g. management, robotics), to more abstract concepts (e.g. Star Wars, Super

Figure 12.1 Examples of games developed to teach software engineering to other students

Figure 12.2 Examples of posters promoting the games and demonstrating creative flair

Mario, the Muppets) or to an entirely original creation (e.g. the McCrindle case and the quest for a government contract).

In recognition of the students' engagement, hard work and achievements, an annual awards day, the SEBAs (Software Engineering Brilliance Awards), is organised whereby teams compete in front of a judging panel comprising academic and industrial members to win prizes, as well as a coveted SEBA, in categories associated with best games, posters, presentations and documentation – software engineering meets *The X-Factor*!

▶ Pedagogic practice

Underpinning the game-based approach described above are a number of pedagogic principles and models in order to support and ensure a quality learning experience and positive range of learning outcomes for the students. The assignment takes on board the 'seven principles of good practice in undergraduate education' identified by Chickering and Gamson (1987) and synthesised from a meta-analysis of 50 years of research on good teaching principles. Specifically the assessment fosters interaction between students and staff;

Figure 12.3 Waiting for the names of the SEBA winners to be announced

Figure 12.4 A SEBA

encourages interaction and collaboration between students; uses active learning techniques; provides prompt feedback; emphasises planning and timings of task; communicates high expectations and quality; and celebrates student diversity with regards to their skills, experiences and ways of learning.

By adopting a combination of project-based learning and problem-based learning (Aalborg University, 2010) students collaboratively work on complex tasks, encountering and applying the central principles and concepts of the discipline to solve given problems and challenges through hands-on activity, in a way that supports a real-world framework.

This approach has demonstrated positive outcomes in relation to student learning in areas of content knowledge, collaborative skills, engagement and motivation and critical thinking (CELL, 2009). The active and experiential learning theory of Kolb is also evident whereby knowledge is created through the transformation of experience via a cyclical model of concrete experience (do); reflective observation (observe); abstract conceptualisation (think); and active experimentation (plan); thereby allowing different learning styles to be accommodated (Kolb, 1984).

▶ **Student experiences**

Post-assignment reviews, formal assessments and lecturer observation indicate that the students engage with and enjoy the assignment, perform well in the module overall and take great pride in their work. Each year the students produce some excellent work, with games showing some great consideration of how software engineering works in practice. Some of their experiences are quoted below:

'I feel I have really learnt from this project, and although a bit stressful at times, it was very enjoyable. It has given me a real insight into the world of software engineering and team management ... I've learnt a lot from my team mates, and I think they have learnt from me.'

JM1 studying BSc Robotics

'The project enhanced my learning abilities due to the fact that I am able to understand the theory and work significantly better when put into practice kinaesthetically. The material in the lectures was brought to life with the ability to relate to the key methods and ideas of project management and software engineering to those faced in the creation of our board game.'

JM2 studying BEng Electronic Engineering and Cybernetics

'[A]nother enjoyable aspect of the project was overcoming the challenge we had set ourself by coming up with a complicated design. Once it was finished I felt a great sense of accomplishment because we had met our own specification.'

NB studying BSc Computer Science

This approach has been recognised as innovative and an example of good practice by the Higher Education Academy, by professional institutes and by industry who have applauded the approach not just for delivering technical knowledge but by further developing the soft skills of the students which they regard as being so important for employment. The work has also provided a rich experiential base for students to use when being interviewed by employers for work placements.

Transferability

The pedagogic approach of developing board games through a structured series of deliverables has excellent transferability for learning subject knowledge, developing soft skills and enhancing digital creativity to other science and technology subjects, as well as to arts- and humanities-based subjects. The process and deliverables described above can be used just as effectively to create, for example, a game about Ancient Rome, protein synthesis or the learning of a foreign language – the project, problem and process just require some imagination and modification in relation to terminology and emphasis.

Reflections

Of all the teaching and learning activities I have used during my career, this approach has been one of the most rewarding, not only in terms of its effectiveness for engaging students in the learning process but also because it has provided me with the opportunity to positively engage with students individually from the beginning of their learning experience. Interestingly, each cohort exhibits their own defining characteristics and team dynamics.

This is not to say, however, that the process is an easy one. There are challenges for both staff and students, and the activity requires a significant time investment for it to run smoothly, as well some financial and material resource for games production. Although the overall educational basis of the assignment has remained consistent, modifications have been made to the process each year, based on staff experience and student feedback. These include liaising with the disability officer to identify students who may need additional support; administering a light-touch Belbin test (2012) so students can consider the type of team player they are, as well as their likely strengths and weaknesses when working in a team; and having trial team sessions, enhanced by sweets and chocolate, prior to formalising assignment teams!

Additionally, although there is an emphasis on independent learning, the activity requires continual engagement with the student teams in terms of providing timely feedback for each deliverable, to ensure that they are functioning as they should, and for patching up the occasional team meltdown!

13 Teaching with assessment, feedback and feed-forward: using 'preflights' to assist student achievement

Brian Whalley (NTF 2008)

Keywords: learning outcomes, troublesome knowledge, sticking points, preflights, feed-forward, feedback, criterion-referenced assessment

Brian Whalley is Emeritus Professor at Queens University Belfast, where he spent most of his working life in the School of Geosciences. He is now Visiting Professor at the University of Sheffield. Although retired, he continues his research in glaciology and mountain geomorphology. He has interests in fieldwork and Technology-Enhanced Learning, is currently engaged in an 'Enhancing Fieldwork Learning' project and is a trustee of the Field Studies Council.

'Assessment for education', rather than 'examination of learning', is the core concept for teaching and learning at any level. As such, it needs to be linked to the planned learning activities and associated with stated 'learning outcomes'. Beetham (2007) defines a learning outcome as 'an identifiable change that is anticipated in a learner' and making explicit the linkages between learning activities, which includes assessment and statements of outcome. It is part of John Biggs's (2003) concept of 'constructive alignment' that can be applied to any element of teaching, such as a piece of practical work or a subject topic or a full module. Thus, there should be alignment of activities, assessment and feedback.

This essay proposes that by linking several ideas and educational devices, such as constructive alignment, criterion-referenced assessment, feedback and feed-forward, we can help, and improve, student performance.

One important approach to improving alignment is to investigate the students' needs before any summative assessment. Teaching may elicit a student comment such as, 'I'm so stupid, I just don't understand/see what you mean', and some students may be reluctant to ask for help. Various studies have shown the importance of tackling students' difficulties at an early stage in their academic journey. Paying attention to, and tackling, some of these difficulties can be addressed by way of small tasks, 'preflights', performed before a major piece of summatively assessed work.

Several ideas are used in this integration. For an activity, especially if challenging, there is likely to be a topic that presents a difficulty – troublesome knowledge, threshold knowledge, sticking points. An identified troublesome topic can be presented as a short test or exercise as a '*preflight*'. Feedback is given and this provides '*feed-forward*' before students embark upon the main task. In this way students' difficulties can be addressed before a summative assessment takes place. Indeed, students may not realise they have a problem until they are faced with it. Hence, it is best to tackle this early by building problematic items into forms of assessment.

Assessment criteria are made explicit before students perform the preflight check so that they can use their prior knowledge and results, via feedback and feed-forward, to enhance performance. The assessment criteria, transparent to the student, again help in understanding the question or problem.

▶ Threshold concepts and troublesome knowledge

A threshold concept can be considered as akin to a portal, opening up a new and previously inaccessible way of thinking about something.

(Meyer and Land, 2003)

The idea of threshold knowledge associated with threshold concepts, suggested by Meyer and Land, is often linked to Perkins's 'troublesome knowledge' (Perkins, 2006). Meyer and Land suggest that negotiating a threshold concept usually encompasses some knowledge that causes difficulties for a student, and what may be difficult for one student to understand or perform may not be for others, and usually is easy for the expert. This is especially common where students arrive at university with a wide variety of educational backgrounds. Things that might be troublesome, of the '*I can't see how you do this*' variety, may be easily overcome by demonstration or explanation, perhaps as part of peer learning. Once overcome or understood, the 'aha' moment is accessible; confidence is gained and no longer a '*sticking point*'.

▶ Just-in-time teaching and 'preflights'

The concept of just-in-time teaching (Novak et al., 1999) involves a 'preflight check' or 'warm up' before a lecture or practical session. Preflights act as a pre-assessment contributing to understanding and providing feedback, so enhancing understanding. It is in the preflight that the sticking point is tackled. A general procedure for devising and incorporating preflights into teaching might be:

▶ Identification of what sticking point is to be covered by the preflight and how it is to be accomplished by students. Preflights typically should be relatively short, perhaps 5–10 minutes. The topic selection is important and the concepts of 'troublesome knowledge' and 'sticking points' are used to help formulate the task. For some students it might not be a problem but it provides a check for both students and tutor that the sticking point is overcome.

▶ Decide how provision of 'rapid' feedback is provided, for example e-mail and Twitter can be used effectively.

▶ Establish how the preflight will be incorporated into assessment (summative or formative) in a criterion-referenced assessment scheme.

▶ Criterion referencing

Criterion referencing helps students identify what is required of them, rather than what they believe is needed, and should be made transparent to students from the outset (Rust, Price and O'Donovan, 2003), showing students not only what is needed to fulfil the task but to show where to concentrate effort.

Marks for preflight activities should be criterion-referenced, and this then becomes part of the process of informing students about desired performance and accomplishment. Using criterion referencing with preflights in this way is a form of 'feed-forward', giving students an indication in what direction they have to go and where to spend the time and effort before they start. Further discussion on my use of criterion referencing, formulating criteria via spreadsheets and e-mailing material to students, is available in Whalley and Taylor (2008).

▶ Practical implementation of preflights

This example, of the development of a poster, was used in a second-year, first-semester module on geomorphology for 70 physical geography students in which six practical tasks were to be completed. A preflight was designed and set for each task.

Step 1: Identify the sticking point. Students had not done a computer-generated poster before so they were given brief verbal instructions which were also placed on the module website. Include the preflight in the criterion-referenced mark scheme.

Step 2: Inform students of the overall task, including deadline, submission details and mark scheme: 'Design and produce an A4 poster to illustrate the geology of the field trip area'. Even though the task was quite straightforward, the sticking point was that they had never produced a poster before and had to set it up rapidly. Experience shows that students lose marks because they leave things until the last minute and they don't know how long things take until they have had the experience.

Step 3: Establish the preflight task, explaining that it should take only about 10 minutes to complete: 'Produce a basic poster but only include title and background'. Students were required to submit this within 2 days in order to be able to move forward. The preflight's brevity is important as it shows the task is not onerous. Many students will complain about the shortage of time. However, when they see that they get 5 percent of the marks for just starting, they do see the value. In later preflights they might not be marked, but by then they would have seen that the preflight system was for their benefit.

Step 4: Students were able to email me for points of clarification and were encouraged to discuss their ideas with their peers. Emailing their poster file to the module's account was also used as an implicit test of their digital and information literacy.

Step 5: The preflight was marked, with 5 percent of the total available for the assessment. This not only provides an incentive but also demonstrates to students the value of understanding the assessment criteria. The assignments were divided into a few (6–10) elements. Each element indicated the maximum mark possible, helping to indicate the effort required. Marks were part of a regime of criterion referencing.

Step 6: Feedback was provided rapidly, and as soon as the deadline had passed. Instant feedback is essential if students are going to be able to use it to feed-forward into their next task. Thus preflights, and other elements, should be designed so they are not onerous for the tutor, allowing efficient marking and speedy responses.

Subsequent preflights for practical work elements took the same general form, although the nature of task was different.

Further examples of the use of preflights are shown in Table 13.1.

Table 13.1 Examples of preflight activities used in a second-year geomorphology module

Objective 1	To define terms and units (stress, strain, tension, compression)
Sticking point	That such terms have strict scientific and engineering meaning that was not part of their prior learning
Preflight activity	Students look up the terms and send them in the text of an email
Results/feedback	Emails could be scanned very rapidly for compliance and the terms could then be used in a subsequent lecture or practical. A general response was all that was required to alert them that these concepts would soon be used
Objective 2	Setting up a spreadsheet to calculate an expression involving fractional powers
Sticking point	Students were not as familiar with spreadsheets as they thought they were
Preflight activity	Different values of the variables were sent to each student, who had to email the answer calculated
Results/feedback	Each student was sent their individual answer, calculated by some simple scripting via a spreadsheet. Students had to work out whether their calculated answer was correct and, if not, why not. Collusion was avoided because each student had been mailed a different set of values
Objective 3	Introducing students to HTML scripting
Sticking point	For students with no programming experience, the concept of writing script can be difficult; instructions have to be explicit
Preflight activity	I demonstrated how to write some simple HTML and save it as an index.html file. They then had to write some of their own
Results/fededback	Students could see for themselves immediately how they were progressing and what the file produced on their web browser. They thus produced their own feedback and the task gave them a sense of achievement

Now these preflight tasks are simple, but they are probably not trivial for students. As such, preflights, and their associated elements, should be aligned to the objectives of the exercise or lecture and hence the learning outcomes. Preflights can also be set up as group or peer-group exercises. Indeed, the '*peer instruction*' methods can be usefully employed here; some of Mazur's (1997) problem examples are similar to those in Novak et al.

(1999). Students might need to practise a task, and preflights can allow space for experimentation before a formal assessment. In this way preflights can guide students to an end product, and within a given time period, such as that allocated for completion, for example, of a laboratory practical.

Preflight scenarios need not be used for every activity, or indeed at every opportunity, but when they are, because they set only a small challenge, students should be able to see where the activity fits into a larger whole in a progressive manner as feed-forward.

▶ Conclusion

Students have many problems in their academic lives, especially in the early stages at university. Tutors' identification of troublesome knowledge or minor sticking points in modules is valuable in helping students to overcome some of their difficulties. Preflights are a useful way of getting students to tackle such sticking points and so enhance their learning. The design process helps students link taught and practised elements to learning outcomes and to criterion-referenced assessment, of which preflights can be a part.

14 Ongoing challenges in cross-disciplinary teaching: a case study from statistics

Paul Hewson (NTF 2012)

Keywords: threshold concept, statistical literacy, learned helplessness, undergraduate research

Paul Hewson is an Associate Professor in Statistics at Plymouth University. He worked in the medical device industry and local government prior to taking an MSc in Applied Statistics and a PhD in Statistics (part time). He researches applications of Bayesian Statistics and currently edits the journal *Teaching Statistics*.

One commonly held aspiration of higher education is to foster a sense of independent learning (Leathwood, 2006). This is a challenging goal in a mass education system and that challenge is amplified when learners have to work outside their field of interest. Cassidy and Eachus (2000) highlight the importance of students perceiving that they are mastering a subject; but it can be difficult to attain this sense of mastery in subsidiary subjects. Every discipline brings with it a set of norms and conventions, which need to be understood yet are rarely set out explicitly (Becher, 1994). This essay examines the particular challenges in developing critically independent learners when this other subject is an enabling subject of limited *intrinsic* interest to the student. Statistics serves as a powerful case study; most or all undergraduate programmes in science and social science require learners to demonstrate some ability in interpreting the world through quantitative data.

▶ From parody to reasoning

This essay contends that statistical methods courses are often a parody of learning. Various procedural tasks are assessed for little obvious reason other than being easy to assess. The procedures are selected by pedagogic inertia, from standard material in dated textbooks, with little thought. This parody obscures concepts that should be mastered and certainly does not reinforce how quantitative reasoning advances knowledge in the learners' chosen field of study. Our own work, however, has followed the statistical literacy movement. By listening to students attempting to conceptualise statistical methods we have gained insights from a community of learners that informs our teaching design. Although still travelling, the end goal is clear. We need clarity on the relationship between 'statistics' and epistemology. To demonstrate the relevance of 'statistics' to the advance of knowledge we need to design courses that advance knowledge in their own right.

▶ Threshold concept: inference

Meyer and Land (2003) describe threshold concepts as ideas that transform perception of a subject, and indeed refer to ideas that can seem alien or counterintuitive. Statistical inference – the way we make statements that apply to a world beyond a particular dataset – is a striking example. Inference is sufficiently troublesome that statisticians do not agree on which philosophy to use. The arguments are well set-out elsewhere (Harlow, Mulaik and Steiger, 1997); the point we make here is that statistics exists within a philosophy of science framework. It seems to us to make little sense *unless* that framework is understood. Yet that is exactly what many try to teach – isolated procedures that 'fit' different problems. Educational silos dictate that philosophy of science belongs on philosophy degrees; mathematical statistics on mathematics degrees, and what we leave most scientists and social scientists with is a dated bag of a procedural knowledge that is a poor fit for many problems they encounter. Crucially for the learning process, this ragbag is not self-justifying in its relevance. Indeed, many simple heuristics applied to data analysis do not validly match any philosophy of statistical inference, and this is rarely explained to learners.

▶ Innumeracy?

In passing, we note one challenge around quantitative methodology in the UK, namely the prerequisite mathematical ability of many undergraduates. Simply put, many courses recruit undergraduates with only a grade C pass in GCSE mathematics. This requires study of the foundation (lower)-tier standard UK mathematics qualification to age 16. In turn, this puts pressure on curriculum design. Additional challenges include cultural issues around maths phobia and related attitudes towards numerical skills, even amongst those studying science degrees. These issues are well argued elsewhere, and rather than deal with the considerable angst expended concerning the mathematical abilities of students, this essay will draw attention to the quantitative skills of their lecturers.

▶ Statistical illiteracy

Notable publications show that many academics demonstrate consistent and major misunderstandings of statistical philosophy when publishing their own research. McCloskey and Ziliak (2008) have reviewed publications in eminent epidemiology, economics and psychology journals and contend that 'publish or perish' pressures almost encourage a culpable misunderstanding of statistical philosophy. Ioannidis (2005) reviewed medical publications, reaching a similar conclusion (with a paper entitled 'Why Most Published Research Findings are False'). Vaux (2012) has highlighted very simple fundamental misunderstandings, such as the need to replicate findings from different experiments. One charitable explanation is that academics have some heuristic for interpreting the results from a study, and use formal statistical methods to confirm this after the fact without appreciating the flaws in what they are doing. It is therefore rather unsurprising that so many introductory statistics textbooks, training students in the same procedures, signally fail to develop the underlying philosophy. The ultimate parody is that we regard research as designing and conducting a study and 'statistics' as the mere selection of a suitable 'Statistical Hypothesis Inference Test' to pass some pre-publication ritual.

This is what we do in our research; this is what we teach our students.

▶ Statistical literacy

It is reassuring that considerable work has been done on the fundamental problem of learning statistics, often labelled statistical literacy. We have articulations of what statistical education should be about; for example, 'Guidelines on Assessment and Instruction in Statistical Education', published by the American Statistical Association (Aliaga et al., 2005).

Nevertheless, it is striking that this remains a statistician-written document. If statistics are fundamental to epistemology, other professional bodies (biologists, economists, psychologists, and so on) ought to be queuing up to endorse such a document.

These endorsements should come with caveats, for example the guidelines include a learning outcome that states learners should know 'when to seek help from a statistician'. This may well be sound advice, but has the feel of 'learned helplessness' (Firmin et al., 2004) and in this context speaks more to the agenda of selecting and applying procedures rather than to an agenda of fundamental understanding. If statistics is fundamental to how we advance knowledge, then we simply *cannot* be required to seek help from a statistician to appreciate this. To give one specific example, scientists and social scientists need to be clear that random allocation in experiments is what lets us conclude causation.

We fully accept that knowing what we don't know is a valid learning outcome. Higher education should not be a stopping point, it should be a transformative process that changes the way we see the world. That we may continually need to develop and refine our understanding should be a given; it is just that by becoming independent learners we are better equipped to see when and why we need to learn more and have a wider range of choices as to how we develop. This may or may not include consulting a statistician. The obvious concern is that by building learned helplessness into the curriculum goals we reinforce the idea that statistics is someone else's subject and will design curricula that limit agency.

▶ Student engagement

Our experience is consistent with the argument that a lack of attention to foundational concepts, an excess attention to procedures combined with learned helplessness is a major problem in learning for many students. Yes, it is rare to find students with maths beyond 16 and common to find maths phobias. But the parody of learning does little to demonstrate to these students that they ought to become more numerate. Why should students learn methods if they aren't core to advancing knowledge? Perhaps students are realising, by various subtle signals, that we don't actually need statistical methods and statistical courses really do become a strange hurdle – only needed by those who will end up on a publication treadmill. At one time we used papers featuring fundamental errors in statistical methods as a core teaching technique.

'Benefited from being able to understand the principles behind the working rather than book-bashing formulae which hold no real gain in understanding.'

First-year science undergraduate

'This is key to understanding the limitations of statistics'.

Healthcare Masters student

Whilst we see many benefits in exposing the underlying concepts, without care this approach can become counterproductive:

'What's the point of me learning this stuff if you can get away with that sort of ****?'

First-year science undergraduate (on understanding flaws with a paper published in the *New England Journal of Medicine*)

Statistics is an approach to thinking which has to be used by many, but only studied to PhD level and beyond by a few. Finding flaws in its application is therefore not surprising and in our hands can readily become a sterile endeavour. Currently we are edging towards following Root and Thorne (2001), who highlight the potential for community-based statistics projects to provide a route to learning about statistics. There are obvious challenges in implementing such an approach and disciplinary silos provide barriers for adoption in the UK (what if one project doesn't cover some vital procedure?). A way of addressing these concerns could be by adapting what Spurrier (2001) describes as a 'capstone' course; students offer statistical effort for working researchers. This ensures that procedures are learnt within disciplines but perhaps does not afford room for the philosophical and epistemological fundamentals that might be possible on a community project.

▶ Conclusion

Both the expansion of higher education and, in the UK, the increases in student fees invigorate debate on the very nature of higher education. Is it, as implied by the UK National Student Survey, a consumer product designed to produce employees for the knowledge economy? Or is it, as implied by the US National Survey of Student Experience, a transformative process that alters the way learners see the world?

The former vision may well imply that designing courses for easy and objective assessment is desirable. The latter supports the argument that we should facilitate some wider kind of statistical agency amongst learners. Our journey into statistical literacy started with critique and debunk of published work. However, if we really believe that you need statistics to learn about the world, our students tell us that we should provide authentic learning opportunities to advance knowledge whilst learning the technical skills. Community projects, or capstone projects where fundamental knowledge is advanced at the same time as learners gain mastery of the skills of the trade, can demonstrate both the importance of the subject as well as their abilities to function in their chosen disciplines.

15 Demystifying statistics: bring your imprimatur ... to the laughter

Andy Field (NTF 2010)

Keywords: statistics, humour, engagement

> Andy Field is Professor of Child Psychopathology at the University of Sussex. He has published over 70 research papers and 17 books about either children's emotional development or the teaching and learning of statistics, including the bestselling, award-winning 'Discovering Statistics using SPSS/R/SAS' textbook range. Various teaching awards, including from the British Psychological Society, and his website, that pokes fun at the apparent 'scariness' of statistics by housing it in 'statistics hell' (based on Dante's Inferno), reflect his unorthodox teaching of statistics.

Honey, it's getting close to midnight, And all the maths [*sic*] are still in town.

> Iron Maiden, *Bring Your Daughter ... to the Slaughter*

▶ Statistics is hell

Statistical methods are the backbone of scientific disciplines as diverse as psychology, economics and business, management, sociology, medicine, health sciences and sports sciences (to name but a few). Statistics is a core knowledge area within my own discipline, psychology (QAA, 2007), and statistical literacy is a key transferable skill (Field, 2010). Outside academia, it has never been more important to be skilled to evaluate the 'fact and figure' bombardment from politicians, journalists, the workplace and advertisements (Field, 2010). Most students on non-statistics degrees fail to see the transferable skill that statistics offers. One study looked at the attitudes of 279 students from diverse backgrounds (66 per cent from Bachelor of Arts degrees, 17 per cent from science degrees, 7 per cent from economics and 5 per cent from education) who were all enrolled on a second-year psychology module. It showed that only 7 per cent thought that statistics was generally useful in life and only 16 per cent saw the relevance of statistics to their psychology module (Gordon, 2004).

Teaching statistics to non-statistics majors poses a unique set of challenges. The main barriers are (Conners, McCown and Roskos-Ewoldson, 1998): motivation, statistics anxiety, performance extremes (students tend to 'get it' or not) and retention of the material. To some extent, the last two problems will be eased by addressing motivation and anxiety. Although in the case of statistics these barriers are particularly high and topped with barbed wire; motivation and anxiety are ubiquitous challenges.

Many people who teach statistics to undergraduate social scientists can regale you with tales of students who are anxious, bored, unmotivated and see statistics as a form of torture foisted upon them to satisfy the sadistic urges of their evil professor. Studies estimate that anywhere between one-third and four-fifths of students experience uncomfortable levels of statistics anxiety (DeCesare, 2007; Onwuegbuzie and Wilson, 2003). Statistics anxiety causally decreases performance (Benson, 1989; Onwuegbuzie and Wilson, 2003), whereas positive attitudes to statistics and motivation improve performance (Schutz et al., 1998). Statistics anxiety has a knock-on effect for motivation in that it is likely to make students give up when confronted with challenging material (Paxton, 2006).

▶ What's so funny about peace, love and understanding?

Statistics is often taught passively through equations and dry examples, but many people, myself included, have tried to make statistics more engaging and less scary through using humour and lively examples. Like many others (Berk, 2003; Friedman, Friedman and Amoo, 2002; Garner, 2006; Kaplan and Pascoe, 1977; Lesser, 2001; Lesser and Pearl, 2008; Neumann, Hood and Neumann, 2002; Pyrczak, 2009), engagement is at the heart of my face-to-face teaching, my books (Field, 2013; Field and Hole, 2003; Field, Miles and Field, 2012) and my website, which pokes fun at the apparent 'scariness' of statistics by being housed in an environment known as 'statistics hell' (based on Dante's *Inferno*).

Humour can take the form of jokes, cartoons or songs (Lesser and Pearl, 2008); Lomax and Moosavi (2002) produced a cornucopia of statistical songs, jokes, stories and raps that could be used in teaching compiled from their own experiences, online searches and emails to 183 members of the statisticians' special interest group of the American Educational Research Association. They conclude that these techniques reduce anxiety, motivate students and foster a deeper level of conceptual understanding.

> How 'bout them co-relators, ain't they just so ...
> Wi' they Pearson product moment an' they Spearman rho?
> Them coefficient co-relators, they ain't metaphoric,
> Studyin' dichotomies by means tetrachoric.
> How 'bout them co-relators, ain't they fine?
> Get they linear relations where they ain't no line.
>
> A rap by John Konopak (cited in Lomax and Moosavi, 2002)

Visual images can also be useful; for example, to explain the idea that an 'outlier' can be a real data point, Neumann et al. (2002) show students pictures of entities that have unusual characteristics (e.g. a boy with an extraordinarily long tongue, and an oversized rabbit).

Like others, I have found a place for attention-grabbing songs (Lesser, 2001), videos (Berk, 2007), demonstrations (Lesser and Glickman, 2009; Lesser and Pearl, 2008) and examples (Berk, 2003; Pyrczak, 2009) in my teaching. I find it particularly useful to embed a lighter tone within the examples themselves. Teaching statistics through examples and analogies to which students actively relate enables them to anchor statistical ideas to their own experiences and develop their own conceptual sense of what they have been taught (Field, 2010). I use the freedom that statistics offers for creating examples that address student-relevant questions such as 'Do people smell horrible after three days at a rock festival?' 'Does the "beer-goggles effect" (i.e. finding people attractive when drunk) differ in men and women?' 'Are looks or personality more important when speed dating?' 'Does soya lower your sperm count?' 'Are horoscopes accurate?' 'What mischief would we get up to if we had a Harry Potter-style cloak of invisibility?'

▶ Does humour work?

None of the examples I cite are inherently amusing, it is more that they grab students' attention and offer a platform to construct amusing stories and hypothetical situations around them. I wouldn't necessarily advocate the exact stories that I construct or the way that I deliver them: you have to find your own voice. However, to inspire you the Consortium for the Advancement of Undergraduate Statistics Education (CAUSE) website contains fun cartoons, jokes, songs, poems, quotes and videos.

The effort may well be worth it: humour motivates the student to learn (Lomax and Moosavi, 2002) and 'humanise' the lecturer, making them seem more approachable, which fosters openness in the teaching environment (Friedman et al., 2002). However, unpicking whether humour is universally useful is difficult. There is the highly subjective nature of humour with which to contend, and whether you care about humour helping retention, or reducing anxiety and helping engagement. In terms of student perceptions of the course, humour can improve ratings of the lessons and lecturer (Garner, 2006); 96.6 per cent of students want an 'ideal' teacher to use humour (Epting et al., 2004) and the use of humour is positively related to student evaluations of teachers' effectiveness and appeal (Bryant et al., 1980). Chapters from humorous textbooks are rated by students as more enjoyable (Klein, Bryant and Zillmann, 1982).

Finally, in a qualitative study of the effects of humour on psychology students' attitudes to their statistics class, 47 per cent reported that humour reduced anxiety and lightened the mood and 45 per cent said that it helped maintain their attention (Neumann et al., 2002). Other studies echo the finding that humour can be useful in reducing student anxiety generally (Berk, 2000; Schacht and Stewart, 1990) and when used in test situations (Berk, 2000; Berk and Nanda, 2006).

In terms of learning outcomes, there are some promising findings:

1 humorous videos produce significantly better recall of information compared to videos without humorous inserts (Garner, 2006);
2 compared to lectures with no humour, specific concepts presented humorously were better remembered 6 weeks after the lecture (Kaplan and Pascoe, 1977);
3 GPA-matched groups of psychology statistics students who sang humorous-jingle versions of definitions remembered them better than students who read them. (VanVoorhis, 2002)

However, Bryant et al. (1980) found that humour was associated with effectiveness in male, but not female, tutors. For female tutors the use of puns had a detrimental relationship with effectiveness. It would be interesting to revisit this study in a contemporary context, because the results are likely to reflect outdated societal attitudes. Also, humorous textbooks have been shown not to improve learning, interest, persuasiveness and the desire to read more (Klein et al., 1982).

'I'm lying on the floor and laughing. It's so great to have a book like this which is uniting a kind of absurd humour and really insightful explanations.'

▶ Bring your laughter ... to the slaughter

A potential danger of the creative examples that I use is that they stray too far from statistics. Lesser and Pearl (2008) suggest that fun should not be perceived as frivolous and unrelated to the course. To some extent I disagree: as a tool for reducing anxiety and making students feel engaged with the material I think some irrelevant fun is no bad thing. If a student feels relaxed and good about the course they are much more likely to engage with the 'serious' content. In the aforementioned study by Neumann et al. (2002) only 18 per cent of students produced statements suggesting that the relevance of the humour was important. There is also research (not specifically from statistics) showing that educational films achieve better learning outcomes in children when they contain unrelated humorous inserts (e.g. *The Muppet Show*) compared to when they containing non-humorous or no inserts (Zillmann et al., 1980).

Nevertheless, in recent editions of my textbooks (and lectures) I have taken a leaf from Lesser and Pearl's book and mixed in examples of real, but bizarre, research. These examples act as a framework for both amusing comments and discussions about research design. Some examples are studies that showed that pornography use is related to infidelity, looking at the evolutionary function of gossip, whether Friday 13th is really unlucky or whether Bonn Scott or Brian Johnson is the better of the two AC/DC singers.

Berk also warns against offensive humour, which he views as detrimental to learning (Berk, 2003, 2007). He sensibly advocates avoiding put-downs, sarcasm and ridicule, and straying into sensitive topics. He also advises steering clear of profanity, vulgarity and sexual innuendo, which are all areas into which I stray. Humour is a very personal thing: I am often struck by how unfunny I find some of the 'humorous' things that other statistics teachers use; conversely some colleagues find my textbook vulgar and not remotely funny. It has been banned at a Tehran book fair because of its 'lively' content. This brings me back to finding your voice, and that voice needs to reflect the culture of your university and the students who attend it.

Humour can be a thin wire on which to balance.

'It's 12:15 midnight and I can't put my statistics textbook down. I'm really falling in love with statistics and I have you to thank for that.'

16 Performing critical thinking?

Stella Jones-Devitt (NTF 2012)

Keywords: critical thinking, performance, unlearning, play, risk-taking

Stella Jones-Devitt is Head of the Centre for Leadership in Health and Social Care at Sheffield Hallam University. She is renowned for her commitment to critical thinking and in using innovatory approaches that animate learning and inspire creative and critical thinking.

I believe that development of critical thinking abilities is paramount for students' success and effective engagement in higher education. The term 'critical thinking' was first articulated by Glaser (1941) as an educational construct premised as an individualised cognitive skill. Subsequently, critical thinking has oscillated between two competing principles; either as a theory-dense concept with little practical application or, more popularly, as an over-simplified skills-based tool for problem solving. According to Angeli and Valanides (2008), critical thinking has been conceptualised primarily in terms of dispositions and skills (Ennis, 1996; McPeck, 1990); however, others have acknowledged a broader conceptualisation of critical thinking which goes beyond the dispositions/skills debate by exploring critical thinking as a social process or performance (Alston, 2001). The following definition (Jones-Devitt and Smith, 2007) captures my approach to critical thinking:

> Making sense of the world through a process of questioning the questions, challenging assumptions, recognising that bodies of knowledge can be chaotic and evolving; ultimately with the aim of continually improving thinking. (p. 7)

Whilst critical thinking continues to evolve, so does the concept of the university. Barnett (2012) indicates that higher education is in a time of unprecedented continuous change or supercomplexity. Johansen (2009) explains this challenge in terms of living in a 'VUCA' world – an environment that is volatile, uncertain, complex and ambiguous. Volatility – both economic and political – creates rapid shifts in our usual environment, leaving us to cope with uncertain futures, complex systems, ambiguities and resultant 'wicked problems'; those thorny items which, according to Brown, Harris and Russell (2010), have no obvious solutions, since any attempted resolution generates further issues. Arguably, this creates the need for both individuals and organisations to make sense of as much as possible to feel secure; hence the growing interest within higher education in the notion of 'critical thinking' as one possible method.

This corresponds with the tension between two primary ideas of contemporary higher education: the ascendant market model which sees it as a sector of the skills-based economy and the contrasting – arguably diminishing – view of the university as a social institution with a variety of public functions. Olssen and Peters (2005) define higher education as immersed fully within a neoliberal ideology of individualism, deregulation and reduced state intervention, dominated by the notion of performance outputs. Within the context of the marketised university, Paul (2004) describes three common facets that underpin the majority of critical thinking teaching in higher education: first, he claims that the majority of higher education institutes do not have a cogent view of what is meant by 'critical thinking' beyond use as a business cliché; secondly, this lack is not acknowledged because higher education institutions believe that – as they are peopled by academics – they already understand critical thinking concepts and assume they teach students adequately; thirdly, he argues that lectures, rote-learning and short-term study habits are the norm for much teaching and learning in higher education. It is within this neoliberal context that critical thinking has flourished into a heavily outputs-driven and skills-based approach that, I contend, is neither critical nor really about effective thinking.

▶ Unlearning in order to think critically

My dissatisfaction with the way critical thinking is facilitated in universities as a skill set led me to explore how to construct alternative perspectives. As well as the voluminous critical thinking literature, I drew upon my sense of discovery as a young art student and considered how to re-engage in that process. For inspiration, I revisited some of the ideas espoused by Gropius (1919) within the *Bauhaus Manifesto* and identified two key principles, comprising:

▶ avoidance of all rigidity; priority of creativity; freedom of individuality, but strict study discipline;

▶ encouragement of friendly relations between masters and students outside work; therefore plays, lectures, poetry, music, costume parties.

Central to these principles is the notion of encouraging 'unlearning' characterised by finding a core essence of thinking, released and liberated from prevailing knowledge and power. Bauhaus master Johannes Itten (1919) defined this as to:

> free the creative powers and thereby the art talents of the students. Their own experiences and perceptions were to lead to genuine work. The students were to free themselves gradually from dead conventions and to take courage for work on their own.
>
> (cited in Tierney, 2010: 437)

These concepts clarified matters for me regarding the need to create a learning environment in which experiment and play are encouraged yet built around a safety net of collaborative engagement; one in which learners can unlearn collectively, to enhance their critical thinking approaches within the complex and ambiguous 'VUCA' world defined by Johansen (2009).

▶ *Performing* critical thinking

The following two examples represent my approach to developing learning opportunities that animate critical thinking processes from within a culture of experiment and play.

So what? Snakes and Ladders critical thinking game

This is Snakes and Ladders with a difference: the ladders and snakes are separated from the board and participants make critical and collective decisions about what each moveable ladder (enabler) and each moveable snake (inhibitor) represent, dependent on the context of the scenario presented (Figure 16.1). Players conceptualise what the 1–100 squares represent and consider if there is significance to specific numbers. An additional layer of complexity is introduced as participants are provided with a set of task cards about a particular issue, which can be prescribed or – ideally – generated by participants themselves in a preparatory session. Upon landing on a snake or ladder, one participant selects a task card and completes the task within a time-limited period, after which all other game participants form a consensus view to decide whether the individual has earned the right to stay or move, as judged by the quality of their response. This process has been designed to engage learners in performing collaborative critical thinking rather than as pure application of analytical and cognitive proficiencies; the latter so often expected when critical thinking 'skills' are imparted.

At one level, it engages participants to develop effective negotiation and group working skills, yet it also scaffolds the process of 'unlearning' in relation to challenging expectations of what formal learning processes should be and encourages participants to take risks by considering rules which can be adapted or even abandoned, provided that changes are justified and agreed by all players. The value of this game relates to its wide utility, as it can be used across many disciplinary areas and with staff and students at many academic levels. One student describes it as:

'Great fun, but really helped me to think.'

It appeals to a wide variety of learning approaches, as it integrates visual and linguistic forms of critical thinking into the curriculum. Amongst multiple applications, it has been used to consider causes of health inequalities with final-year nursing undergraduates, to examine the role played by gender in educational attainment by second-year education studies undergraduates and also used to consider effective leadership infrastructure with senior university managers. It can be used as a problem-solving tool for anything from straightforward decision-making to examining complex subject matters in a variety of contexts. It aligns with the work of Vygotsky (1978) as a process exploring the zone of proximal development, in which distance between learners' ability to perform tasks collectively with peer support and individuals' ability to solve problems independently is blurred and reduced, leading to increasing reciprocal autonomy.

Figure 16.1 The Snakes and Ladders critical thinking game

Launch of Critical Thinking in Higher Education: a Manifesto for Action

My belief in the power of critical thinking as a shared social process led me to create this *Manifesto*, designed to a turn my vision of critical thinking into reality by seeking wider engagement in ideas, testing those thoughts in experience and considering what might then be possible if making collective changes. I launched the *Manifesto* at the University Learning and Teaching Conference, underpinned by the following principles:

▶ Critical thinkers are made not born
▶ It should be a force for social change
▶ Effective critical thinking is a collaborative process
▶ Critical thinking is fluid, complex and evolving
▶ It seeks to challenge prevailing wisdoms and ways of knowing
▶ Critical thinking concerns constructive sense-making
▶ It is an immersive and long-term process
▶ Critical thinking has meaningful application and utility
▶ All universities should embody critical thinking principles and practices as minimum requirements for an effective educational experience
▶ Critical thinking should utilise literal, visual and kinaesthetic approaches
▶ It should be an inclusive process in which all can engage

I introduced the *Manifesto* as a mechanism to move critical thinking from the margins of the university into the mainstream. There are risks when making something explicit when its previous essence is its very edginess; however, I was conscious of the inoculation that can occur when challenging subjects like critical thinking get 'boxed in', rendering them contained. Inoculation in this context comes from the work of Roland Barthes (1972), who suggested that allowing small amount of dissension within an institution warded off awareness of its fundamental problems. The *Manifesto* is work-in-progress, designed so that it generates debate and adaptation, thus recognising that critical thinking is an evolving *performance*. It was launched by an animated presentation[14] and a Bauhaus-type leaflet rather than as a formal educative process. Again, my intention is to use process, rather than knowledge, to challenge ourselves to unlearn rigid habits that arguably block new ways of thinking.

▶ Successes, lessons learned and wicked problems

Interestingly, many successes have resulted from aspects of critical thinking which started on the margins; hence, involvement in a Critical Thinking

Research Cluster and small staff development project which engaged staff in new ways of working that resulted in changes to a University Learning and Teaching strategy and significant capacity building. The 'So What' critical thinking game has proven successful in engaging students and staff to explore complex issues from the position of, at worst, novelty and, at best, by 'unlearning'. The impact of the *Manifesto* is too early to assess. There are many lessons being learned whilst initiating the *performance of* critical thinking rather than skills-based approaches, including: that creating a willingness for unlearning takes time, trust and engagement; convincing others that longer-term gains can outweigh short-term outputs; that developing an ethos of risk-taking is essential for effective learning and teaching. The primary wicked problem concerns operating collaboratively in times of individual sovereignty: perhaps there has never been a better time to show the value of *performing* critical thinking?

17 Best practice in assessment and feedback: neglected issues

Peter Hartley (NTF 2000)

Keywords: *programme assessment, assessment strategy, feedback*

Peter Hartley is now an independent higher education consultant and Visiting Professor at Edge Hill University, previously Professor of Education Development at Bradford and Professor of Communication at Sheffield Hallam University. His national projects (JISC/HEA) have included e-portfolios, employability skills, work-based learning, computer-aided assessment and audio feedback. He has promoted the use of new technology, including educational software – *The Interviewer* and *Interviewer Viva* – and *Making Groupwork Work* with the LearnHigher CETL. He co-edited and contributed to *Learning Development in Higher Education* (2010) and led the NTFS Group Project on Programme-Focused Assessment (PASS).

Academic staff in higher education who wish to improve their professional practice in assessment and feedback are in a much better position than they were ten or twenty years ago. As well as relevant advances in technology (as illustrated by recent initiatives such as the JISC Assessment and Feedback Programme), we can now draw upon a range of evidence-based principles of good assessment/feedback practice. These principles have come from the work of individual scholars (e.g. Boud, Falchikov and Nicol),[15] from major funded initiatives (e.g. the work of the HEFCE-funded Centres for Excellence in Teaching and Learning (CETLs) – ASKe[16] and AfL[17] – and publications by staff associated with these, e.g. Price et al., 2012), and from numerous individual projects (e.g. the work of projects such as Audio Supported Enhanced Learning (ASEL)[18] and Sounds Good[19] on audio feedback, both funded by the JISC). But I argue that we will not fully realise these principles until we resolve three outstanding issues.

Three key issues have been under-researched: the nature of course/programme assessment strategies; the influence of institutions' regulatory and curriculum frameworks; and the nature and influence of systematic personal differences in student responses to feedback. We need a more concerted attack on these issues over the next few years if we are to fully capitalise on all the valuable developments highlighted at the beginning of this essay.

▶ Course/programme strategies

The significance of course/programme strategies has been highlighted by the outcomes of recent NTFS (National Teaching Fellowship Scheme) Group Projects, especially PASS[20] and TESTA.[21] Both these projects investigated the nature and impact of course or programme assessment strategies, but with different starting points and approaches. Both projects reflected concerns about the nature of dominant assessment practices in UK higher education.

The PASS project team started from the premise that Programme-Focused Assessment (PFA) is a strategy which can resolve or alleviate many of these current problems and issues. The project aimed to explore and test this proposition (Hartley and Whitfield, 2011). TESTA started from the investigation of specific assessment and feedback practice on a range of courses (Jessop, El Hakim and Gibbs, 2011) and a concern for the course or programme 'assessment environment' (Gibbs and Dunbar-Goddet, 2009).

Both projects uncovered important limitations in existing course/programme assessment strategies. In validation documents and course handbooks, these strategies are often rather cursory and limited. They may simply use the assessment-grid approach suggested by the QAA, which identifies where learning outcomes are covered in specific modules. This may demonstrate that learning outcomes have been covered, but is unlikely to show how well the course develops and integrates the overall programme outcomes. Perhaps more importantly, existing assessment strategies may be based on inappropriate or even misleading assumptions. For example, TESTA exploded a number of 'assessment myths', including the finding that increased variety of assessment methods, which is usually taken to be a 'good thing', could be counterproductive in some situations.

In the first year of our PASS project, we found very little innovation which reflected PFA, defined as follows:

The first and most critical point is that the assessment is *specifically designed to address major programme outcomes* rather than very specific or

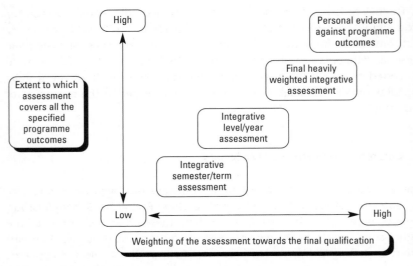

Figure 17.1 Varieties of Programme-Focused Assessment

isolated components of the course. It follows then that such assessment *is integrative in nature*, trying to bring together understanding and skills in ways, which represent key programme aims. As a result, the assessment is likely to be more authentic and meaningful to students, staff and external stakeholders.

PASS Position Paper[22]

This can also be represented as a diagram – see Figure 17.1. To adopt PFA, you need to move to the top right of this graph. This figure reflects the fact that there are types and degrees of PFA. What they all have in common is their concern with desired programme outcomes rather than very specific task or module outcomes.

The good news is that there is evidence of change and development across the UK higher education sector. PASS identified key examples, such as the Peninsula Medical School and the BioSciences and Mathematics courses at Brunel University, where PFA has delivered important improvements to both the student learning experience and to academic teaching staff. Most of these innovations are relatively recent, so long-term impact is difficult to assess at the moment. However, evidence to date suggests that PFA can lead to impact of various types and at different levels, as summarised in Figure 17.2.

The quality of an innovation based on PFA does seem to depend on clear educational aims and objectives, the coherence and commitment of the

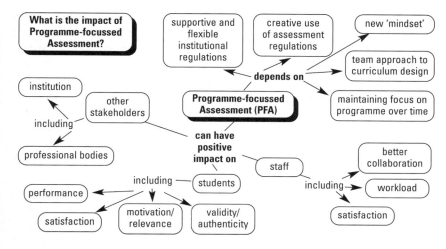

Figure 17.2 The impact of Programme-Focused Assessment

course team, and the necessary support from institutional regulations and frameworks, as discussed below. Based on these and other examples, PASS developed a workshop format which can be downloaded, adopted and adapted by course teams to introduce the main principles and consider them in their own institutional context. TESTA has also developed a methodology which can be used by course teams and institutions and which has been used by the Higher Education Academy in one of its Change Academy initiatives.

▶ **Regulatory frameworks**

We piloted the PASS workshop in a number of UK higher education institutions. One very common discussion point that emerged was the nature of the modular framework and the underlying regulatory structure, which could impede innovation in assessment. These modular systems promised flexibility to enhance lifelong learning, but they may not have delivered on this promise while restricting innovation in integrated and coherent assessment. These structures may have implications for assessment, which undermine particular strategies. For example, the development of slowly learnt aspects of 'graduateness', such as academic literacies, may be lost, ignored or only serendipitously acquired within fragmented course structures.

One of the most interesting sets of case studies to emerge from PASS is the analysis of courses at Brunel University, which have taken advantage of a new regulatory framework introduced in 2009. This framework allows courses to redesign their provision using a mixture of 'study blocks' (teaching and study periods with only formative assessment), 'assessment blocks' (assessments of more than one study block) and conventional modules (where study and assessment are delivered completely within the module). Different courses have used this new flexibility in different ways and report *inter alia* that it can reduce assessment workload while increasing student engagement and understanding of broad programme outcomes. Institutions which are prepared to consider working around or outside the limitations of a 'strict modular system' can develop assessment regimes which are much more satisfying and meaningful for staff and students alike.

For an example emerging from the TESTA project, Jessop, McNab and Gubby (2012) investigated how the format and structure of degree specification documents influenced course/programme approaches to assessment. These documents obviously reflect institutional rules and regulations, but are they based on the most appropriate pedagogic principles? Their main finding was that the documents focused the attention of programme leaders on summative assessment, and that this was usually narrowed down to module assessment. This had particular implications for the use of formative assessment:

> The invisibility of formative assessment in documentation reinforced the tendency of modular programmes to have high summative demands, with optional, fragmented and infrequent formative assessment. Heavy workloads, modularity and pedagogic uncertainties compounded the problem.

Whereas much innovation in assessment (e.g. from initiatives like REAP, or Re-Engineering Assessment Practices) focuses on changing modules or individual assignments, fundamental change depends upon course/programme teams implementing coherent assessment strategies within institutional frameworks, which allow subject-specific innovation. But even this may not completely transform learning for all our students.

▶ Student differences

Any coherent strategy on assessment must include appropriate guidelines and a framework for feedback, but this raises my third issue. Current guidance on 'good feedback' tends to treat students as a homogenous group. But how significant are the differences between students, and how can we best characterise their different approaches? And how far do we take account of changes over the duration of the course? For example, Ali, Ahmed and Rose (2012) found significant differences between the reactions of psychology students to the feedback they received. First-year students were the most satisfied and third-year students the least, suggesting that we need a developmental strategy to fully satisfy student needs.

Some of our own early research demonstrated that, despite some rather cynical comments from tutors about student motivation, there was significant evidence of students behaving as 'conscientious consumers' – keen to obtain a 'good degree' and therefore act as critical consumers of a service, but also 'conscientious' in their enthusiasm for their subject area and learning for its own sake. They saw feedback as both a way of improving their performance and increasing the chances of achieving that good degree, but also as a way of developing themselves as learners (Higgins, Hartley and Skelton, 2002).

Subsequent research by Richard Higgins (unpublished PhD thesis) focused on the reactions of individual students to tutor feedback. Using Repertory Grid Technique to arrive at the students' own constructs regarding feedback comments, he found that most student responses could be summarised using six common bipolar constructs, which were applied to tutor comments:

1 Comment is helpful – Comment is unhelpful
2 Comment is praising me – Comment is punishing me
3 Comment is personal – Comment is impersonal

Students differentiated between comments they felt were directed at them as individuals from comments, which seemed impersonal and could have been written about anybody's work.

4 Comment is about conceptual aspects of my work – Comment is about technical aspects of my work (such as grammar and spelling)
5 Comment is implicit – Comment is explicit
6 Comment encourages me to reflect on my work – Comment does not encourage me to reflect on my work

Four of the six constructs were generally viewed as 'positive' at one end of the construct pole and 'negative' at the other. Students had positive views of comments rated as helpful, personal, about conceptual aspects of assignments and as explicit. Conversely, the students held negative views about comments rated as unhelpful, impersonal, about technical aspects of assignments and as implicit. There were more complex reactions to constructs 5 and 6, reflecting the emotional implications of praise compared with punishment and the difficulties of engaging with reflection.

Although this research did identify common constructs and reactions, perhaps the most interesting finding was the different ways in which some students *applied* these constructs and the way that this reflected other aspects of their personalities and role behaviour. The student with positive feelings of self-esteem and self-efficacy was likely to see themselves as an 'apprentice' in terms of the tutor/student relationship and would respond to feedback as a positive opportunity to reflect upon and improve their performance. The student with low or negative self-esteem/efficacy would anticipate more 'punishment' through the feedback process and their chances of using it for self-improvement would be low. While the importance of emotional responses to the assessment processes have been long recognised, we have not sufficiently employed conceptual approaches, which allow us to fully understand the range and consequences of different responses. Further research and interventions in this area should be a priority over the next few years, e.g. using the concept of mindset from Dweck, as piloted by Glasgow University's Centre for Confidence and Well-Being.[23]

▶ **Conclusions**

This essay has identified three neglected issues in assessment and feedback practice. Confronting and resolving these issues will not be easy and will require institutions and course teams to adopt a critical view of the long-term and probably unintended consequences of their course frameworks and supporting regulations. Alongside this we need more to pay more attention to the variety of student responses to their assessment and develop course structures that enable students to fully benefit from feedback at all levels.

18 Assessment strategies for developmental and experiential learning: successes and challenges

Anita Peleg (NTF 2012)

Keywords: formative assessment, continuous feedback, experiential learning, learning by doing, live projects

Anita Peleg is Senior Lecturer in Marketing at London South Bank University. Prior to academic life she worked in export marketing, public relations and market research, expertise that she has brought to her specialist teaching areas. Her research interests focus on marketing education and she has presented and published papers on graduate employability, skills development, marketing ethics and moral education at seminars and conferences in the UK. She recently co-authored a chapter on 'Ethics and Social Responsibility' in a new book, *Marketing: Theory, Evidence, Practice.*

According to Chalmers and Fuller (1996), assessment does not merely measure achievement but drives learning and development, providing feedback and enabling critical reflection. In this essay I demonstrate how formative assessment can be a key opportunity to inspire and engage students and develop their learning.

As opposed to summative assessment, where student work is awarded a final grade, formative assessment provides feedback and stimulates reflection at a point when adjustments can be made. This gives students the opportunity to demonstrate learning by improved performance.

Here I describe and evaluate examples of two modules, Public Relations (PR) and Market Research (MR), where students take on the role of consultants to work on live or quasi-live case studies. I show how experiential learning (Kolb, 1984; Rogers, 1996), 'where learning takes place when students

... experience directly or indirectly the subject matter' (Rogers, 1996: 113), is developed by continuous feedback to enable reflection and improve performance along the way.

This marriage between formative assessment and experiential learning supports Kolb's Experiential Learning Cycle (Kolb, 1984), where students' learning develops through four dynamic and interactive stages:

▶ *Abstract conceptualisation*, where the student is encouraged to acquire knowledge and understand the theory through lectures and additional reading
▶ *Concrete experience*, where the students experience the creative process of planning and executing their projects facilitated by the tutor with continuous feedback
▶ *Active experimentation*, where feedback and reflection enable students to develop creative skills and practise techniques such as writing and presenting a speech for PR or facilitating a focus group in market research
▶ *Reflective observation*, where students critique their own performance, suggest ways to improve and understand what they have learned

The formative assessment activities for each module are described in Table 18.1.

I consider four main activities to be critical to success:

▶ practical live projects
▶ developing creativity
▶ embedding employability
▶ constructive formative feedback

▶ Practical, live projects

Key to experiential learning is anchoring solutions in decisions justified and supported by theory and research. Through live projects, developed throughout the semester, students are encouraged to apply theory and utilise secondary data to formulate and justify real-world decisions and their execution. Students work with internal departments at London South Bank University (LSBU) or external companies that they know, or they identify situations through secondary research where their PR or MR services are needed. In MR many like the freedom to choose a project that interests them, and enjoy the challenge of working with a live client, such as the LSBU student services. In PR students are particularly engaged by the exhibition and the

Table 18.1 Experiential learning and formative assessment activity for Market Research and Public Relations modules

Market Research – Undergraduate Level Five	Public Relations – Undergraduate Level Six
Aim: to develop the ability to devise and carry out effective market research and to critically analyse performance. Students attend lectures and seminars. Lectures build knowledge of academic principles. Seminars guide students through phases of development with continuous feedback enabling reflection on both process and outcome of their activities.	**Aim**: to develop and execute a PR campaign through creative ideas and creative communications tools, presenting the campaign through an exhibition and dramatic role-play. Students attend lectures to develop academic knowledge and practical skills workshops. Students are guided through the different phases of the PR process through workshops, presentations and continuous feedback.
Project examples	**Project examples**
Students research LSBU careers and employability service to understand usage and experience.	Students devise a PR plan and develop PR materials for the LSBU Language Centre.
Students research reactions to a new breakfast-menu offering for Pizza Express.	Students develop a PR campaign for a cruise liner after the sinking of a competitor's cruise liner.
	Students develop a campaign for AfghanAid to raise awareness for civilian victims of the war in Afghanistan.
Phase One	**Phase One**
Students meet with client or tutor in-role and gather secondary information to understand the background and context of their study and to identify the specific research objectives. They present this first phase for formative feedback and a formative grade. They reflect on the feedback and further develop their study objectives.	Identification of a need for communication through secondary research. Students meet with the representative of the organisation or the tutor (in-role) to discuss the communication requirements and objectives.
	(continued overleaf)

Table 18.1 *continued*

Market Research – Undergraduate Level Five	Public Relations – Undergraduate Level Six
Phase Two Students develop a research methodology in classroom workshops and present a full research proposal for both formative and summative assessment. This mirrors the process in industry where the research agency a proposal to their potential client.	**Phase Two** Submission of a written campaign plan for formative assessment. Following written feedback and a formative grade, students revise and improve their campaign plan prior to execution.
Phase Three After feedback, reflection and adjustments they execute the research. Classroom activities facilitate development of their data-presentation and analysis skills.	**Phase Three** Students are invited to practice specific PR skills in workshops such as: writing press releases, speech writing and delivery, event planning, digital communications, feature articles, newsletters, etc. Each student perfects one skill for summative assessment.
Phase Four Students write a research report, including a full analysis of results for summative presentation to their client. Finally, they write a critical reflection of the limitations and errors in the research, proposing amendments to the methodology. This demonstrates what they have learnt about the research process, allows them to learn from their mistakes and improve performance in their final-year research project.	**Phase Four** PR Exhibition. Students display their PR materials and use drama and role-play to demonstrate one activity of their campaign, e.g. a press conference, radio interview or special event. They express the messages of the campaign in a creative and memorable way, consistent with their campaign plan. Feedback facilitates submission of a full report, including campaign plan and portfolio of materials developed.

130

dramatic role-play that is required of them. This role-play sometimes results in dramatic changes in student mood and performance; 'little lights go on' in previously disengaged students; students develop previously unknown practical communications skills whilst experiencing the live delivery of creative communications activities.

▶ Embedding employability

Both MR and PR students endorse the approach as influential in gaining employment. Particularly useful are the understanding of real-world processes, the practical skills gained and the ability to devise and analyse strategies.

'The mix of academic theory and real-world projects within the unit kept it fresh, current and engaging. PR was not something I knew much about nor had I considered it as a career path until I took this unit. I've now been in the industry for almost six years and have Anita to thank for that.'

Graduate, BA Marketing

In the postgraduate PR module embedding employability skills goes a step further and assesses students through an oral exam in the form of a mock interview for a PR role. Their summative assessment requires submission of a CV and covering letter and attendance at two interviews, including the oral presentation of a campaign plan. Formative assessment takes place at two points. First, students develop their CV-writing and interview skills with the Careers and Employability Service. They also submit a campaign plan proposal for feedback prior to the interview.

▶ Opportunities for creativity

In the undergraduate PR module, the exhibitions and role-play encourage creativity and innovative communications techniques. In the exhibition students are tasked to dramatise and role-play a particular PR activity from their campaign plan. The aim is to communicate the messages of the campaign by creating an exhibition space to facilitate the role-play. For example: students holding a press conference for a cruise liner transformed their exhibition space into the dining area of a cruise liner, and assessors attended the press conference in the role of journalists seated at the dining tables. In another example students role-played a seminar for travel agents, hosted assessors as travel agents in a round-table interactive Q&A session, decorated the space with posters and information, served national food and played national music. Other examples involve the creation of digital presentations, creation of web, Facebook and Twitter pages, news clips, webcasts and podcasts. Creativity is developed through the group process of brainstorming, encouraging innovative ideas and ensuring that students consider the diverse range of communication tools available to them.

> 'The exhibition is so different from anything we have done before, it was creative and fun.'

> 'The press release, speech writing and event-planning workshops were particularly useful to help us prepare.'
>
> Exchange students, 2012

▶ Formative feedback

For deep learning to succeed, Kolb's (1984) experiential approach depends on the tutors' constant feedback and questioning, challenging assumptions and driving reflection throughout the semester. Where students work in groups, collaboration invites development and sharing of ideas. Writing and presenting proposals and campaign plans for an indicative grade and constructive feedback drive the student to use knowledge and theory to support planning, carry out critical analysis and improve output. Practical workshops develop specific PR communication skills, facilitating practice and experimentation with written, oral, visual and digital communications. This in turns bolsters confidence and improves both the learning and the achievement of the student.

> 'It's good to get a second chance; it makes me feel that I can get a higher grade, if I put in the work.'
>
> BA Marketing Student 2007

▶ Critical challenges

Different students with differing needs; ensuring critical learning

Perhaps the greatest challenge is dealing with students' diverse learning styles, cultures and abilities. Some are more academic learners, some more practical, others creative and/or reflective. Some are passive learners accustomed to a teacher-centred approach; others find applying the theory delivered in lectures to justify tactical plans particularly challenging. Kolb (1976, 1984) and Honey and Mumford (1982) identify different styles that need addressing. Some interpretations (Fleming, 2001) suggest that students receive instruction tailored to their learning styles, while Stahl (2002) suggest that the learning-styles approach risks labelling students and limits their learning. However, Kolb (1976, 1984) emphasises the need for students to engage with all types of learning to be effective.

Formative assessment can challenge and guide students at different stages of a learning cycle, to brainstorm new ideas, develop criteria for decision making, apply academic principles and concepts or analyse alternative actions and justify decisions taken. Challenges to the oversimplified use of experiential learning by Young, Caudill and Murphy (2008) and Brennan (2012) suggest that this nudging around the cycle can avoid surface learning and ensure analytical and critical learning. This requires deep commitment and involvement from the tutor to encourage the use of feedback practically and creatively.

Non-attendance

In the case of the modules described here, the benefits of formative assessment rely on attendance. This can be a challenge when students have conflicting family and work responsibilities. A schedule of 'client' meetings can be helpful, requesting response and reflection to feedback, communicating via electronic means, such as Skype, and in some cases a summative grade linked to attendance may be necessary. However, where students select projects that interest them they are more likely to take responsibility. Moreover, in my experience, where students have contact with real clients, whether internal or external, their engagement and sense of responsibility grow and most attendance issues disappear.

Group cohesion

Where experiential learning is carried out in teams, group discord often impedes learning. Students often fail to understand how group work enhances learning through 'shared experience' and 'co-operation and sharing of ideas and solutions' (Zhao and Kuh, 2004). This is a perennial problem eased by allocating both individual and group tasks as part of a project. For example, in PR the group must collectively develop the ideas and activities for the PR campaign plan but each individual takes responsibility for the execution of one activity. This could be writing a speech for a press conference, writing a feature article, role-playing a radio or TV interview, etc. In MR prior agreement of individual roles within the group, group contracts and agreements can be helpful. In both cases feedback can facilitate identification of group processes hindering student learning and facilitate greater cooperation.

▶ My approach – a summary

I believe that student engagement is best achieved through creative, interactive and practical learning. Through experiential learning students understand how to apply knowledge, and are motivated to acquire and use it repeatedly. The approach described here advocates the role of teacher as facilitator, nudging and challenging students around different stages of a learning cycle. Students describe it as 'nurturing' and 'encouraging'. Continuous feedback from peers and teachers must be positive and constructive so that students are not discouraged but clearly understand what is required to improve performance. Thus formative assessment will challenge the student throughout the learning period, develop confidence in making, justifying and executing decisions and enable experiential learning to succeed as a developmental learning tool.

19 Developing and assessing professional competence: using technology in learning design

Luke Dawson (NTF 2012) *in association with Ben Mason*

Keywords: technology-supported learning, contextual leaning, work-based assessment, professionalism

> Luke Dawson is Professor of Dental Education, Oral Diseases and Director of BDS programmes at the University of Liverpool School of Dentistry. He is interested in how early-stage clinicians develop expertise and how this can be enhanced through the development of innovative technology-supported 'assessment for learning' designs.

Medical disciplines provide a rich environment for the development of innovative designs in assessment because many different formats of assessment are used, for example multiple choice questions (MCQs), essays, Objective Structured Clinical Examination (OSCE), oral presentation and portfolio. Furthermore, each assessment has to be deployed in a manner that ensures validity, reliability and defensibility. However, this assessment-intensive environment is also acutely subject to the educational impact of the assessment because, as we observe, 'regardless of the curriculum objectives, students in a learning programme will follow the examination programme' (Vleuten, 1996).

The corollary of this is simple: get the assessments wrong and you are likely to get the learning wrong. In 2009, data from dental-school student focus groups suggested that our approach to assessment was having the wrong educational impact. Our learners were tending to focus on accruing knowledge and being able to perform skills, rather than the intended outcomes of synthesis and understanding, i.e. 'they knew a lot' and 'could do a lot' but had little concept over 'why they were doing it'. Clearly, this was not the ideal. Coincidentally, we were also aware that the General Dental Council (GDC) were working on a new document, *Preparing for Practice* (GDC, 2011), that would detail the learning outcomes required for the professional registration of our graduates. This document moved the assessment of two compensatable domains – 'knowledge' and 'skills' – to a situation that required the non-compensatable, longitudinal continuous assessment of 150 outcomes across five domains, including professionalism.

▶ Analysis of the problem

Naturally, a significant change to professional requirements would need an equally significant change to assessments. Even the most transient voyage into the literature indicated that we needed to improve the alignment of our assessments to the intended outcomes (Biggs, 1996), as well as improve their contextualisation (Rumelhart and Norman, 1981). However, what was less obvious was how to manage the valid, reliable, defensible and longitudinal continuous assessment of 150 outcomes, while maintaining the appropriate educational impact. Indeed, how could this even be achieved by an ever-shrinking and overburdened workforce? Our solution was to embrace technology, something that we believe is essential to consider in any modern learning design.

We opted for a design-based research approach (Brown, 1992), and used it develop a design capable of addressing the problems, including how to: (1) develop practical skills; (2) assess professionalism; and (3) integrate currently available assessment approaches.

The development of practical skills

Our traditional approach to develop practical skills was grounded in mastery (Chambers, 1993). Recent evidence, however, would suggest 'enhancing performance' is a better approach (Ericsson, 2004). In this paradigm, following focused and *deliberate* practice within a domain, the performance of the learner improves until it becomes automated. Upon 'automation', the individual loses conscious control and therefore is no longer able to make 'specific intentional adjustments' without external observation and feedback (Ericsson, 2004). From the perspective of the learning design these data suggest that we needed to: (1) embrace longitudinal assessment for learning strategies (Black and Wiliam, 1998); (2) monitor skills development at the level of the individual tasks; and (3) ensure the delivery of appropriate feedback (Nicol and Macfarlane-Dick, 2006) at the level of the tasks, to drive changes in self-regulated learning processes (Butler and Winne, 1995).

The assessment of professionalism

In 2009, the only formal assessment of professionalism within our programme was knowledge! The assessment of professionalism is difficult and issues include: passing students with ethical behaviours but unethical attitudes (Rees and Knight, 2007); agreement over what constitutes unprofessional behaviour (Ginsburg, Regehr and Lingard, 2004); and the unwillingness of teachers to take responsibility for their judgements. We concluded that: (1) the longitudinal pattern of professionalism is likely to be a more reliable indicator than a series of spot assessments; (2) longitudinal judgements would need to be triangulated and accumulated to produce the composite pattern; (3) judgements needed to be made by multiple staff; and (4) judgements over progression would need to be made by a panel to circumvent the problem of staff not willing to take personal responsibly (Albanese, 1999). This same approach could then be employed for the assessment of all skills.

Available models

A number of work-based assessment tools with good predictive validity have been developed (Norcini, Arnold and Kimball, 1995; Prescott et al., 2002). The common principles that underpin them are that they link: structured feedback to the learning objectives; have systems for scoring performance based on expected standards; enable clinical development through a combination of assessment, external feedback and targeted training; and enable informed longitudinal qualitative judgements (Prescott et al, 2002; Norcini et al., 1995). However, they were designed to be used with a small number of trainees, on a discontinuous basis. Therefore, we needed to design a new approach that integrated their essential nuances, but could be used continuously with large numbers of students.

▶ The learning design

Our solution was to amalgamate existing work-based assessment tools into an integrated format, and develop it onto a mobile device linked to a central database or 'Core'. We then designed two bespoke assessment modules linked to the 'Core' through the outcomes. One is web-based for 'paper-based' assessment, the other iPad-based, for work-based assessment (i.e. in our case, the clinics). With this design, staff were only required to score what they observed, and by using it on every clinic the longitudinal pattern of development could be triangulated and assembled with time. In addition, through using a rating-scale criterion referenced to the developing independence of the learner (Crossley et al., 2011), at the level of each component of the task being undertaken, immediate learner feedback could be provided, driving required changes to learner self-regulation. Furthermore, a centralised design enabled decisions over progression to be made by a single panel using data from hundreds of triangulated assessments from up to 30 different staff in all 150 outcomes, rather than one-off spot tests. This approach consequently increased the reliability and defensibility of the panel decisions.

Moving forward, we further developed the Core by mapping the required learning outcomes from the GDC (and/or any other stakeholder such as the Quality Assurance Agency) to the programme Aims and Objectives. This allowed the design to be used as a powerful curriculum-mapping tool, able to demonstrate where every outcome was taught and assessed, as well as instantly return the current progress of each student.

Finally, by designing a new electronic Exam Database system that linked its questions to the Core, we were able to present individual developmental profiles facilitating self-directed learning, development, and the production of validated transferable skills portfolios to employers.

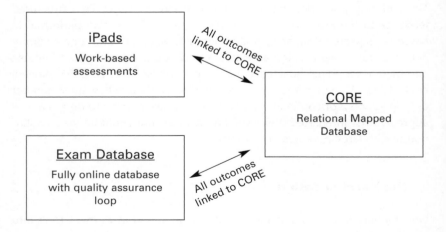

Figure 19.1 The final technology-supported learning design

Each learner has a personalised interface to view the organised, triangulated, multi-source data. This enables reflection upon their developing performance in any of the 150 outcomes, in real time. Furthermore, progression judgements are based on longitudinal development patterns in multiple domains, comprising hundreds of data points, compared with single assessments.

The additional benefits of the design included: full triangulation between all assessment formats; automated assessment blueprinting (i.e. mapping to learning outcomes); and teacher calibration.

▶ Evaluation of the learning design

We have evaluated the design from three perspectives, those of the students, staff and its inherent transferability across disciplines.

Students

The students have embraced the design, and responded enthusiastically to invitations to participate in its further development through focus groups and surveys.

Table 19.1 Examples of qualitative feedback from student evaluation of the learning design

Question	Student comments
Are there any ways in which the design has shifted the way you think about developing as a dentist?	'The continual reflection, and the ability to see your data as you progress are definitely the way forward for development'. 'Definitely. The design encourages self-assessment and a mature way of doing so'.
What changes to your learning style have occurred (if any) by having your data immediately available?	'The ability to reflect immediately after clinics in your own time has a huge advantage for long-term development'.
Do you see further uses of the design outside dentistry?	'Absolutely. I believe the design can be useful in any learning process'. 'The design is a tool not only for dentists, but a new way of continuous professional development. It is the modern way of approaching learning and reflection. It can provide the employee's profile and experience. It is the way forward'.

Table 19.2 Data from staff evaluation of the learning design (n = 25)

Statement	Agree with statement (%)	Disagree with statement (%)
The grading system gives students feedback on the quality of their clinical work	91	0
The grading system allows students to see areas in which they need to improve	90	10
The clinic form highlights the importance of a more holistic treatment, taking into account professionalism, time management, communication, etc., to the students	82	5
I feel I could easily defend my grading on a particular item of treatment if required	73	9
Overall I prefer the new version of clinical assessment	85	10

In addition, the design has had a dramatic effect on our National Student Survey scores, with the domain of assessment and feedback increasing from 40 per cent satisfaction to 90 per cent since 2009. Moreover, there is good evidence that the design is significantly improving student performance, evidenced by the fact that in 2012 all final-year undergraduates sat and passed their examinations for the first time in the last 20 years.

Staff

The results of staff surveys (n = 25) suggest that staff are also happy with the design.

Furthermore, we have been able to defend progress decisions at the highest levels of university scrutiny.

Transferability

The design is modular and can be applied to any situation where the aim is to demonstrate that an outcome has been met. Although it was developed in dentistry, we are currently working with veterinary, medical, chemistry, engineering, life sciences and even our own human resources department to adapt aspects of the design to their required purposes.

▶ Conclusion

The symbiosis of technology and pedagogy has enabled the Liverpool School of Dentistry to harness the positive educational impact of assessment. We can now longitudinally assess multiple domains at once, providing instant feedback to students, resulting in self-assessment and individualised learning. Decisions can be proven to be valid, reliable and defensible. All assessments are blueprinted and triangulated to reveal a true 360-degree appraisal of any student or cohort, at the touch of a button. Importantly, through the correct utilisation of technology, this new design actually results in a reduction in staff administrative time, enabling focus on the student experience.

Ben Mason is Lecturer in Educational Development, having worked in the Liverpool Dental School since 2008. He is interested in curriculum design and the use of mobile technologies to enhance the student experience.

20 Building curriculum internationalisation from the bottom up

David Killick (NTF 2000)

Keywords: *internationalisation, curriculum, communities of practice, change*

After several years teaching overseas, David Killick joined Leeds Metropolitan University in 1991. Having held several roles there, he now provides institutional leadership in academic development. David is committed to internationalisation in higher education, and has presented and published widely on cross-cultural capability and global perspectives in the curriculum. His current research interests are focused on links between internationalisation and equality and diversity in higher education.

In the 1990s we had barely coined *internationalisation*;[24] the sector was, to greater or lesser extents, working with more limited *international* strategies, focused on recruiting international students and, possibly, developing offshore provision. Some might wonder how much has actually changed in terms of many institutional priorities, notwithstanding ambitious mission statements. But there are positive stories to tell, and this one is in the main a story of curriculum internationalisation shaped within communities of practice (COPs) (Wenger, 1998a), in which colleagues' educational and social justice concerns outweigh institutional drives for marketisation or global positioning.

▶ Beginnings

At the start of the millennium, working with a colleague who is now an internationally recognised expert-advocate in internationalisation (see, e.g.,

Jones, 2010), I set out to produce guidelines to facilitate the internationalisation of our undergraduate curricula, interpreted as introducing 'cross-cultural capability' and 'global perspectives' through changes to content and delivery. I had worked with international educators in Australia and the USA, establishing an international student exchange programme, and had seen excellent examples of work at modular level and in service learning contexts (Killick, 2007) which seemed to enable students to transform their horizons and perspectives (Mezirow, 1997; Mezirow and Associates, 2000).

I sought volunteers to inform the development of our guidelines, and the new COP included colleagues from:

- a range of disciplines
- equality and diversity
- widening participation
- international student support
- our university chaplaincy

The chaplain introduced us to the work of the Development Education Association, and a related project embedding sustainability at Bournemouth University (see, e.g., McKenzie et al., 2009). Intelligent, critical and open discussions led to the production of an initial set of guidelines in 2003. Through subsequent work with course teams, some revisions were made, and a published version became available (Killick, 2006).

Explicit reference to the guidelines became a requirement of course annual quality reviews, and of the approvals process for new courses (for a project report, see Jones and Killick, 2007). It is a moot point whether this (unanticipated) top-down driver for what had been a bottom-up initiative was a blessing. Among colleagues there were many enthusiastic adopters, but others cited 'managerialism' as an inhibitor.

The bulk of the naysayers, though, fell into two camps – those who professed that cross-cultural capability and global perspectives bore no relationship to their subject, and those who were 'already doing it'. The second group were the more difficult to move.

Outcomes

The guidelines comprise a rationale and summary of related concepts, followed by a series of 'key questions' about how a course addresses/achieves a number of objectives – two examples will serve to illustrate these.

How does the course:

- ▶ seek to incorporate the knowledge and understanding brought to it by students from diverse backgrounds?
- ▶ make students aware of the global impacts of professions related to the subject area?

Despite advising that 'consideration of the key questions should be approached as a developmental process rather than simply an audit of existing practice', several responses were more audit-like and did not evidence a significant developmental process (though many did). In retrospect, a better phrasing of questions might have helped, perhaps especially with those in the 'already doing it' camp, shifting from:

- ▶ How does the course ...

to

- ▶ How could the course better ...

Nonetheless, and importantly, in addition to advances in specific courses, the project achieved at least three important outcomes. It:

- ▶ brought the discourse of IOC (Internationalisation of the Curriculum) into the academic community of the university
- ▶ was a sufficiently significant project to advance the discourse in the sector (several conference presentations, publications, and requests to share the underlying approach with other institutions flowed directly); and
- ▶ significantly enhanced my personal COP, and with that, my development and confidence as an internationalisation practitioner/advocate.

This last point was an important factor in convincing myself to embark on a PhD. My broadly phenomenological study into the lived experience of students engaged in a variety of international activities brought to the surface narratives in which participants evidenced, in varying ways, developments in their self-identification as 'global citizens'. This reflected other research into 'study abroad' outcomes (too numerous to cite, but some excellent examples can be found in Savicki, 2008).

A rather surprising and significant finding for IOC, however, was that many of the richest experiences for these students occurred in encounters with others who were not members of the host culture and/or were peripheral to the international activity itself (Killick, 2012). This finding, while not invalidating the power of being temporarily located in new and 'foreign' spaces, did point me back to the question of how IOC could help bring similar transformative learning to the majority of students, for whom the home campus remains their university experience. How could the formal curriculum support students to cross borders and encounter the diverse others which make up the student body?

▶ Change

The end of the curriculum review project and the completion of my PhD more or less coincided with a change in our senior management team, and a related shift in institutional direction and identity. Colleagues as long in the tooth as myself will be familiar with the kinds of structural change that follows in the wake. Some will also identify with the angst which can follow when our individual academic identities feel under threat, especially when a shifting institutional identity is itself riding a tide of uncertainties surrounding a globalising and marketising higher education (Bauman, 2005; Barnett and Di Napoli, 2008; Fanghanel, 2012). However unsettling, the reimagining of our institutional 'scape' (Appadurai, 1997) required a new approach to IOC. Our original project had reached its end, and internationalisation generally had moved to a less peripheral position in the UK higher education landscape. Given how much work we had already committed to it, the question which emerged was how to mainstream IOC; how to embed its objectives and aspirations rather than continuing to frame it as a separate agenda.

From my institution's broader strategic change agenda emerged a large-scale project to 'refocus' our undergraduate curricula. This was to involve structural changes and the introduction of graduate attributes; with that came an opportunity – could we define one of those attributes to embed our IOC work? Again, this called for bringing together a new COP from across the institution – this time drawn mainly from our Teacher Fellow network. In the light of experience, as well as reviewing our IOC objectives, we enjoyed intense debate on process. What process would best serve to set the IOC objectives within the disciplinary contexts of a course, and be resistant to a tick-box approach?

Working on these projects with so many colleagues has proved one of the richest professional spaces I have ever experienced. Their commitment and willingness to share honest stories of disappointments offset by the joys of small steps forward continue to help keep my glass half full in turbulent times.

▶ **Impact**

Notwithstanding the tension inherent in a prescriptive aligned curriculum, and a constructivist learning paradigm, Biggs's influential notion of constructive alignment (Biggs and Tang, 2007) led us to identify learning outcomes as the most likely mechanism for embedding IOC across diverse subject areas. After a considerable amount of critical, passionate and energising discussion, a new guidelines document emerged, now formulated around embedding a global outlook (Killick, 2011).

Perhaps the most significant feature of the document were the examples of how existing learning outcomes might be modified to embed an aspect of a global outlook while retaining their primary subject focus. Interestingly, lengthy discussions often produced quite subtle shifts, which often also served 'only' to make explicit what was intended but not expressed in the original. Examples by way of illustration are shown in Table 20.1.

While some found this easier than others, aspects of a global outlook have now been written into course and module learning outcomes across our undergraduate curricula. There is space here to quote only a few from revised module specifications. These, hopefully, offer a flavour of how students will experience our work to fit their development to the turbulent world(s) they will inhabit.

At the end of this module, students will be able to:

'critically appraise the World Health Organisation's health priorities in both a national and international context of healthcare policy and prac-

Table 20.1 How learning outcomes can be modified to reflect internationalism in the curriculum

Original	Modified
Students will be able to: analyse market opportunities in the international business environment	Students will be able to: analyse market opportunities in contrasting international business environments
debate the ethical responsibilities of science in society with reference to current issues	debate the ethical responsibilities of science with reference to current issues in a multicultural society
present key findings from an individual research project to a professional audience	present key findings from an individual research project to a professional audience whose first language may not be English

tice, evaluating the role of nursing and other healthcare professionals within a globalised context.'

Leadership, Management and Enterprise, BSc Mental Health Nursing

'Develop and evaluate inclusive approaches to teaching and learning, including strengthening global and local dimensions in the taught curriculum.'

Professional Studies, BAH Primary Education

'Evaluate the cross-cultural contexts of a variety of music genres.'

Music in Context, BA Music Production

'Demonstrate a critical understanding of relevant concepts, theories and methods in landscape architecture and an awareness of their relevant social, economic, environmental and cultural contexts through study of a chosen topic.'

Critical Study, BA(H) Landscape Architecture

'Present an appreciation of Animation Principles appropriately for an audience of diverse cultures and first languages.'

Animation Principles, BSc(H) Computer Animation and Special Effects

'Introduce the fundamental issues and principles within the water sector both in the UK and overseas.'

Hydraulics and Water Engineering, BEng(H) Civil Engineering

'Critically examine the labour and product market restrictions utilised by global sports leagues.'

Sport Economics and Finance, BA(H) Sports Marketing

▶ Conclusion

As our first-year students embark upon these 'refocused' courses, we must capture their learning and assessment experiences, and the global outlook to learning that these facilitate. Above all, this will provide an indication of the creativity of colleagues in embedding internationalisation in their curricula, which, however top-down the drivers, can always only ever be achieved through bottom-up commitment.

The various projects focusing on IOC in which I have been engaged have demonstrated to me how much can be achieved at module and course level, with or without institution-wide initiatives. I believe there is scope for other academics to enhance the global relevance and inclusivity of any course, and in the current UK approach to higher education programme design, small changes to learning outcomes have tremendous potential to help your students make their way in their future worlds.

21 New horizons and old challenges for distance learning: bridging the access gap in African universities

Basiro Davey (NTF 2012)

Keywords: *distance learning, higher education, dual-mode universities, Africa, Ethiopia, Nigeria*

Basiro Davey has been developing distance learning at the Open University, UK for more than 35 years, specialising in health sciences, infectious disease and public health. Since 2009 she has mentored Ethiopian and more recently Nigerian academics in distance-learning pedagogy and curriculum design in intensive writing workshops in Africa.

Demand for higher education has risen across Africa since the 1990s, and although university provision is rapidly expanding, many African universities turn away thousands of qualified applicants every year. The sector cannot keep pace with increasing demand just by building new campuses, and a chronic shortage of faculty staff in many subject areas further constrains the provision of tertiary places. In this essay, I reflect on prospects for closing the gap in university access through distance learning (DL) in Nigeria and Ethiopia, using methods developed over 30 years of teaching experience at the Open University (OU) in the UK. In the process of scanning these new horizons, I consider the many challenges to delivering high quality DL undergraduate programmes in Africa, many of which echo experiences during the early years of the OU.

▶ Background

A brief history of my involvement in DL capacity-building with African academics gives the context for this article. In 2009–10, the OU and the Ethiopian Federal Ministry of Health (FMOH), with UNICEF, the African Medical and Research Foundation (AMREF) and the World Health Organisation (WHO), began collaborating to upgrade and extend the knowledge and competencies of Ethiopia's 33 000 rural Health Extension Workers (HEAT, 2012). I led teams of OU colleagues to mentor Ethiopian academics and health professionals through residential workshops in DL pedagogy and curriculum design, and together we developed an extensive curriculum of theory modules drawing on OU experience of teaching adults at a distance. OU teams with experience of the Ethiopian programme (myself included) also led in-country workshops with Nigerian academics from seven universities in 2012, using the same methods as in Ethiopia.

We supported participants in directly experiencing the intense academic collaboration required to produce high-quality DL modules. We helped them devise clearly framed learning outcomes, demonstrated how a structured template paces students through manageable two-hour study sessions, emphasised the need for a narrative structure, the value of engaging illustrations and activities with 'built-in' student support, and the role of formative self-assessments to build confidence in distant learners.

Mentoring these Ethiopian and Nigerian academics has been among the most rewarding experiences of my career. It informs the following reflections on the prospects for increasing university access through DL methods in these two countries, and by implication in most of Sub-Saharan Africa. The quotations included below are from questionnaires completed by participants after these workshops (N and E codes identify the nationality of respondents).

▶ Challenges to distance learning in Africa

The practical constraints that explain why most DL resources in Africa are still largely produced in print include frequent power cuts, unstable or inaccessible internet and inadequate technical support for online study (Olakulehin, 2008; Wright, Dhanarajan and Reju, 2009). Although mobile phones are widespread in Nigeria, large areas of rural Ethiopia lack mobile phone coverage and neither country has expertise in m-learning.

Unaffordable course fees and the cost of PCs and laptops are additional barriers. Postal delivery of study materials may be impossible or unreliable; for example, Nigerian students on DL programmes often travel to host universities to collect their course resources.

In addition to these structural problems, academics in our workshops revealed several personal and professional difficulties in producing quality DL study materials. Their most persistent challenge was developing the 'conversational' writing style typical of DL texts and activities. It jarred with the didactic mode of instruction familiar to African academics more used to lecturing hundreds of students with PowerPoint slides and handouts offering 'facts' for memorisation.

> 'Keeping the language and flow simple was not a simple task. Module writing is such a demanding task and needed more time than I thought initially.'
>
> (E13)

> 'The job is very tasking and for you to ask someone to develop a module of this nature – honestly, not all persons in tertiary institutions can do that, because it needs time, it needs additional funding and you have to be dedicated.'
>
> (N4)

A cultural issue that made collaborative working tricky was reluctance to critique each other's drafts or suggest improvements, especially where the commenter was junior to the author whose draft was under review. Some academics had limited knowledge of word processing, and I learned to check discreetly after discovering a senior lecturer retyping tracked comments because he didn't know how to accept or reject them. Slow typing speeds made long writing periods arduous.

Assessment to encourage learning as distinct from assessment for credit was another unfamiliar concept. Abandoning multiple-choice styles and writing self-assessment questions that support critical thinking and reinforce key points was a new technique that most initially struggled to grasp, but soon learned to value.

Despite these intrinsic difficulties, there was also real enthusiasm in the workshops. Participants tackled the challenges of writing for DL with interest and accepted our support with appreciation. Most rewarding of all, they quickly embraced the student-centred approach:

> 'It's essential that your materials are interactive so that you carry them along and talk with them and put yourself in their shoes and appreciate where they're coming from.'
>
> (N6)

These reflections underline the need for specific training in DL pedagogy and curriculum design, which very few African academics tasked with producing DL programmes have received:

'Most [of us] have passed through the traditional classroom teaching learning process and have limited understanding and poor attitude towards distance learning.'

(E7)

They also needed more time for innovative work. Most DL resources are generated in dual-mode universities by academics who also carry heavy face-to-face teaching workloads.

'Instructors are often overburdened with routine duties; so there must be clear incentives to work on such issues including using the DL teaching materials for academic promotion.'

(E13)

This comment hints at a general feeling that DL teaching is undervalued by academic colleagues who do not appreciate the skill required to produce high-quality DL modules, or perhaps fear the consequences if DL methods became more widespread.

'Most do not like to come out from the traditional way of teaching [i.e. classroom-based teaching]. Some feel that they may lose their jobs if distance learning is expanded.'

(E2)

'Some of our senior colleagues they don't want these changes [because] they may be left out of the system.'

(N5)

Entrenched opinion within the African university sector that DL offers 'second-class' education reminded me strongly of attitudes towards the OU in the 1970s. Sir Walter Perry, the first OU Vice-Chancellor, noted:

'Most of my colleagues in universities regarded my move to the Open University as a sign of incipient senility. They did not believe that education through the media could conceivably work ... I had to persuade them that there would be absolutely no compromise on standards.'

(Perry, 1976: 32)

African academics now face similar opposition to DL:

> 'Challenges include low value and attitude for distance learning, considering it as inferior compared to formal education.'

(E1)

Current suspicions about the effectiveness of DL methods often assert that African students find self-directed study alien, preferring 'respected professors' delivering lectures face-to-face. For example, Basaza, Milman and Wright (2010: 88) noted that 'Ugandan culture tends to be a verbal or talking culture; thus, students feel pressure when they are expected to read and write for extended periods of time.' The Ethiopian Minister of Education made exactly this point to OU colleagues in 2009, acknowledging that Africans don't like DL but may be forced to embrace it in order to meet the country's aspirations for higher education. But Nigerian and Ethiopian academics already engaged in DL feel that negative perceptions are slowly being overturned by the quality of DL resources:

> 'It has even started changing their mindset that distance learning is a second class system of education, because nowadays even conventional students are looking for distance learning materials from our distance learning students and this raises their confidence in distance learning.'

(N2)

> 'Improved access to quality, standardised training material is the most important benefit. Even regular students ... will immensely benefit if they access such a material as a side reference.'

(E13)

▶ The future for distance education in Nigeria and Ethiopia

Nigeria and Ethiopia have the two largest populations in Africa – 167 million and 84.7 million, respectively – and their 'young' median age structure (17–18) is one driver of increasing demand for university places. Both countries have rapidly expanded their university provision. For example, nine new Nigerian universities were founded in 2011–12, bringing the total to 124 institutions. In 1999 there were only two universities in Ethiopia; by 2012 there were 31, including 13 new campuses.

However, this ambitious building programme cannot keep pace with demand. Ethiopia has not published data on the number of qualified applicants turned away, but at least 500 000 qualified Nigerian students fail to get a university place each year. The Nigerian Minister of Education, acknowledging that enrolment is 'abysmally low' compared to student demand, admitted that:

'It is worrisome that less than 15 per cent of candidates who annually apply for admission into Nigerian universities are admitted.'

(Alaneme, 2011)

Against this background, Nigeria has recognised the potential of DL programmes to widen university access, particularly to employed students with family responsibilities. The National Open University of Nigeria opened in 2001–2 and within ten years had an enrolled population of 32 400 students, all studying at a distance. Six dual-mode Nigerian universities have also established DL Centres or Institutes accredited by the Nigerian National Universities Commission (NUC), and although most of their students still attend campus-based education for some courses, the future is clear to DL academics:

'It means almost everybody can access university education at every nook and cranny of Nigeria if it is done through the e-Modules. You don't have to abandon your job to actually acquire a university education.'

(N6)

'Existing universities have never dreamt of meeting the number of applicants that apply for courses and this kind of learning will liberate us, will liberate the education system, liberate the universities.'

(N1)

By contrast, in 2010 Ethiopia abandoned its earlier intention to create an Ethiopian Open University, enrolling 1.6 million students by 2017 (Ethiopian Embassy, 2007) and the Federal Ministry of Education (FME) briefly banned DL programmes altogether (Daniel, 2010). The government acknowledged that 'Open and distance education remain hardly developed' in Ethiopia (FME, 2010).

But there is a new cadre of educators in African universities who can see the potential for DL resources and methods to influence traditional university teaching for the better, as the OU has done in the UK:

'If they will seek my opinion, then I would even advocate to let them get these modules, because it will enhance the teaching in our tertiary institutions, not only in distance learning but in other conventional universities.'

(N4)

Despite many challenges, these academics are heading enthusiastically towards new and not so distant educational horizons.

22 Kinds of international: internationalisation through engagement with one another

Jane Spiro (NTF 2010)

Keywords: *creativity, engagement, growth, identification, ownership*

Jane Spiro is Reader in Education and Teaching of English to Speakers of Other Languages (TESOL) at Oxford Brookes University. She has run programmes worldwide in academic literacies, language teacher education, creative writing, literature pedagogy, testing and assessment, including in Hungary, Poland, Mexico, India and China. Her publications include: *Storybuilding* (2007), *Creative Poetry Writing* (2004), *Changing Methodologies in TESOL* (2013) and stories for and about language learners published in Germany, Italy and the UK.

This essay is written from the perspective of a higher education educator who, for 30 years, has been passionate about the notion of students as international participants, long before the rhetoric of 'internationalisation' entered university mission statements. It aims to tell the story of how the landscape of higher education has gradually transformed in its response to international students, illustrating the way in which this impacted on learning and teaching.

'International' is here deemed to describe students studying in a higher education context that differs from their pre-university education, and is thus likely to be in a second language or culture. I shall illustrate a shift in view of the international student as economic resource, to a view of the whole university as an international environment committed to mutual listening and learning from one another. What this means in concrete terms will be illustrated by four projects conducted in a post-1992 university, in which home and international staff and students became equal participants in learning from one another. The projects offer a template for developing mutual learning opportunities that can be adapted to any subject discipline or teaching context.

▶ Kinds of international: higher education approaches

The 'economic rationalist' views the international student as a commodity and economic resource: 'the more foreign students pay a high tuition fee, the higher the economic return' (Knight and de Wit, 1995: 11). This has been described as the 'marketisation' of universities, 'forced into the market place' (Dixon, 2006: 320) by economic imperatives, and thus into competition with one another for international students. Even the term 'international' has been repositioned semantically to mean a non-EU student paying full fees. Teichler (2004) notes that the debate has tended to focus on 'marketisation, competition and management in HE' and hardly at all on notions of mutual learning, 'such as knowledge society, global village or global understanding' (Teichler, 2004: 23).

The Russell group university where I was teaching in the late 1980s adopted such a marketised approach to international students, both in policy and in practice. The recruitment policy for international students was vigorous, with vibrant recruitment of non-EU students on government scholarships, particularly to postgraduate taught and research programmes. However, their presence in increasing numbers triggered no revisiting of pedagogy, curriculum, or approaches to student engagement within their subject disciplines.

Instead, international students who struggled within their subject disciplines were referred by their subject tutors to the Language Centre. This lack of explicit planning for the non-indigenous student, and the assumption that all acclimatisation and academic issues had at source language differences, led to a number of challenges for the students: from the deciphering of tutor feedback to difficulty in formulating a viable doctorate topic; from social problems such as isolation during the Christmas period, to feeling excluded by native English speakers in seminars and discussions.

There is ample testimony to show that these experiences were not atypical. The 'Teaching International Students project' (HEA, 2011b), as an open story-sharing forum, showed that students experience challenges from induction through to the completion of their studies, which are hidden and unaccounted for within traditional subject disciplinary approaches. For example, terms used by higher education educators as self-evident, such as 'independent learning', 'criticality' and 'reflective writing', were found, in listening to the international student voice, to be problematic and opaque (Spiro, Henderson and Clifford, 2012). Jankowska (2011: 811), for example, describes her own experience of 'distancing' from her teachers, requiring her to 'find my own way' too early in the study process, before she felt she had the resources she needed to continue. Grant and Manathunga (2011) found that supervision relationships were unclear and undefined; and that international students did not necessarily build support networks with their peers that crossed cultural boundaries, even where tutors felt they had generated group work to encourage this (Leask, 2010). Loneliness and isolation emerged as significant factors in the experience of the second-culture student (Erichsen and Bolliger, 2011). In short, what was assumed might be acquired simply through exposure to a higher education environment, proved to be very real challenges.

As a support tutor in the Language Centre, in 'listening' to international students I came to see that their experiences were those of all students making a transition from one learning culture to another; and that it was we as higher education educators – not they – who needed to be clearer about academic assumptions and conventions in order to make them transparent for learners. It became clear their concerns needed to be addressed not just by a specialist unit but also by everyone who cared about universities being places of inclusion, opportunity and empowerment.

▶ Internationalisation through engagement with one another

Simply 'being' in an international classroom does not in itself lead to engagement with or deeper understanding of others. It is possible to remain personally unchanged while travelling physically or virtually across cultural borders, identifying 'international' as simply 'distance from home' (Mohanty, 2003: 204). This section describes four projects in which cultural differences became significant learning opportunities, and both international and local students had equal share in the exchange of knowledge.

Project 1: Co-producing poems, stories and songs

English literature students on a 'Literatures in English' module were asked to find a partner with a first language or learning background different to their own (Spiro, 2010a). They discussed texts that mapped the crossing between cultures and languages – examples are shown in Table 22.1 – allowing the students to exchange stories of their own experiences crossing cultures – whether this 'crossing' was school to university, adolescence to adulthood, home country to a new country/culture, one language to another. All students were able to relate to this sense of passage and transition in some way. They then wrote a joint creative text that captured what was shared and what was unique in some way. These shared experiences could be written as two intersecting voices, as poem, song or story; but both had to feel equally visible in the text and accompany it with individual reflections on the writing process and what had been learnt.

> Ghana is my homeland
> But
> I am also a daughter of France.

In her individual reflections, Joanna explains her words:

> 'The conjunction 'but' is important to show the fact that I belong to both countries: 'but' is isolated to show the ambiguity I feel when it comes to explaining where I am from.'

> (Joanna)

What emerges are explanations that offer windows into home language and illustrations as to how students have learnt from one another in making this personal knowledge explicit to others.

> 'I saw some of the others had difficulties with talking about their feelings or beliefs, i.e. from Japan or Germany. They would not restrain themselves from expressing their emotions when having a conversation, but when it came to writing, they wanted the text to sound more formal, hence, not including what they were actually thinking about.'

> (Charlotte)

whilst another student acknowledges the change in her own assumptions:

> 'Before I conducted the study, I had very closed mind about learning, I had never thought in such detail about how each person may have different characteristics and skills.'

> (Malgorzata)

Table 22.1 Poems crossing cultures

Poem	Cultural transition	Themes emerging
John Agard *Listen Mr. Oxford Don*	The poet proudly rebukes the 'Oxford don' directly in his own variety of Guyanese English, revealing the inadequacy of standard notions of 'correctness'	Being empowered or disempowered by using the standard language in comparison to a regional variety
Ee Tiang Hong *Tranquerah Road*	The poet walks down a road in Malacca, Malaysia, and reveals how the buildings each reveal part of the history of colonisation	Colonisation and its impact on language, architecture and education
Anna Akhmatova *The City that I Have Loved*, translated from the Russian by Richard McKane	The poet yearns for her lost city using gentle metaphors of childhood	Homesickness and memory; links between home and childhood
Louise Bennett *Colonization in Reverse*	The poet describes her experience of moving to the UK, as compared to UK colonisers moving to Jamaica	Migration and moving home
Czesław Miłosz *My Faithful Mother Tongue*, translated from the Polish by the poet and Robert Haas	The poet describes his struggles about choosing to use or not to use his mother tongue in his poetry	Language choice, and the personal and political power of the mother tongue
Nagesh Rao *I Am a Door*	The poet describes the dilemmas of belonging to two cultures	Being bicultural/bilingual: a personal identity that straddles more than one culture

Project 2: Exchanging languages

Students with mother tongues other than English were supported to run a one-hour language-sharing session open to staff and students at their institution. The languages shared included Turkish, Arabic, Spanish, Ukrainian, Polish, Hindi, Mandarin and Japanese. Topics selected included the Mandarin dragon icon; the differences between three Ukrainian and Russian sounds; and Hungarian ways of saying 'hello'. The sessions were attended enthusiastically by staff, administrators and student peers and resulted in a Language Exchange notice board for students to meet and exchange languages:

> 'There's a language exchange notice board and I noted down the name of a Japanese guy, I hear Japanese and it's interesting to listen to it, if I get more time we can meet up, he wants more time practising English and I want to practise Japanese.'

> (Dan)

Similarly, international students became empowered to recognise and formalise their language knowledge and skill; the Mandarin student offered a weekly Mandarin language lunchtime class adopted by the university and open to all.

What was significant was the opportunity for students to become experts and demonstrate this expertise beyond their own discrete student cohort. It empowered them to recognise their home culture as a source of unique knowledge, which had value to others.

Project 3: Sharing teacher values online

Teachers of English worldwide were invited to share online critical moments or incidents in their careers and explore the underlying values and beliefs which made them significant. 'Critical incidents' were defined as a significant moment in which they felt something changed, or was learnt (Tripp, 1993). In so doing, teachers from different cultures and contexts recognised parallels between one another. They identified differences in their approach to discipline and student control; and similarities in their experience of teaching as a vocation. They were surprised to see similarities in the status of the English language teacher in different countries and cultures, and similar constraints in funding, resources and professional conditions of service.

Over several cohorts, these statements have been shared between groups so that 'long lists' have emerged of shared beliefs and priorities cutting across year groups. Hence this data grows from the single identity of a teacher, to an ever-broadening community of practitioners, for example:

> 'The online discussion board has been providing excellent studying views; we can not only learn from tutors in uni, but also learn from students, who are from different countries, or English students but currently teaching in other countries.'

> (Nan)

'When I work with others I feel needed, I really feel I have something to contribute, I like it … I found I learn more by talking to other students.'

(Eloise)

The experience made the UK-based students more aware (Spiro, 2010b, 2011):

'There is no English without other countries. Britain is nothing without other places.'

'In France it's really regimented, you have real respect for the teacher.'

'I heard about the Chinese school entrance exams – people from Oxford couldn't do them – they set the bar so much higher/the competition is so much higher.'

'In Germany too – the students were really hard-working.'

'In contrast to the system here – you think if you don't do homework, who cares?'

Project 4 Paired learner profiles

Undergraduate students on a 'Language Learning and Creativity' module were asked to find a partner with experience of a different language or culture. They drew up a series of questions, and wrote a report, which elicited the story of how their partner learnt the language and experienced the crossover between cultures.

Their partnerships included: the discovery that peers from the African continent (Ghana and Nigeria) spoke three or more local languages; an understanding for the first time of the challenges for parents and relations who had moved to an English-speaking country later in life; the appreciation for the first time of peers' skills in their mother tongue – one was a songwriter in Japanese, another a poet in Arabic, another had exhibited a painting in a Polish art gallery.

'In order to know your culture you need to get out of it. It has to be something new just to shock'.

(Chris)

'It just seems to me that a lot of people go to a lot of trouble to learn

English and change culture ... not many English people would go to the same trouble.'

(Jenny)

'I have been made to re-evaluate my perspectives a little. A good example is how easily some western people such as myself fall into the trap of assuming that everyone agrees with me.'

(Dan)

▶ What does transformation look like? How can the university make a difference?

What transformation really 'looked like' for these students was a shift in their understanding of themselves and their peers. The international students were able to place themselves at the centre of learning, finding their languages, skills and stories recognised as inspirational; the students who had not travelled from their home culture or language, experienced change in their own assumptions and expectations without physical travel. Shared tasks, guided questions that elicited stories, thematised discussion that teased out parallels and differences, a forum for sharing linguistic and cultural knowledge, all provided a structure through which students and teachers learnt from one another and shifted the balance of power, placing the international student at centre stage.

In a survey of 100 undergraduate international and home-based students, after a year of shared/paired tasks across cultures and languages, all but seven felt that the university played a role in their development as global citizens and 97 articulated positive views relating to ways in which the university had transformed them:

'It enables me to meet people from all over the world and enjoy life with these people and understand their background.'

'It raises awareness of the diversity of the world.'

'I've learnt to see everybody as one/to adapt to other cultures/have an open mind/be open to international information/ feel a part of being human.'

These are large claims, but they pinpoint the shift that has been made in the higher education sector's response to the international student. They suggest that the pedagogy needed to make academic conventions and culture transparent and meaningful to international students is important and helpful for all students. I have come to understand that this is indeed so. I have also learnt that the challenges of the international student are those that everyone in the university sector needs to confront. Yet there are challenges in this: how can a changed sensitivity be framed, taught and assessed, and is it indeed desirable to do so?

I have recognised that we have as much to learn about our own culture and practices from the international student, as the reverse. It is through encounters with international students over three decades that I have come to understand our own organisational culture. These approaches reflect the repositioning of the international student as part of an international community to which all university participants are members. I, along with many higher education educators, have learnt that the challenges of the international student are those that everyone in the university sector needs to address, because these are the challenges of being human.

PART 3
Engaging students

... in the process of learning and discovery   167

... its wider influence   191

23 Doing, being and becoming: an occupational perspective on enabling learning

Rayya Ghul (NTF 2008)

Keywords: *enabling learning, occupational perspective, scaffolding, transformative education*

Rayya Ghul is passionate about people's potential for transformation and positive change. After 20 years as an occupational therapist in mental health settings she joined the Allied Health Department at Canterbury Christ Church University as a lecturer in occupational therapy and is now Programme Director for the Postgraduate Certificate in Learning and Teaching (Higher Education). She is widely recognised for her work on transformative learning and the Contexts of Participation Critical Thinking Tool.

▶ **Beginning: connecting to my own discipline of occupational therapy**

I have this very strong memory of being in a lecture hall, looking out at 80 occupational therapy students and feeling very bored. If I was that bored, how must they be feeling? It was my second year of teaching, having previously worked as an occupational therapist in mental health, and I was teaching a module someone else had written, *Psychosocial Aspects of Disease, Illness and Disability*. I was passionate about my profession and eager to transmit my knowledge and passion to my students. However, personality and jokey overheads only held their attention for short periods and I was unsure how I could improve my teaching. I was lucky enough to do a postgraduate certificate in higher education at my university and was introduced to the idea of *enabling learning* rather than delivering content, and that fitted somewhat better to my previous work as an occupational therapist. Enabling is our core skill!

I began to consider how my specialist knowledge could help me think through ways to enable my students' learning. From an occupational perspective, 'doing' is the primary engine of change. We regard humans as 'occupational beings', by which we mean that there seems to be an inherent imperative towards being occupied in some sort of meaningful activity – all types of which we call 'occupations' (Wilcock, 1998). Not only are we impelled to participate in occupations, gaining comfort from carrying out familiar ones, but also we are constantly creating interesting new occupations in which to participate. We appear to dislike being bored. For some reason, as a species, we have not been satisfied with the simplest level of activities to ensure survival, but have created a vast and complex array of things to do and built structures to support every conceivable occupation. Each of us born into a part of this structure can, through participation, quickly acquire some degree of the knowledge and skills to develop as a human being without having to possess them at birth.

This understanding of the interdependence between our sociocultural structures and ourselves gives rise, in occupational therapy, to a theory that the ability to engage in, or perform, an occupation is predicated upon a good fit between the person, the occupation and the environment (CAOT, 2002). Here's a simple example: if a person who uses a wheelchair wants to enter a shop the shop must have level access.

There is also recognition that change takes place over time. This complex relationship between the person, the occupation and their environment is constantly open to adjustment, and this is where the skill of the occupational therapist comes in. You want to be able to set just the right challenge so that the person's skills are improved and they become more capable and independent. That might require adapting the occupation through the way it is set up and carried out, or adjusting the environment to facilitate success. Too much assistance or ease and the person stays the same or is bored; too much challenge and they become demotivated or disheartened.

We could say that transformation is a natural state for humans. We are continuously changing because we are always engaging in something and that is how we develop; we're hard-wired that way. Changes might be imperceptible or dramatic, negative or positive, but it is a constant process of becoming anew. *Doing* produces a new experience of *being* through which a person *becomes* the next version of him or herself. The occupational perspective produces a rather different ontology of the person (see Figure 23.1) from conventional psychological models, which tend towards essentialism.

Along with the theories and tools from education, I set out to create transformative learning opportunities for my students.

Birth—*Doing—Being—Becoming—Doing—Being—Becoming—*
Doing—Being—Becoming: repeat: Death

Figure 23.1 An occupational ontology of the person

▶ Enabling learning: pain management

My first experiment was a day with 25 students learning about chronic pain management. Teaching this generally includes the anatomy and physiology of pain, the psychology of pain, drug treatments and psychological interventions. Unlike acute pain, chronic pain is not associated with a treatable injury, may not even be a result of injury, and is considered a syndrome in its own right. Although drug treatments have a role in pain management, psychosocial methods are far more effective, but this is counter-intuitive and can be considered a form of 'troublesome knowledge' (Meyer and Land, 2003) for learners. Understanding why this is the case is dependent on learning about the Gate Control Theory of pain (Melzack and Wall, 1965), a threshold concept (Meyer and Land, 2003) in chronic pain management. The theory is extremely hard to grasp and even harder to explain, so this seemed like an ideal opportunity to consider how I could enable my students' learning.

I planned the day's activities by visualising what students would be *doing* to create the *experience* of understanding the Gate Control Theory (the *'being'* element), thereby enabling passing through the conceptual threshold. At the point of explaining the model I needed the students to be highly motivated to listen hard and engage with the concept – but how to bring them to the point where they really wanted to know how various nerve cells in the spinal cord acted as 'gates' to pain?

Rather than giving the students information about the different ways that pain manifests itself and some of the more puzzling aspects such as phantom limb pain or the occasional absence of pain in severe injury, I reasoned that as everyone has experienced pain I could scaffold the students' learning through eliciting their own stories of pain. Using a large whiteboard, I went round the room and asked each student to share their experiences which I wrote up on the board. As I had hoped, the stories demonstrated different aspects of pain. The students became relaxed and interactive as they told and listened to the stories. I then added any missing elements and drew attention to all the differing and contradictory aspects of pain.

I then put the students into groups of four and gave them a task. They role-played scientists in a top university who were developing a theory that could explain how pain worked. This theory had to be able to explain all the differing and contradictory aspects of pain. With a sheet of flipchart paper and some coloured markers they had to produce, in 30 minutes, a poster to present at the annual conference. They were encouraged to be as imaginative and fanciful as they wished. Observing the groups, it was clear that they were highly engaged with trying to solve the puzzle of pain and becoming more and more interested in the solution. The presentations were hilarious,

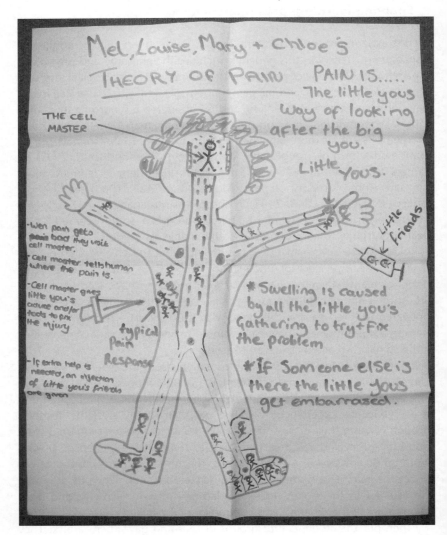

Figure 23.2 An example of student theories of pain

with some students explaining how aliens orbiting earth controlled pain mechanisms, while others presented a 'Cell Master' theory of pain.

To date the session has run six times, with different groups and never with the same explanation, and only once producing a theory that was close to the Gate Control Theory (the 'Canal Lock' Theory). However, each time the students finished the exercise they were extremely curious about what theory *could* explain pain. Consequently, when I finally explained Gate Control, they were easily able to grasp, appreciate and apply it.

I went on to try out other ways of designing learning with a precision fit.

▶ Enabling learning: contexts of participation

In 2003 I had the chance to redesign a module on *Psychosocial Aspects*. Reflecting on it through using the concept of constructive alignment (Biggs, 1996), I could see that teaching discrete elements of psychology and sociology and then expecting the students to magically bring these together in the assignment was an impossible task for all but the most talented student. I reasoned that if this were the ultimate aim we would have to reconsider the entire module content and to ensure that it was made clear how it related to occupational therapy. I created a diagram from the different elements and my colleague, Ian Marsh, suggested it be made with moving parts and a critical thinking tool: Contexts of Participation (Ghul and Marsh, 2013) was born (Figure 23.3) – although at that point the students called it the 'Wheel of Fortune'!

Used in conjunction with powerful narratives from historical footage of disabled people, and with real service users coming into the classroom, students were challenged to engage with the realities of what makes up the barriers and enablers to participation in life for marginalised and disadvantaged groups. The use of emotional and provocative material was deliberate. Our students became fascinated by the relationships between discourse and practice and their assignments showed high levels of critical thinking and reflection for the first year. This tool went on to be developed further through a mini-project grant from the Higher Education Academy (Ghul and Marsh, 2009),[1] and its use is now being explored with students from other health and social care disciplines, as well as education.

▶ Enabling Learning: Developing the Reflective Practitioner

Reflective practice is an essential element of health service education and is

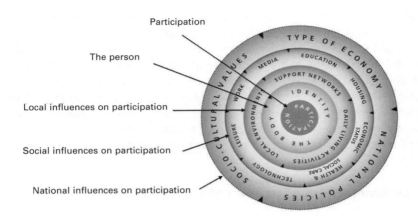

Figure 23.3 Contexts of Participation (Ghul and Marsh, 2013)

generally encouraged through the requirement to write reflective logs while out on practice placements. Despite this, the level of reflection had been poor, with most students complaining that they didn't see the point or found the activity nothing more than a task of compliance. In 2009 I proposed a third-year module on reflective practice so students could develop their skills and appreciate its power. Having previously researched the topic as part of my MA Educational Studies, I again thought about what the students would be *doing* to have the experience of *being* critically reflective and *become* reflective practitioners.

The students were asked to select a reflection they had completed on a second-year placement. Each week, part of the process of reflection became the theme for a day's experiential workshop – on, for example, 'thinking', 'feeling' and 'values' – and they were also introduced to concepts such as their orientation to reflection (Wellington and Austin 1996). After each session they updated their reflection. The assignment required them to submit their original and updated reflections as appendices to an essay in which they reflected on what they learned through the process of updating.

This module is currently being formally evaluated through research on four cohorts of students, but informal feedback suggests many students found the module personally transformative. An unsolicited email from a graduating student said:

'The "Developing the Reflective Practitioner" module completely changed the way I approach life situations and has made me feel ready to cope with any challenges that lie ahead.'

▶ **Final thoughts**

I think that the most important aspect of the way that I engage students in their own learning process is the constant search for that precision fit between what they are doing and the intended learning outcome. Thinking about the experience, the *'being'* element in detail allows me to use both reason and empathy to design for learning to take place. Using educational concepts such as constructive alignment and threshold knowledge help to focus that experience sharply towards the intended learning outcome. For me, that is the *becoming* element. When that is successful, the students can see the relevance and trust the process.

As an educator, it can be unsettling to work in this way because one must not only create the means for the experience to take place but then stand back and trust the students to engage in the process. Working as an occupational therapist and watching someone relearn basic life skills is a good training for only intervening when necessary. However, seeing someone take control of their own learning and reap the benefits is worth the discomfort of letting go a little. Students can have the space to become more knowledgeable and capable.

24 Learning together through student–lecturer collaborative enquiry

Will Curtis (NTF 2011)

Keywords: *collaborative enquiry, assessment feedback, employability, student–lecturer enquiry, learning together, students as researchers, Education Studies*

> Will Curtis joined the Centre for Lifelong Learning at the University of Warwick in 2013 where he leads the 2+2, part-time degree and certificate programmes. His research interests include post-16 learning cultures and identities, further education transitions, Finnish higher education, assessment and feedback and radical democratic education. He has written five books for undergraduate students and is currently Secretary of the British Education Studies Association.

Interest in the value of student–lecturer collaborative enquiry in educational research has risen since the start of the twenty-first century. Much of the literature has focused on its pedagogic potential, highlighting student ownership of their learning and subsequent improvements in engagement and academic performance. I instigated two projects in which teams of students and lecturers undertook research in Education Studies departments in UK universities. Both projects explored current higher education practices and considered opportunities for innovation – the first in assessment feedback,[2] the second in employability.[3] This essay reflects upon the immense potential of this model of research – as a means for learning together – expanding horizons and enhancing practice.

▶ Student–lecturer collaborative enquiry

Recent years have witnessed considerable interest in strategies that encourage students to take active roles in research – in particular, as a means of enhancing educational provision. The notion of students as 'agents of change' (Kay, Dunne and Hutchinson, 2010; Fielding, 2001) has gained increasing currency, with many educational institutions encouraging their students to play an active role in the research, evaluation and development of new assessment, curriculum and resources. As well as improving educational provision, evidence suggests significant benefits for participating students. Bland and Atweh (2007), for example, have suggested that fostering 'students as researchers' can lead to greater student engagement and improved academic performance.

The approach we took in both projects involved students engaging in collaborative enquiry alongside lecturers. Collaboration enables teams 'to share their expertise, to clarify and refine their own thinking through the process of sharing, and also to learn from one another' (Kotsopoulous, 2010: 129). The use of student and lecturer collaborative research has become increasingly widespread over the past decade – particularly in schools (Fielding, 2004; Bahou, 2011), but also in universities (Seale 2010). Bahou (2011) identified some common features of collaborative enquiry projects in the literature. Among these, she indicates that staff–student collaborative projects aim to 'enhance the conditions and processes of learning and teaching' (2011: 7). In the UK, Michael Fielding has been the most influential advocate for both 'students as researchers' and student–staff collaboration. He makes a particularly strong case for the latter as promoting opportunities for 'radical collegiality' (Bragg and Fielding, 2005), 'mutual responsibility' and 'energising adventure' (Fielding, 2012: 53). Specifically, he argues that successful student and lecturer partnership can open up creative and democratic spaces and the 'promise of intergenerational learning' (*ibid.*).

▶ Two approaches to student–lecturer collaborative enquiry

Both projects employed a student–lecturer collaborative enquiry approach to examine current practice, identify common perceptions of students and lecturers, and to consider strategies for enhancing provision. The first project[4] – 'Assessment Reassessed' – concluded in January 2012 and was funded by ESCalate (the Higher Education Academy Education Subject Centre). The project entailed developing three research teams – each consisting of three students and one member of staff. Each team visited two other institutions to conduct research with students and lecturers on other Education Studies courses. Each team was semi-autonomous – developing their own research design based on project aims and research questions. The project identified a number of common assessment strategies. It established common concerns around mechanistic processes, lack of reliability and a perceived lack of value of much written feedback. All respondents recognised the potential benefits of more democratic and collaborative models of assessment feedback, but all regarded institutional structures as barriers to implementation.

The second project[5] – 'Employability in Education Studies' – began in autumn 2012 and was funded by a Higher Education Academy Collaborative Teaching Development Grant. This larger project involved six teams of students and lecturers from two universities. Each team visited two UK institutions on two occasions during 2012–13. Unlike the earlier project, all students and lecturers agreed a common approach to data collection and analysis prior to the commencement of fieldwork. As such, the semi-autonomous teams of 'Assessment Reassessed' were replaced by a consistent overall approach – in relation to fields of enquiry, methods and targeted respondents. Early findings indicated wide variations between courses: some Education Studies degrees explicitly focused on preparing students for primary PGCE, some provided information and opportunities in a wide range of educational employment, and some had little emphasis on employability. Students desired more accurate and meaningful pre-course and in-course employability information and more opportunities for placements and work experience practice.

▶ **Learning together and expanding horizons: reflections on the process**

Both projects had explicit aims to consider the value of student–lecturer collaborative enquiry and to identify characteristics of effective practice. Without exception, all participating students and lecturers found the experience tremendously positive. Grouped around notions of learning together and expanding horizons, a number of factors proved particularly noteworthy:

▶ **Negotiating and maintaining teams**: One of the more challenging aspects of the process was to develop coherent and balanced teams. As we have written elsewhere (Curtis et al., 2012), collaborative relations were dynamic, situational and (often) contested – as each member's roles were refined, adapted and developed. Balancing differing skills and interests required sensitivity and careful negotiation. Successful team relations depend upon 'a commitment to shared resources, power, and talent' (John-Steiner, Weber and Minnis, 1998: 776). To move beyond pre-existing roles, these commitments needed to be made explicit and repeated throughout the process. A measure of both projects' success is in the positive nature of team relationships during and after fieldwork.

▶ **Challenging taken-for-granted 'expertise'**: To facilitate teams in this shared commitment, we needed to diminish pre-existing roles of 'expert' and 'novice' – that define, to a greater or lesser extent, student and lecturer institutional identities. We found that within-team conversations eroded these roles fairly rapidly. The longer projects lasted, the more all participants acknowledged that students have 'access to a rich knowledge base within their own practices and experiences' (Ainscow, Booth and Dyson, 2004: 130). Lecturers, without their scripted lecture notes, became more fallible and human. With each research visit, students became more prepared to take ownership of the process and to lead various fieldwork and dissemination activities. For instance, one student presented her own work from the project at a national Education Studies conference.

▶ **Authenticity of co-researcher relations**: The research enabled students and lecturers to develop relationships outside the confines of traditional lecturer–student environments. Removed from the constraints of assessment relations and regimes, we found more trusting, humane and authentic ways of communicating with one another. We were working together on real, meaningful activities – to uncover new knowledge in areas relevant to our practice and new opportunities and innovations.

▶ **Bridging gaps**: Not only did both projects bridge gaps between students and lecturers, they also encouraged connections between participants at different institutions – student–student, student–lecturer and lecturer–lecturer – revealing a wide range of common and divergent experiences. Moreover, students and lecturers had the opportunity to interview senior management, including head of school and dean, and these conversations started to bridge gaps in perception and experience between policy and practice.

▶ **Accessing 'hidden worlds'**: One of the more commonly articulated student perspectives was surprise at the messy and imprecise nature of educational research and evaluation – the complex and fuzzy nature of qualitative data collection and analysis. Similarly, in the assessment feedback project, students got the chance to see behind the apparent objectivity of marking criteria and grading descriptors, to reveal the subjective, tentative and problematic processes involved in providing marks and feedback.

▶ **Empowering learning identities**: Students reported that the collaborative research process impacted positively on their identities as learners. The opportunity to visit other institutions afforded insights into how other universities, courses, lecturers and students work – developing informed perspectives from which to reflect on and evaluate experiences on their own courses. Students became active, engaged co-producers of knowledge and meaning. Working with their lecturers to evaluate and develop existing practice made them feel their viewpoints were valued, meaningful and influential. Taking part in fieldwork, data analysis and disseminating findings enhanced transferable 'academic skills' and resulted in greater confidence and authority.

▶ **Transforming practice**: Findings from both projects have impacted on curriculum development at host institutions. Through a variety of dissemination workshops, presentations and papers, these findings are reaching wider university audiences – offering student–lecturer interpretations of key aspects of contemporary higher education provision. In addition, as the above indicates, taking part in the process has shaped the learning and teaching perceptions and practices of the students and lecturers who took part in both projects.

▶ Conclusion: enhancing practice through student–lecturer collaborative enquiry

During both projects, we encountered challenges in terms of building and sustaining student and lecturer research teams, most notably in occupying the dual roles of student/co-researcher and lecturer/co-researcher. It is difficult to 'recruit' students from a wide range of interests, experiences and levels of attainment; giving rise to a danger that student–lecturer collaborative enquiry creates a 'self-selecting elite'. Experiences were very divergent. Some students wanted greater opportunity to lead and shape research activities, while others tended to rely heavily on the experience and expectations of lecturers. At times, lecturers reported feeling exposed in accompanying 'novice' researchers into the field. Despite these challenges, all participants found the collaborative research process engaging, stimulating and empowering. Our experiences from the two projects suggest a number of approaches to develop effective student–lecturer collaborative enquiry:

▶ Involve students in the initial drafting of the research bid

▶ Articulate the value of the research on practice/improving student experiences

▶ As a group, explore the characteristics of 'good'/effective fieldwork prior to the first visit

▶ Ensure all students feel that their ideas are taken seriously and shape data collection and analysis

▶ Use more than one research team and include 'group events' in the research schedule to facilitate conversations between teams at various points throughout the process

▶ Encourage continual dialogue between members of each research team – about their feelings and expectations, frustrations and fears, different and changing roles and experiences of working with other students and lecturers

▶ Advise all participants to keep a reflective diary on the process of working in a collaborative team

▶ Be conscious of how shared experiences impact on relationships with students who were part of the research and their peers who were not

▶ Suggest students use fieldwork data for their own independent project

▶ Ensure that all participating students are given opportunities and support to participate fully in a range of dissemination activities.

25 Creating space for student autonomy and engagement through partnership and letting go

Colin Bryson (NTF 2009)

Keywords: *student engagement, students as partners, graduateness*

Colin Bryson, Director of the Combined Honours Centre at Newcastle University, has had a long career working in UK universities as a lecturer and educational developer. He has been researching on student engagement for some years and is currently the Chair of RAISE. He adopts the model of students as partners in every way he can.

For my first 20 years as a higher education teacher I always tried to be an innovative educator, but within the context of a rather teaching-centred orientation (Kember, 1997) – echoing the values and beliefs of the system into which I had been inducted. I researched on my academic subject, precarious employment, and linked that to being an active trade unionist. These were two areas I felt passionate about, not my teaching or students. And then something changed. I discovered student engagement (SE).

SE is the sense of being and the will and disposition to 'become' rather than 'have' (Fromm, 1977) that enables persistence, personal and educational development, and transformational learning (Perry, 1999). Each student is unique – in what they bring to HE in terms of goals, aspirations, values and beliefs and how these are shaped and mediated by their holistic experience whilst a student. SE is constructed and reconstructed through the lenses of the perceptions and identities held by students and the meaning and sense a student makes of their experiences and interactions.

In 2003 I was given responsibility for developing more independent learning among undergraduates in a large business school. Senior managers desired this for the expedient reasons of extracting more and different contributions from the staff. I had some reservations about the pedagogical implications of reducing contact time and support and so took what was an unusual step at the time – I decided to consult the students.

▶ Researching

I conducted focus groups covering 60 students, asking broad questions. The student view on independent learning was negative; 'you are pushing us away'. However the revelation that emerged was SE, or a lack of it. The students described that in stark, emotive terms: 'no one knows my name here, I am just a number'. Another worrisome trend was the degree of trans-actionalism, what we called 'false' engagement; *every mark counts*. This powerful evidence compelled me to find out more, and to become an advocate of promoting SE.

There was surprisingly little research in the UK that was really about SE. An exception was Mann's (2001) notion of alienating forces in higher education impacting negatively on students. The international literature was much more fruitful, particularly from Australia (e.g. Krause et al., 2005). So was the long tradition of work in the USA on the impact of college on students (Pascarella and Terenzini, 2005) and Kuh's development of the National Survey of Student Engagement (Kuh, 2008). We assimilated these ideas to argue that SE is holistic and socially constructed (Bryson and Hand, 2007).

Further research, including a longitudinal study following students throughout their degree, has added to our understanding (Bryson and Hardy, 2012). These studies emphasised Tinto's (2003) point that the social is as critical as academic engagement. I have also explored the connection between SE and 'graduateness'. The leading commentators argue that it is the integrated development of the whole person (Yorke and Knight, 2006) that enables higher-level graduate attributes (Barrie, 2006) and the initial formation of a graduate identity (Holmes, 2001). In fostering that development, it would appear to bear a remarkable resemblance to experiences and processes associated with high SE (Kuh, 2008). This promotes the rather radical notion that it is not the 'knowledge' gained but the *learning process* that is key, and the extra- or co-curricular is rather crucial in offering authentic opportunities to gain 'practice'. Learning in the 'subject' is important as it draws and maintains the student's interest and offers intellectual development.

Somewhere along this journey the Researching, Advancing and Inspiring Student Engagement (RAISE) network[6] was created. As co-founder and inaugural chair I sought to define and map SE conceptually (Bryson, 2011). This exercise did show the importance of separating the dualism of 'students engaging' with 'engaging students'.

▶ Putting it into practice

Although this clarion call from students was changing my own values and promoting a radical new approach, coming to Combined Honours (CH) at Newcastle in 2008 presented a new opportunity. Students study two or three subjects from a long list in CH; 4500 combinations are possible, with nearly everyone on their own unique pathway. Previous student feedback was grim: the worst NSS (National Student Survey) scores in the university, a sense of alienation and unfair discrimination, lack of belonging and identity and a real failure of systems such as personal tutoring. It seemed impossible to change much in the curriculum because it is taught 'out there' in the academic schools.

Therefore I decided to invite the students to identify what the big issues were and what solutions they proposed. There were quick wins, such as changing the name of the degree as they felt the former name rather pejorative. We introduced a new model of Staff–Student Committee (SSC); student-led and with elected representatives with their own constituencies. We co-manage annual cohort surveys (with 80 per cent participation) to identify issues. We have Student Forums on specific issues to which all 400 students are invited. The Combined Honours Society was reborn. This is completely student-led and promotes the social and community-fostering agenda with a growth of membership to 30 per cent from 2 per cent.

The SSC proposed peer mentoring and we developed such a successful scheme that the whole university is now adopting this for all students. The mentors run transition and induction, and have taken over from personal tutors in large measure. We introduced Peer Assisted Study Support leaders and a system of graduate mentors to support students with ongoing transitions. Students and I have also co-designed modules. We introduced a final-year independent project with features such as peer assessment, a reflective interview, and a very negotiable remit for topic and criteria. The fifty or so students who are involved in CH roles can undertake further co-designed modules, in which they are guided and assessed on their development and reflection through practice.

These approaches appear to have enhanced SE very strongly for some (who become 'super-engaged' and involved) and quite well for others. The

NSS overall satisfaction score rose to 96 per cent. Those who do get involved report an enhancement of graduate attributes.

Is this substantial progress, then, to the epitome of SE? And what is that? Is that a learning community as advocated by Perry, where mutuality flourishes, or some form of partnership?

▶ Partnership

The concept of partnership needs unpacking. In my industrial relations past, I have always been wary of the notion of employee partnership, not only because there is never an equal distribution of power, even at the collective level, but also because the goals of employer and employees are nearly always different and often conflictual. There have been attempts to power-share and achieve industrial democracy, but that involves collective power (i.e. between union and employer), for example co-determination. True democratic participation – the cooperative – is very rare.

In higher education the goals of educator and students are mutual, although power is not shared equally. My initial attempts have features of co-determination, of co-design and co-creation – close to the top of the 'ladder of student participation' (Bovill and Bulley, 2011). I am less sure that they are co-production (McCulloch, 2009), but may be on a par with attempts to do that elsewhere (Neary, 2011), although for my students the majority of their curricular and broader experience is 'traditional'.

A confusing tension and ambiguity in the SE debate is that the national bodies see SE as collective representation (e.g. HEA, 2010). This may be one aspect, but is too narrow. Wenstone (2012) argues for an approach of democratic representation broadly across the institution in synchrony with partnership at the level of individual. She acknowledges that this will require democraticisation in staff structures too!

At the unit of degree it seems possible to do both. There are some practical constraints. Students taking this much responsibility and ownership is demanding for them and involves steep learning curves. Should we offer (more than intrinsic) reward for these challenging roles, and to attract more take-up of opportunities? Peer tensions arise too, as students do not have, inherently, 'the authority of office' or 'credibility' that staff have. Are there limits to areas that students should be partners? Student turnover offers renewal but discontinuity. Heterogeneity needs to be embraced, but what level of engagement and participation in a democratised HE community should be *obligatory*? Can one opt out? These are challenging questions, but should not deflect us from pursuing partnership and seeking solution with the students.

▶ Reflections

I conclude with some reflection of the impact of this agenda on staff and on me. It involves both a change in values and beliefs *and* on practices. It involves consciously letting go. That entails giving a lot of trust. It can be frustrating, standing back and feeling you are letting the students 'flounder'. It involves a lot of investment of time and effort. But it really is worth it. For years I worked hard in an environment where both students and staff were alienated and disempowered – and that was much more frustrating. In a relatively short period, adopting holistic SE and partnership working has been really emancipatory for all parties. Even senior management have noticed. It has tremendous reward for me. Working in partnership with engaged students is a true privilege. It has transformed my own engagement as an educator and had a very positive impact on so many of the students. Adopting this ethos across higher education would be so beneficial and offers a rather better and more valuable purpose to all within and beyond higher education.

26 The student-professional

Laura Ritchie (NTF 2012)

Keywords: *music learning, professional practice, experience, self-belief, self-regulation, reflection*

Laura Ritchie is Teaching Fellow in Music at the University of Chichester, UK and a performing cellist. Her research interests lie in self-efficacy beliefs and the self-regulation of musical learning. Laura has an unquenchable optimism and thrives on enriching the lives of others through her teaching and music.

A month after graduating from my Masters degree, I landed my first hourly-paid job as a private music teacher. I suddenly found myself in a situation where I was left alone in a room with a new student every half-hour. I was expected to know how to teach a range of ages and abilities how to play my instrument.

Musicians can teach privately without a formal teaching qualification or even any training. Although an experienced performer, I had no guidance, practical experience, monitoring or mentoring in teaching, save what I had gleaned from the teachers who taught me to perform, and there is no set curriculum to draw upon to teach specific musical instruments. I floundered, and saying that this experience was a steep learning curve is an understatement!

This experience was what motivated me to develop tailored Instrumental/Vocal Teaching programmes at the University of Chichester. My aim was that no student would have to wait until after graduation for an invitation into the professional field to gain experience.

▶ Instrumental/Vocal Teaching (IVT)

IVT students at Chichester gather a wealth of real-world experience through modules in which they are expected and entrusted to own, and lead, their learning inside and outside the classroom. These students develop individual, and group, teaching strategies, deliver workshops in schools, prepare public events on campus, and shadow and support other professionals with larger regional performances. A 2012 graduate began teaching right away, explaining:

> 'I've been teaching privately since the month after graduating, and have started teaching for the Music Service. I was surprised at how fast I got a job.'
>
> Emily, IVT graduate

Even in the early stages of the course when learning about teaching and musical interaction, my students are actively engaged in both simulated and real-life situations where they are responsible for creating and delivering music lessons. Many aspects of learning about teaching, though described here in relation to music, still directly apply to other disciplines:

- planning
- robust and engaging content
- flexibility
- acute perception
- effectiveness of delivery
- attention to student needs

When students have freedom, and permission, to take charge of their learning, lecturers and teachers must tailor learning experiences actively and cannot rely on a ready-made template for teaching. IVT modules introduce methodologies and concepts to ground understanding, discussing teaching material and musical repertoire, and enabling progression, and how layers of technical learning involve both mental capacities and physical coordination (Barry and Hallam, 2002). Students present and explain how to produce the first sounds on their instruments, teaching one another. They learn new instruments and prepare for performance exams to experience the fun, frustration and accomplishments of a beginner musician.

We explore our own self-efficacy beliefs about capabilities to carry out a given task (Bandura, 1986; Ritchie and Williamon, 2011a). These beliefs are important for any teacher or learner, and impact upon students' goals, the complexity of strategies that they use, perseverance, well-being and achievement (Ritchie and Williamon 2011b; Ritchie and Williamon 2012; Zimmerman, 2000). The realisation that beliefs develop through achievement and experience encourages my IVT students to be active participants in class. Integrating an awareness of students' self-beliefs and developing knowledge contributes to building their identity as budding professionals.

In learning a musical instrument or singing, solely understanding theory, concepts and processes cannot substitute for experience, and my students recognise this:

> 'Whist university is great for allowing students some respite between school and the grindstone, there needs to be a preparation for the rest of their life – few of them will be able to spend life in the cloisters of academia.'
>
> Craig, current third-year student

Students see the value in practical learning, are motivated to engage, and are often surprised by their own achievement.

▶ Setting the stage for practice

To gain a tactile understanding of teaching and learning music, each of my students take responsibility for their learning choices throughout their studies. One example is that every student is asked to design his or her own short-term music curriculum to teach private, one-to-one instrumental or vocal lessons. This requires them to go well beyond basic comprehension to develop deep learning with an engineered, yet real experience.

Students study both the musical (see Hallam, 1995) and academic literature, exploring teachers' reflections and students' thought processes (Atkinson and Claxon, 2000). They seek application of theories about learning styles, methods of learning, and self-belief through discussion, role-play and by examining their own behaviours and experiences. This becomes the backbone for the next stage of reflective analysis.

Self-regulated learning methods help students shape their learning experience and understand how to guide their future students as efficient, productive learners (Zimmerman and Schunk, 2001). Creating carefully crafted situations that teach skills, such as how to arrange the physical setting, approach material effectively, and evaluate learning, are essential to integrate into students' developing teaching practice (Ritchie and Williamon, 2013). Understanding how to self-direct is especially important in musical learning. Private music lessons typically last between 30 and 60 minutes per week, and between lessons students are without teacher contact. The proportion of contact time with the one-to-one music teacher is small compared to the quantity of 'at home' or independent music practice that teachers expect even young students to undertake. Thus, this is a very different situation to a school classroom, where the teacher can monitor and guide the student's learning on a daily basis.

Students recognise that delivering music tuition in this way means that there will be many hurdles to navigate. The instantaneous reactions to learning situations and the need to change tack slightly so the pupil stays on board are not conveyed by 'textbook' learning. Pupils with their own concerns and ambitions create situations where the teacher-professional must act and respond quickly and appropriately, integrating theory into practice.

▶ A dress rehearsal for teaching

After the initial planning, my students engage in peer modelling and teach one another through role-play. This allows experimentation, time to overcome nerves and often includes fun and laughter leading to valuable discussion. The challenge of having both in-depth technical knowledge and the foresight to set achievable goals in their lessons is teased out in the privacy of our class.

Students are individuals and each teaching situation is unique, so the same concept, skill or piece of music might be taught completely differently depending on the needs of the student. Students learn how to communicate good practices, and progress to various forms of demonstration and modelling (Schunk, 1991). The concept that learning can be progressive, with hierarchical goals, instead of a show of willpower or force to conquer a massive task (Thoreson and Mahoney, 1974), is translated to designing and teaching lessons for my student-professionals.

From a musician's point of view this preparatory experience is particularly important, as once in the profession, there are very few opportunities to publicly share experiences and good practice, or to observe lessons given by other teachers. Students inevitably look shocked when I ask: 'How many of you have watched someone else's music lesson?' as traditionally, 'private' music lessons are taught behind closed doors.

▶ Taking the stage with the lessons

Each of my IVT students recruits a pupil, who may be a student or staff member from another department, possibly with little or no previous musical experience. Each situation is different and 'plans' often have to be reshaped and tailored to meet the new pupil's needs. The experience creates a symbiotic relationship benefiting the teacher and pupil. My student teachers gain professional experience interacting with their pupil, and those who participate in the one-to-one learning experience learn music and the new skills of playing an instrument or singing. Importantly for my students, this experience goes along with having the study and class time to be supported in preparing, developing, delivering and reflecting on their teaching skills.

These student-professionals video their teaching, and keep detailed journals on all aspects of their experience; from the planning stages to whether they were prepared for the possibility of fantastic progress or the fact that the pupil might be completely stumped by the planned lesson. Reflecting on lessons is critical, because even if something does not go to plan a great deal can be learned. The more accomplished student teachers mentor those who are still gaining confidence, and the dynamic within-lecture sessions encourage assertive growth, self-discovery and inspirational learning. All are encouraged to be intuitive, flexible practitioners who use critical reflections to enhance their teaching performance (Atkinson and Claxton, 2000).

As lessons unfold, those teaching find their feet and begin realising goals. They become increasingly student-centred in considering and realigning sub-goals for the next lesson, choosing methods that will best enable learning. Guided reflection and discussion are invaluable to develop, reinforce and mentally archive positive achievements, thus building confidence, and there are often 'aha!' moments for the new teachers. In professional teaching situations this dedicated time to reflect is often squeezed out of schedules:

'When you reach that level and your [teaching] schedule is full or too full, your time to step back becomes difficult. Corners may be cut and prep work is reduced. A good professional will be able to draw from experience at short notice but it is better to have a good measure of equilibrium. For a lot of professionals it is trying to keep a consistent balance.'

Erica, Year 3 student (already with considerable professional experience as a teacher and performer)

I enable my IVT students to establish a repertoire of skills and experience within their teaching portfolio. It is not uncommon for IVT students to retain their new pupil as the first in their professional teaching practice, and many secure jobs within the profession well before graduation.

▶ Where do they go from here?

Graduates teach privately, are employed by music services and private schools, run their own performance companies or schools, perform and volunteer. Every year between 10–25 per cent of IVT graduates are employed by the local Music Service, and many others relocate across the country. Emily, a 2009 graduate, spent a year teaching music to Year 6 students in an independent school in North London, teaching 32 private pupils and directing the choirs and musicals. She also teaches 23 pupils at an academy in a challenging school and performs professionally as member of the choir of the church of St Martin in the Fields, London, singing regular services and BBC broadcasts.

Graduates teach, and like Emily, they do this successfully alongside their professional performing. The balance of practical methods and theoretical teaching in the curriculum engages learners within the university and empowers these musicians to be prepared for the demands of private teaching. Rob, an 2007 IVT graduate, went on to establish his own music academy, and reflected on what the theories and practice in the IVT course meant for him as a professional:

> 'Being given the opportunity to teach a student on a one-to-one basis was an extremely valuable experience. The hands-on experience gave us the opportunity to put the skills that we had learned into practice. The opportunity opened your eyes to the real world of teaching and prepared you to think with great creativity and imagination. Now, as a director of my own peripatetic music academy I continually monitor the ways in which the students learn so that our tutors deliver tuition to the highest standards.'
>
> Rob, Director of Music Academy for Schools

The experience gained through IVT embeds the seeds of good practice and paves the way for a future full of music. Craig, who graduated in 2012, plays bass guitar, keyboards, sings and has a successful funk band, concludes:

> 'During my time in Laura's lectures, I was able to indulge in the theoretical and tangible elements of teaching in a very realistic environment. This experience prepared me for my life as a professional peripatetic teacher … without the hands on-experience that the IVT course provided me, my entry into the professional environment would have been very inexperienced. Understanding a skill is just the beginning, delivering and imparting its knowledge is what sets you apart as a teacher in the real world. Thank you for allowing me to practise in a safe and controlled environment; I wouldn't be where I am now without it.'

27 Wanted! Agents of change: enabling students to make change happen in their professional world

Duncan Reavey (NTF 2008)

Keywords: ownership, challenge, creativity, employability, problem-based, assessment, change, professional

Duncan Reavey is Principal Lecturer in Learning and Teaching at the University of Chichester, UK. As well as teaching full-time in primary and adventure education, he is also a Forest School Leader and enjoys stirring things – his latest CPD workshop is called *'Dare you to do it!' Taking risks in university teaching and learning.*

Making significant change happen in their professional world is a challenge for students – but also for university teachers. We need our graduates to have the skills and confidence to make an impact in their first jobs – but we need the same skills and confidence ourselves. Here I explore an innovative, learner-centred, problem-focused pedagogy that engages and excites students – and increases their effectiveness in the months, and years, after graduating. At the same time I reflect on how university teachers have themselves made change happen.

I focus on two very different contexts and, in particular, two very different kinds of students. One context is a ground-breaking, transdisciplinary Masters programme in Environment and Development in South Africa. The other is an undergraduate degree for new primary school teachers in UK. Both programmes aim to offer action-based learning that addresses practical challenges. Both respond to an agenda from employers that demand graduates who are reflective, adaptable and motivated professionals. Both programmes attract students who are excited about the idea of making change happen but have little idea of how to do it.

▶ Addressing real-world problems in South Africa

The now University of KwaZulu-Natal took a big risk in allowing us to create a coursework-based Masters in Environment and Development (Reavey, 1997). Demonstrating a need was easy – the region was desperate for problem solvers who were not constrained by traditional boundaries between disciplines. But persuading staff from 32 different, tiny university departments to work together for the first time was harder. Having a shared end goal – to develop a new kind of problem solver – gave us the focus we needed. From this, the design of the Masters degree followed. The one-year programme started with five weeks in '*The Melting Pot*' for 30 students from diverse academic and professional backgrounds working together to address a seemingly intractable problem. On one occasion this was the imminent closure of a coal mine and the consequences for miners, their community and their small town. Students learned quickly that they needed to understand each other's perspectives if they were to appreciate a complex problem – a lawyer learning wildlife conservation, an economist learning environmental history. Six months later, the final assessment was another problem-solving task: with five days to do it, students used their initiative and any resources they wished (including each other) to propose a future for a controversial informal settlement.

Does it work? Data from graduates at several points after completion highlight benefits of working on real problems with real constraints and real practitioners, and on breaking down barriers between disciplines. Data from employers emphasise a welcome 'paradigm shift in university teaching'.

▶ Challenged to make change happen in primary schools in UK

New teachers need many of these same characteristics. Indeed, the model for the primary education and teaching graduate from the University of Chichester uses words like aspirational, resilient and creative. But how can they develop real-world skills in a training that is necessarily focused on children, curriculum and classrooms? In the same way as the Masters course, we set final-year undergraduates the challenge to make change happen in their professional workplace (Reavey, 2011). In our module '*Creativity3*' which runs for one day per week over 4 months of their final year, self-selected groups of 3–5 students work to provide genuine end products for external clients. Schools and non-governmental organisations (NGOs) come to the university with ideas for projects, and each year around 35 projects happen. Groups are assessed mostly on the outcome/product for external users.

Examples of *Creativity3* challenges have included:

▷ Motivating disengaged secondary-school pupils in literacy
▷ Engaging non-English speaking migrant families with school
▷ Learning approaches to engage children who have a habit of starting fires
▷ Creating calm spaces for special-needs children
▷ Achieving Green Flag status at an inner-city school
▷ Hospital learning for long-term ill children
▷ Helping schools understand how technology shaped the navy

Does it work? Students say:

'I loved it. Really inspiring and got us thinking outside the box.'

'Grew in confidence and will use a lot in my own practice. We could be creative. We could be *individuals*.'

Graduates a year into their first jobs say, for example:

'It prepared me for taking responsibility … and made me feel more confident in tackling issues in school.'

'I learnt to deal with different levels of position – from school governors and heads to other teachers.'

Comments from employers emphasise end products as 'uplifting and fascinating' and stress their need to employ 'motivated self-starters'.

▷ Why these courses worked: golden rules for university teachers

What aspects of these courses led to these very positive outcomes? When we ask them, graduates and current students focus on the aspects set out below. These are broadly the same features that mattered to those creating the courses in the first place, but are often emphasised even more strongly by students and graduates:

▶ use real-world projects
▶ give genuine student ownership
▶ keep a distance
▶ encourage and reward creativity
▶ assess what matters
▶ stop students working too hard

Use real-world projects that matter to external clients

'First-hand experience implementing changes – relevant to real life – it *is* real life!'

Student

At the start, students are presented with a real-life situation full of challenge. Their goal is to achieve a meaningful outcome. Each project is proposed by an organisation, which has a strong interest in the solution so invests valuable time and sometimes money in the work our students do. The students see them as clients whose needs must be addressed directly. If the end results matter to the real world, there is pressure on the students to get it absolutely right – so the students set themselves the highest standards. Invariably the quality of end products is exceptional.

Give genuine student ownership

'The ideology behind *Creativity3* cannot be faulted. It provides opportunities for student teachers to take control, take risks and take the initiative in managing projects which have a real impact.'

Students

Whether it is five weeks full time for a group of 30 Masters students working together, or a day or week for four trainee teachers, the pathway to reaching the solution is their own choice. Students know this. They become discerning in their choice of external support and fiercely focused on getting exactly the inputs they need. They have high demands of themselves and each other because theirs are the decisions and the consequences. In the words of *Creativity3* students who presented at a national student workshop on employability, universities

'would benefit from giving students projects, which encourage autonomy both within and outside the classroom. This seems to work best with large-scale projects where students can truly make change happen in creative ways.'

(Koiston, Goodall and Hughes, 2011)

University teachers must keep a distance – whatever the temptations

'It really felt like the lecturer cared about our project.'

Student

In both the Masters degree and *Creativity3* there is a time each week to reflect. We call it 'Muffins and Mindmaps'. Yes, there are free coffee and muffins, and this changes the way the session works. On the Masters course, it started at 8.00 a.m. on Mondays – deliberately professional. These relaxed interactive sessions provide a chance for students to share news, ideas and concerns with other project teams and tutors. They are used to identify areas where further development is needed to help projects succeed – such as advice on project management, dealing with difficult people, making projects sustainable and understanding how teams work – and to learn from each other. University teachers are present as peers and consultants, giving support while allowing groups to have full ownership. What makes this especially exciting for university teachers is that these projects push them in unexpected directions, requiring them to use all their expertise to the full – very different from other kinds of university teaching.

Encourage and reward creativity

'It's great to be allowed to follow through our own hunches.'

Student

Employers advertise for 'creative' staff but many don't know what they mean by it. Perhaps this is the same in our universities as we continue to be pushed by our students into a deeper understanding of what creativity is. How do we give enough opportunity for creativity in these courses? By setting the right challenges in the first place and by ensuring that university formalities do not constrain us in ways we credit creativity.

Assess what matters

'Our communication skills are now awesome.'

Student

You have a problem to solve. Anything goes. Solve it. This is the way the world works and the format of the final assessments for the Masters degree and *Creativity3*. But once we relax some of the conventions, we need to be open to the consequences. With every kind of teamwork and networking allowed, we need to be sure that we assess clear thinking, understanding, creativity, an effective outcome and an ability to work to deadlines. Employers tell us these are the skills they want, so that's what we test.

Some impacts of projects are unexpected, valuable but seemingly impossible to measure. For example, what if practitioners from the workplace are changed spectacularly by working with our students – but without the practitioners realising it? This has happened, and we have needed to find ways of crediting the students for what they have done. Even when students are asked to signpost evidence of meeting our criteria, we often need to be as creative as them in assessing their achievements formally.

In terms of university grades, students in these courses tend to achieve far beyond their own – and our – expectations.

Find ways to stop students working too hard

'Fun, thought-provoking and all-consuming.'

Student

A big problem is students' high motivation. They work too hard, because working in, and for, the real world matters to them. Perhaps this is our biggest challenge, and we do not have a simple answer. We help students reflect on work–life balance in many different ways and we know that within their groups students help each other through.

▶ University teachers as agents of change: how these courses happened in the first place

This narrative is not 'set within a literature', as one reviewer requested it should be. This is because the teaching and learning decisions I describe were not particularly the embodiment of my, or others, published research. Rather, they came from careful thinking, talk and reflection by university teachers sharing diverse experiences, pushing each other into taking some risks and adapting as we went. Published research was only a small part of these experiences. At the time, students, recent graduates and employers played their part in the development teams.

Would the academic literature on learning and teaching lead us to design courses that are similar to those I describe? It is interesting to map the features of the courses against published research, and the answer is, broadly, yes (Reavey, 2013). But including these references here would give a false impression that developments were informed primarily by the literature. Instead, the evidence base was far wider – practical experiences from many contexts brought by diverse professionals who continue to learn as we go. In fact our learning journey is no different from that of the students who are challenged to make change happen.

28 Authentic partnerships: inspiring professional identity and ownership in students

Ruth Matheson (NTF 2012)

Keywords: *students as partners, engagement, ownership, professional identity*

Ruth Matheson is a Senior Lecturer in Academic Professional Development at the Cardiff Metropolitan University Learning and Teaching Development Unit, Wales. Responsible for the promotion of good practice in learning and teaching, she contributes significantly to partnership working with students and staff, enhancing curriculum design, capturing the student voice and delivering pedagogic development with programme teams.

A recent initiative by the Learning and Teaching Development Unit (LTDU) at Cardiff Metropolitan University introduced '*Team Intensives*', designed to engage both students and academic staff in working with academic developers to enhance curriculum design. Using data on student retention, and from the National Student Survey (NSS) and Destination of Leavers from Higher Education, together with qualitative student feedback, areas for enhancement were identified. This essay outlines the process and outcome of one such project within the Health and Social Care BSc programme and illuminates the significant benefits of engaging students in partnership working for both curriculum development and the personal development of all involved.

Analysis of NSS data indicated a high student satisfaction with the Health and Social Care degree, with 94 per cent of students indicating overall satisfaction on completion of the programme. However, retention figures, particularly within the first year of study, were worrying. This led the academic staff and staff within the LTDU to question whether the content, organisation and structure of the course were having an impact on student retention or whether there were other contributing factors.

▶ The process

Two paid interns were recruited from the second-year BSc Health and Social Care students and subsequently employed by the LTDU to work with myself (an academic developer), students and academic staff to instigate curriculum development.

A tripartite agreement was drawn up, outlining the expectations of the project and indicating a timeline of expected actions and reporting mechanisms. This proved invaluable in ensuring buy-in of all stakeholders and in promoting ownership by academic staff of potential changes to practice. It was agreed that we would adopt an action research methodology (Somekh, 2006), the starting point being the student voice. The interns were given training in the conducting of focus groups, and together we produced outline questions to initiate discussion and explore issues highlighted by the datasets.

Student-led focus groups were carried out with second-year students, exploring their perceptions of the programme and potential reasons for fellow students leaving. The focus groups used an Appreciative Inquiry approach (Whitney and Thosten-Boom, 2010). I cannot overemphasise the importance of this approach in establishing creative, student-generated solutions and in reassuring academic staff that the focus group would remain positive. Appreciative Inquiry directs participants to look at what is already working, how they would dream it to be, identify the stumbling blocks to achieving this and look for creative solutions to overcome these.

▶ Findings and identification of interventions

Our findings are shown in Table 28.1.

The overriding sense of a lack of professional identity was the students' greatest concern.

> The importance of developing a professional identity within a sphere or field has been recognised as vital for professional salience and effectiveness, acting as a key element in both the retention and motivation of the individual. (Baxter 2011:16)

Students commented on the lack of understanding of the general public with regard to the outcome and value placed on the degree. The students also identified that they lacked awareness of graduate employment opportunities within Health and Social Care and this led to dissatisfaction and some-

Table 28.1 Themes arising from student perceptions of the Health and Social Care programme

Expectations	Expectations of the course were different from the reality (less practical than expected)
Professional identity	A need for increased professional identity and pride as Health and Social Care professionals
Volunteering	The importance of volunteering in making sense of the course and future employability
Information	The need for increased information to make informed module choices
Small-group working	The value students placed on small-group working and seminars

times withdrawal. This lack of awareness of graduate opportunities extended to the interns themselves and the need for raising expectations and identifying graduate opportunities became paramount, providing the starting point for the first action. This involved engagement with the Careers Department, contact with alumni to establish graduate destinations, attendance at a national Social Work and Social Care conference, and discussion with fellow students to establish the areas of current volunteering work and thus future employment opportunities.

The importance of gaining experience through voluntary placements was emphasised time and time again in helping students to see the relevance of theory, while providing opportunities for practical application of the theory into practice. Where students had good volunteering opportunities they were able to place the programme content in context and felt that this helped in establishing a sense of identity. They also recognised the benefits of gaining experience through volunteering for future employability. However, students also commented on the difficulty of knowing how and where to secure these placements and time delays in finding this information led to frustrations and dissatisfaction. Participants suggested that an early volunteering 'fair' would assist them in identifying different career pathways and also securing a meaningful experience.

The participants identified that they often chose modules with little consideration of future employability and would benefit from increased awareness of module content. Understanding how modules linked to specific career pathways was seen as crucial to making informed decisions. Previous work had resulted in the production of a website to help students identify the content, teaching methodology, assessment and potential career benefits of modules and had met with a positive response. This solution was well received by participants in the focus group. The interns presented the outcomes of the focus groups to the programme team and identified the potential interventions that could address our findings.

▶ Interventions

1 *The development of a website created by students for students*
The interns identified ten fields within which health and social graduates were employed. These formed the basis of a website created by them to help students develop a professional identity and explore the different graduate employment opportunities available. Each field provided an introduction to the sector (through case studies presenting potential service user groups), identified volunteering opportunities (providing videos by employers and students volunteering in the field), career information and links to agencies, transcripts from employed former students and information on how module choice would benefit preparation for working in the field.

2 *Integration and use of the website content within the current curricula*
The website also provided a comprehensive introduction to the course, providing students with a video from the programme director outlining the course objectives and structure, together with videos introducing each staff member. Podcasts and vodcasts of each module outline the content, teaching and assessment methods and provide guidance on career opportunities offered through engagement with the module. Having the student perspective and guidance from fellow students throughout provides added authenticity (tips on study and placements being particularly useful).

The website has been designed as a living project to be kept current by staff and students within course activities.

3 *Setting up a volunteering fair early on in the course*
October 2012 saw the first Health and Social Care Volunteering Fair. Set up by the Careers Department, this joint venture with the interns, academic staff and LTDU provided first-year students with the chance to meet and explore opportunities with volunteer agencies and organisations seeking volunteers (12 in total) and set up early placements, thereby providing the much-desired practical application of the course.

▶ Evaluation

Much of the existing literature on student engagement in curriculum change focuses on course evaluation (O'Neill and McMahon, 2012). In 2008, Bovill, Morss and Bulley identified that few examples existed in the literature where students are actively involved as co-constructors of the curriculum. In more recent work (Bovill, Cook-Sather and Felten, 2011), they recognise three potential forms of student participation as co-creators of teaching approaches, course design and curricula, identifying benefits to both students and academic staff. Our work with students as co-creators of the curriculum produced comparable benefits.

The experience of working with students in authentic partnerships has been rewarding to all involved. As a Learning and Teaching Development Unit we have had the opportunity to mentor two inspiring students to develop research skills, practise negotiation skills, employ Appreciative Inquiry to develop creative solutions and develop relationships across university departments. The interns have had to work closely with their academic programme team. At times this has presented challenges to ensure that relationships are not brought into any conflict, as the interns were still being taught and assessed by members of the academic staff and that different relationship boundaries occur depending on the role adopted. There is a need to consider how interns deliver their findings to the programme team. The need for a clear tripartite agreement at the outset cannot be overemphasised, so that there is buy-in from all parties and that the views expressed by the interns are seen as collective student views and not their own opinions. There also may be occasions when the academic developer needs to address the programme team on behalf of the interns to decrease any personal involvement.

There was also the need for open communication between the academic developer and staff team throughout the process to establish the nature of the intervention being for enhancement rather than criticism of existing practice. This can be a fine line to tread. Professional boundaries with the interns need to be clearly established when jointly problem solving.

The adoption of an Appreciative Inquiry approach was central to this project to ensure that activities focused on enhancement. This approach can be used extensively within both staff development and student evaluation activities and its use as a methodology should be given consideration in projects of this type.

Throughout the project the interns have fed back their findings and development to the student cohorts, which is vitally important to ensure that students feel that their voice is being valued and that change has resulted from their input. Many of the student cohort produced videos, wrote case studies for the website and provided information regarding their voluntary placements. Alumni have also been instrumental in providing 'after gradua-tion' stories and opportunities within the sector.

For the interns themselves the benefits of this experience can best be summed up in their own words.

'I can honestly say that the work I have been undertaking during my internship has been one of the most rewarding things I have ever done. I believe that by facing challenges such as running focus groups with my peers, presenting findings to faculty and staff members, having to develop a professional attitude to arranging and attending meetings and conferences that I have grown as a person.'

'Through this internship, I have learnt many new skills and have devel-oped both personally and professionally. I have become more involved in my course and with lecturers and professionals in the field and I now have a deeper understanding of the sector, which will help me professionally. I would definitely recommend a student internship as it's very rewarding to see your ideas develop and provide useful resources to support future students.'

The impact on the student interns, now in their final year of study, has been considerable. Both students have changed their dissertation topics, now focusing on the impact on professional identity, employability and course engagement resulting from the curriculum changes made. They have also been invited to present at a national forum and national conference.

29 Learning from the real

Mary Hartog (NTF 2006) and Philip Frame (NTF 2001) *in association with Chris Rigby and Doirean Wilson*

Keywords: *critical action learning, work-based learning, leadership development, organising reflection, peer learning, collaborative enquiry*

Mary Hartog joined Middlesex University in 1990, having worked in local government in management and organisation development. She is currently Head of Department, Leadership, Work and Organisations, in the Business School. She led an innovative Masters programme in self-managed learning on which she based her PhD and continues to enjoy teaching, especially on in-company programmes and as an organisational coach.

Philip Frame is a business school academic and a Senior Teaching Fellow at Middlesex University. He has co-chaired SEDA's papers committee and has acted as an external assessor and examiner for a range of universities. He was instrumental in developing the Association of National Teaching Fellows as the immediate past Vice-Chair. His interests include induction/transition, diversity management, the impact of national teaching awards and employability.

Increasingly universities are becoming engaged in delivering education and training for external organisations and in real situations that have an urgency and imperative. In this case we were asked to work with a local authority to design a leadership qualification for managers facing cuts, redundancies and changes to service provision. Our challenge was to engage practising managers in a new way of learning that would meet their learning needs in leading and managing organisational change.

Here, in reflecting on that experience, we describe the design and delivery of the programme, which facilitates student engagement. We consider how managers experienced the programme and the impact of their learning for themselves and their stakeholders. To date 60 managers, in four cohorts, from social work, youth work and education, have completed the programme.

▶ Learning Design

Our philosophy and design approach for these types of programmes is informed by:

▶ A 'needs'-based approach to adult learning (as opposed to a prescribed curriculum), as identified by Knowles (1985), where programme content is negotiated with participants to reflect the real challenges they face

▶ 'Action learning' (Revans, 1982), which combines 'programme knowledge' or taught learning with 'questioning insights' that emerge from a peer enquiry process, and produces 'real learning', that is, learning from reality of self and others in order to manage their reality

▶ Weinstein (1995), for whom action learning signposts 'a journey of learning and discovery', via work-based projects, which validate learning from real-work challenges

▶ The work of Reynolds and Vince (2004), who provide a critical approach to action learning with peer learning assisting in the 'organisation of reflection', engaging students in a 'critical' exploration of the discourses on leadership, and identifying the impact of organisational power, politics and emotions on the practice of leadership

▶ The use of students' past and current experience to enhance relevance and engagement (Frame and Burnett, 2008).

▶ The starting point

The local authority had commissioned a training and development programme from a consultancy organisation which included a three-day strategic leadership development event, followed by one-day workshops in leading change, team building, performance management, power and influence, coaching and partnership working. Diagnostic and psychometric tools to support learning were also to be used. Our aim was to find a way forward that worked appreciatively with this programme, respecting the investment that the local authority and its managers were already making. We had to be pragmatic whilst at the same time introducing creative and evidence-based learning solutions.

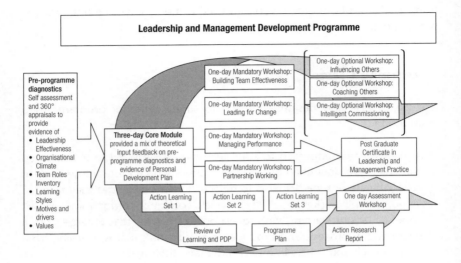

Figure 29.1 The Learning Solution leading to the Postgraduate Certificate in Leadership and Management Practice

▶ What we did

We approached this task as a partnership with the local authority and their training provider to design a postgraduate leadership development work-based learning qualification and utilised their management training programme as its basis. We used the University's Work Based Learning Framework to create what we called a 'wraparound' qualification (Figure 29.1).

We engaged their managers in the design of the assessment process that linked the developmental learning objectives of the workshops with academic learning outcomes of the programme.

We introduced 'action learning' as an opportunity to bring together the learning from the training programme with the qualification process and provide a vehicle for students to undertake relevant work-based projects to fulfil the academic requirements of the qualification.

▶ What's new?

This programme is novel in being designed in partnership with the client and their management development providers, and by linking the different components of the programme: the workshops, psychometric tools and action learning sets, and thereby creating a 'wraparound' qualification using our work-based learning framework and modules.

We linked the modules 'Review of Learning', 'Project Planning' and 'Project' to the action learning sets, and linked the learning and assessment to the goals of the programme, which was '*to develop effective leaders and improve leadership performance*'.

Both the design and the philosophy for learning place the students at the centre of their learning. This is reflected in all aspects of the programme, particularly the assessment, which focuses on their context and the *real issues* they are grappling with in their work experience. As a result, this engaged them as effective co-participants in the learning process and directed them towards addressing, and solving, 'real' organisational issues.

The work of Wenger (1998a) on social learning theory and communities of practice also served to inform the learning of participants, particularly where team learning and collective responses to organisational change were most needed.

Moreover, the learning is both holistic and 'critical', by identifying and valuing the emotional and the political domains of learning that impact their development as leaders. Thus, this provides a *'real'* experience of learning less commonly found in traditional academic programmes.

▶ Action learning and the assignment process

Central to this programme is the use of action learning, where students come together in small peer groups of five and work through assignments linked to their personal development needs and to a work-based project.

▶ The first assignment, a review of learning, involved taking stock and producing a personal development plan. This followed the initial three-day workshop and was informed by a $360°$ feedback tool designed to enable participants to become aware of effective and ineffective leadership styles: students selected eight of their staff to rate their performance across a range of leadership styles.

▶ The second required the production of a project plan, and followed the workshops on team building and 'using your power and influence'.

▶ The third assignment involved a project that each participant identified as being uniquely relevant to their particular leadership agenda and drew on workshop content appropriate to their real-life activities.

▶ **Addressing concerns**

Those who had not experienced action learning before expressed some anxiety about *'what exactly we would be spending three hours doing?'* Additionally, generic fears of redundancies and service cuts were causing anxiety. In our experience, anxiety discourages engagement, so handouts were prepared that provided a focus and a structure for each session, by allocating time to each participant to explore their real and individual organisational leadership issues. This limited the time available to dwell upon these generic issues.

▶ **Creating a safe space for learning**

Integral to our work was our process of 'check in', which we used at the start of every set meeting. This provided an opportunity for each participant to settle down and share with the group real-life experiences and issues which could affect their learning but about which they also wanted to learn, by exploring and seeking help from their peers. This process helped lighten the load that students brought with them. Honest and open sharing created a safe space in which they could engage in the social learning process, as the following feedback testifies:

> 'You know, I am not really used to talking about how I feel about things in the work context. I know it was a learning context. I was with peers which fortunately I felt very comfortable with ... I think I felt very safe in that group.'
>
> Manager, Office Services

> 'Action learning sets were enormously helpful in bonding; there was great deal of honesty and sharing of skills.'
>
> Manager, Safeguarding Children's Services

▶ **Space for working with the real**

In turn, students discussed their work within the set. Typically this would be a messy work-based problem that provided the inspiration for a project. The benefits of such a process are reflected in the following quotation:

I thought the action learning sets were really good. It just gave a forum and space to discuss: some of them were personal experiences as well. I thought that was quite useful because you don't really have time to do that in any other capacity and it gets you thinking as well.

Manager, Safeguarding Children's Services

▶ Organising reflection: critical action learning

Some action learning meetings worked with the sharing of emotions ('delight') and of organisational self-presentation ('putting on a pretence') in the political realm, as the following highlights:

'My (council committee) chair, losing her job and doing the same course as well, and just the delight of not having to put on a pretence on about the quagmire that I think we all found ourselves in, and the learning that went with it.'

Manager, Children's Centre

Here a more critical space for learning was needed, where the focus shifted from action to 'organising reflection' (Reynolds and Vince, 2004). This helped managers address the emotional and political aspects of their learning and their learning from their own experience, and that of their peers.

▶ Participative learning to participative leadership

A major impact on practice was the transfer of the action learning process, encouraging as it does honest sharing of issues and the participation of colleagues in helping to address these, and the application to the performance of the leadership role. As the quotation below identifies:

'The project plan really helped me focus on what I needed to do as a leader to ensure that I supported the staff all the way through ... We have had to do more with less ... I sat them (the staff) down and said, "these are our options. You can either work term-time, you can work reduced hours, what would you prefer?" I could then budget and go to the council and say, "this is what we would like to do".'

Manager, Pre-School Alliance (Voluntary Sector)

▶ Facilitation and teaching

Just as the programme validated a change in leadership style, it also validated, indeed necessitated, a move from teaching in a mainly didactic fashion to learning in a substantially participative manner in terms of both process and content of learning. Necessarily we provided academic input that informed the experiential learning process. For example, the Kubler-Ross Bereavement Model (1970) spoke directly to the experience of loss of services, and was pertinent to the process of redundancy that participants experienced. The work of Fuchs Ebaugh (1988), '*Becoming an ex*', addressed exiting roles and the related issue of identity transition. The work of Goffee and Jones (2006) highlighted questions about authenticity and trust in leadership, posing the question: 'Why should anyone be led by you?' Thus action learning, because of its facilitative nature, provides a synthesis of academic and participant content, with the focus on the latter.

▶ Conclusions

Three key lessons stand out for us:

1 *The power of learning from the real*
   Learning from the real provided an opportunity for students to engage in meaningful learning by placing their concerns and their experience at the centre of learning. This places value on what they bring, which enhances their confidence, and confidence usually produces engaged and effective learners. We are convinced that the greater the confluence between 'lived experience' and academic input, the more likely it is that students will engage and internalise their learning.

2 *The need for facilitators to be supported*
   Learning from the real in this case involved helping students navigate political and emotional issues associated with their roles and organisational work. We recognise and recommend to others that tutors need support to manage this type of work if they are to be effective in leading this process.

3 *The use of structure in action learning sets to reduce anxiety about a new way of learning and development*
   Learning from the real involved a peer-group process, which 'organises reflection' and engages students in 'critical action learning'.

We continue to find these approaches illuminating, incisive and valuable, as do our students, and we recommend others to explore their applicability across disciplines.

'The course gave me the time to reflect on my current practice and identify my strengths and areas for further development. Working on my project has already brought about improvements.'

Manager, Performance and Data

'Taking part in the course gave me a real insight and understanding of different management and leadership styles, which has benefited not only me, but my team too. The course has improved my confidence as a leader.'

Manager, Community Participation

Chris Rigby is a Senior Lecturer at Middlesex University and a Management Consultant. His special interests are in professional identity and career transition, and the role of mentoring.

Doirean Wilson is a Senior Lecturer at Middlesex University and an Organisational Coach, with a special interest in the respect agenda for effective and productive diversity management.

30 Looking at the mirror in the suitcase: encouraging students to reflect on their professional learning journey

Anna Lise Gordon (NTF 2012)

Keywords: *initial teacher education, student teacher, reflective practice, transformational learning, creative writing, professional portfolio*

Anna Lise Gordon taught modern languages in schools in London and Surrey and was a Local Authority Advisory Teacher for modern languages before moving into initial teacher education at St Mary's University College, London. She is currently PGCE Secondary Programme Director, leads the MFL PGCE programme and is a member of the national Executive Council for the Association for Language Learning. Her current research focuses on resilience of early career teachers.

An initial teacher education (ITE) course should inspire a love of learning in student teachers, so that these teachers of the future are both prepared for and positive about the inevitable challenges of their chosen career. However, the learning of student teachers can appear somewhat mechanistic at times, as they grapple with the constant pressure to balance the demands and requirements of the university-based part of the course and the related school-experience placements. As teachers are required to 'reflect systematically' (DfE, 2012), there is a need to consider reflective practice as an integral and creative part of a student teacher's professional development. As such, university teachers need to be innovative in their approaches to inspire student teachers' love of learning and to have a positive influence on their developing professional reflective practice.

On the last day of the Postgraduate Certificate in Education (PGCE) course each year at St Mary's University College (Twickenham, London), the cohort of secondary student teachers gather together to celebrate their achievements. One student teacher representative from each subject group is invited to peep inside a suitcase to see the 'ideal' teacher ...

... inside the suitcase is a mirror, a final reminder that reflective practice lies at the heart of the initial teacher education programme and will be central to their ongoing development as qualified teachers in schools.

This essay considers three specific examples of relevant and engaging learning experiences, developed over time and in collaboration with colleagues, to engage student teachers in taking ownership of their own learning, as well as focusing on the learning of their pupils in schools.

▶ Impact Review Sheet (IRS)

An understanding of the difference between potentially mechanistic reflective practice on the one hand and deeper reflective learning (Barnett, 1992; Schön, 1987), which leads to personal and professional transformation in the longer term, is central to the Impact Review Sheet (IRS) developed by the PGCE team for use by student teachers. As Pring (2004: 16) states, 'Training in a particular skill may or may not be educational, depending on the extent to which it opens up the mind and contributes to that growth as a person', and the IRS is subtitled 'Impact of university-based work on my progress as a teacher ... now and in the future'.

The idea behind the IRS is simple. Student teachers are provided with a template on which to note their immediate reflections after each university-based session in the left-hand column. They are then encouraged to reflect further on the sessions in the light of their experiences in school in the right-hand column.

Clearly, these reflections evolve over time and student teachers are encouraged to use different-coloured fonts to indicate at what stage in the year the reflections in the right-hand column were made. In this way, it is possible to track and monitor the impact of the university-based sessions on the student teachers' overall development. A review of the IRS for each student teacher is also an integral part of the tutorial programme throughout the year.

An example, drawn from a student teacher's reflections in his first term of the PGCE course, illustrates the potential impact of the IRS. The initial reflection on the university-based session is provided first and then an arrow indicates subsequent reflections. These reflections will undoubtedly continue to evolve as the student teacher moves into a second school placement.

'Interesting session on working with a teaching assistant (TA) – I hadn't realised how many TAs there are in schools these days! I need to think more about working effectively with them'.

(September 2012)

'I observed a TA in my placement school and he seemed a bit unsure of his role and always left quickly at the end of the lesson. As I'll be teaching the class, I need to try and liaise with the TA so we can work together well.'

(October 2012)

'The TA was surprised that I wanted to chat and was a bit defensive at first, but I stressed that I needed to learn from his experiences of working with particular pupils and that helped. I always give a plan to the TA in advance now, annotated with notes specifically for him, and he even stays after the lesson to review the lesson and to plan for next time!'

(November 2012)

▶ Portfolio of Evidence

Student teachers must provide evidence of progress, in line with the Teachers' Standards (TS) (DfE, 2012), often in the form of a file or e-Portfolio of Evidence (PoE) for each standard. As part of our aim to develop a deeper level of reflection with student teachers, we have adopted a more critically reflective approach to the presentation of evidence. Initially, the student teachers are concerned about the perceived extra work but, over time, come to appreciate the value of reflecting in greater depth. As one student teacher commented:

'My initial thought when we heard about the PoE was that it was yet another piece of paperwork and it duplicated our profile ... but the penny dropped in about February when I realised that the PoE gave us an additional point of reflection, beyond simply ticking off standards on the profile, and it really encouraged us to think about what we are doing and why, so we can plan the next steps of our learning as a teacher.'

The sequence for the presentation of evidence is as follows:

▶ For the PoE, student teachers are required to consider a series of questions, designed to take a holistic view of the Teachers' Standards, acknowledging that there is likely to be overlap between standards for many pieces of evidence. For example, 'How effective have you been in setting high expectations to ensure that the needs of every pupil are met?' The student teachers provide a PoE at three key points in their school-based experience, so the process of gathering and reflecting on evidence is cumulative.

▶ Student teachers respond to each question (in no more than 250 words) and provide a maximum of five pieces of *annotated* evidence to illustrate their work for each question. These annotations are crucial and the distinctive feature of the PoE, as they allow the student teacher to demonstrate a greater depth of critical analysis and informed reference to relevant literature than would typically be the case with a folder of evidence. In almost all cases, the range of evidence and the level of criticality in the annotations increase at each stage in the sequence, as the student teachers gain in experience and learn from the developmental process.

▶ A distinctive feature of the sequence is peer review of the PoE at each stage, and the student teachers receive a range of structured feedback from peers and tutors. This is used to inform a final reflective comment by the student teacher who also sets targets for the next PoE.

▶ By the end of the PGCE year, students have three PoE files to illustrate their progress as a teacher and the impact of both university- and school-based experiences. They are also skilled in the selection of relevant evidence to further illustrate their progress as newly qualified teachers and beyond.

▶ Creative writing as a tool for reflection

In another attempt to move beyond technical-rational approaches to reflective practice (Brockbank and McGill, 2007; Dymoke, 2008) and respond to Bolton's (2010) encouragement to use creative writing as part of reflective practice, I am exploring this further with student teachers. The purpose of using creative writing is to offer the opportunity for alternative insights and understandings by the student teachers as they deconstruct and reconstruct their experiences in a creative way, and a range of activities is used, including free writing, metaphors, poetry and storytelling.

Just a few examples of the student teachers' metaphors about learning to be a teacher provide an insight into the challenges they experience, but they almost always offer a note of positivity, too:

'It's like deep-sea diving, both frightening and rewarding to explore the depths.'

'It's a bit like nearly drowning several times on a marathon swim, but with lifeguards who won't let you go under'.

'It's like childbirth – painful and traumatic, but worth it in the end!'

Similar themes emerged in haiku poems (17 syllables, in 3 phrases of 5, 7 and 5, respectively) composed by the student teachers towards the end of their second school placement. For example:

> 'Finish line in sight
> Tired, but feeling positive
> I made the right choice.'

> 'Enthusiastic
> Supportive environment
> Where learning happens.'

> 'An exhausting race
> Finally nearing the goal
> And the goal moves!'

▶ The journey ahead

It is perhaps the last line of the final haiku example which best illustrates the importance of reflective practice. The educational landscape is one of constant change and uncertainty, as teachers respond to a number of external pressures, and part of the responsibility of ITE must be to prepare student teachers to manage these challenges. Student teachers, who are equipped for the journey with a suitcase of reflective strategies and a mirror, are ready to face the joys and challenges of teaching and develop as lifelong learners.

The thoughts of a fictional character in Giles Foden's novel, *Turbulence*, reflect the experience of a student teacher in many ways:

How in a world of disintegration and endless renewal – a continuum, a world of flow – one must find one's own rhythm exactly by recognising the incompleteness of the melody.

(Foden, 2010: 315)

As teachers in higher education, the approach taken to developing reflective practice must promote opportunities for student teachers to discover their own 'rhythm' to sustain them in their teaching career.

My thanks are due to the PGCE (secondary) team and student teachers at St Mary's University College for their contributions to this essay.

PART 4

Employability: moving on

31 SOARing to success: employability development from the inside out

Arti Kumar (NTF 2005)

Keywords: SOAR, self as threshold concept, behavioural competencies, career adaptability, transferable model

Arti Kumar MBE has worked with employers, staff and students over several years to develop and author innovative approaches and resources that enable individuals to become effective and productive, personally, socially and professionally: for example the *SOAR* model is influential in the UK and overseas. She is an Association of Graduate Careers Advisory Services (AGCAS) Lifetime Achievement Award winner and a Fellow of the Higher Education Academy (HEA) and the National Institute for Careers Education and Counselling (NICEC). She currently works independently on projects, and coaches and trains.

Employability is often approached in academia as a subject to be debated, defined and theorised. In a complex, unstable global economy, a disconnect in terminology and perspective between different stakeholders is inevitable, so this academic tendency may dissipate energy that could more simply and pragmatically be focused on the results that students need to achieve. Even where beneficial results-driven initiatives are being implemented, I propose that the typical focus on skills-development and work-related opportunities may still miss a vital complementary dimension. That dimension starts from the pragmatic need of all students to understand themselves more analytically, for example to ask themselves:

▶ What strengths and development needs do I bring to opportunities in learning, work and life in general?

▶ What beliefs and attitudes drive my performance and behaviour in different contexts?
▶ What should I do in order to be(come) effective and productive in a complex, competitive, changing world?

To engage students in this process of 'mindful being and becoming' requires pedagogy that is not addressing the subject of employability as such but foregrounding the developmental needs of each individual *Self* from a student-centred, inside-out perspective. This approach leads educators to ask different questions:

What concepts, tools, techniques and environments engage and enable students to:

▶ identify, critically appreciate, articulate and demonstrate their strengths *with explicit reference to behavioural competencies required for success in learning and work*?
▶ engage developmentally with opportunities and experiences within and outside formal curricula?
▶ generate informed aspirations that can be implemented and (re)evaluated?

Inherent in these questions are employability-linked person–environment interrelationships: the intrapersonal world of *Self* interacting with the interpersonal world of *Opportunity* recursively generates, tests and modifies *Aspirations* and produces certain *Results*. These interrelationships determine each individual's pathway through a life-career. Through my National Teaching Fellowship project I developed the acronym *SOAR* into a framework that conceptualises 'career' as 'lifelong and life-wide learning', defined not so much by occupational titles but by the portable skills and values that are the unique possession of each individual (Straby, 2002).

SOARing to Success (Kumar, 2008) amplifies and translates modern perspectives on career into constructively aligned design and delivery mechanisms that enable students to develop a broad range of interlinked behavioural competencies, as a foundation for lifelong and life-wide learning. SOAR aims to engage all students in a structured and supported process of personalised, humanistic and holistic development across all levels of study.

The model has since been embedded in a revised institutional curriculum (CRe8) at the University of Bedfordshire (Atlay, Gaitán and Kumar, 2008). CRe8 advocates personalised, realistic, reflective, active, interactive and collaborative methods of teaching, learning and assessment in order to develop professional attributes and identities, without sacrificing subject knowledge and/or technical expertise. Lessons have been learned from contextualising SOAR pedagogy in undergraduate programmes and from action-researching its impact on MBA international students in terms of *SOARing for Employability* (Kumar, 2012). It has also transferred to other contexts in the UK and overseas.

Since the impact on students has been extensively documented in previous publications, I focus here on recent evaluations with staff that indicate further how SOAR best creates personal agency in the self-development of employability attributes.

▶ *Self-concept*: a threshold concept in employability development?

I invite readers to consider the proposition that focusing attention on Self leads to learning outcomes that have the characteristics of a threshold concept, 'akin to passing through a portal' or 'conceptual gateway that opens up previously inaccessible ways of thinking' (Meyer and Land, 2006). The characteristics that help us recognise a concept as '*threshold*' (central to the mastery of a discipline) are identified as *bounded, integrative, troublesome, irreversible, excursive* and *transformative*. Self-assessment is key to SOARing for employability in some ways outlined below.

Self-concept is *bounded* in the sense that it occupies its own conceptual space. *Self* within SOAR is also a psychosocial, *integrative* construct. As one MBA tutor observed during a recent discussion:

> 'The SOAR model demands internal integrity between its four elements, and also external integration with real-life socioeconomic conditions.'

Animating and contextualising the Self-Opportunity dynamics in SOARing is essentially a process of person–environment adaptation, which is fundamental in career construction theory:

> For human beings, adaptation to social life implicates all core and peripheral roles. As they design their lives people must adapt to expectations that they work, play and develop relationships ... From this perspective, an occupation is a mechanism of social integration or connection, one that offers a strategy for sustaining oneself in society.
>
> (Savickas and Porfeli, 2012: 1)

An important point to note is that SOAR resources are congruent with the concept and recommended scale for 'career adaptability' (*ibid.*, p. 11), consid-

ered essential for developing the generic attributes of resilience, resourcefulness and flexible planning necessary for occupational transitions in an unstable global economy.

A university employability project manager has evaluated SOAR with 100
sports degree students in a first-year core module, *Personal Development for
the Sports Industry*:

> 'Focusing on "Self" in the first instance I found to be absolutely the right
> approach with students who were arriving to us with varied backgrounds
> and often fixed ideas of what they would eventually like to do after graduat-
> ing … They particularly commented on how the SOAR model had helped
> them reflect in a much deeper and detailed way, and how this had really
> helped them reconsider their future opportunities in a much more informed
> manner. They often began to recognise new opportunities they had not
> previously thought of. The effect this then had on them in terms of planning
> their own personal, academic and career development was significant.'
>
> Doug Cole, Buckinghamshire New University, 15 October 2012

The SOAR ethos of treating 'self as hero in the journey of life-career' is *integrative* of all aspects and stages of the journey, where individuals self-reflect
as autonomous beings capable of self-regulation and self-actualisation (e.g.
self-audit: 'It's my journey through life – am I in the driving seat?', Kumar,
2008: 37–40). Accepting that each of us is 'response-able' (capable of choosing our response to situations) may be *troublesome* in that we must take our
fair share of responsibility for life-career events. SOAR pedagogy requires
students to self-assess their engagement with and development through

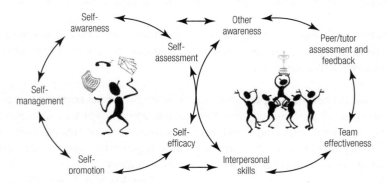

Figure 31.1 Driving behavioural competencies towards personal and interpersonal
effectiveness, based upon a concept of reciprocal causal relations between self-
evaluation, self-monitoring and achievement

opportunities within and outside formal curricula and creates ownership of personal aspirations, decisions and plans. Feedback shows the process typically increases their confidence and self-efficacy beliefs. Research findings show a correlation between people's high internal locus of control and high self-esteem (e.g. Rotter, 1966). Such personality factors, once instilled, are *irreversible* – they become the foundation for creating and managing personal futures.

Confidence is also enhanced when students recognise strengths that arise from the interlinked combinations and permutations of their *Motivation* (interests and priorities), *Ability* (skills, attributes, talents) and *Personality* (styles of interaction with others and with different situations). Educators can use SOAR resources for Self-*MAP*ping to provide a sense of direction, destination and intention for students' personal and collective learning journeys. Unlike other tick-box, bolt-on skills audits, these resources are informed by (and expressed as) employers' requirements for behavioural competencies (as in UKCES, 2010). Students are challenged to develop and demonstrate effective and productive behaviours that are important in current learning as well as future employment. They critically appreciate that self-promotion needs to be evidenced by examples to demonstrate how their generic and specific attributes align with the job they aspire to. The relevance of recording broader achievements in (e)portfolios is further supported by the Higher Education Achievement Report (Burgess, 2007).

Enhancing self-awareness involves an *excursive* learning journey as Self develops, interests, aspirations and circumstances change. Educators may facilitate a linear collective direction within curricula, by engaging students in the process of enhancing self- and social awareness linked with opportunity-awareness, exploring options, testing specific aspirations through experiential learning and evaluating the results they achieve for further cycles of SOARing. However, each personal journey will have deviations, revised and revisited learning intentions – and reaching any given milestone will be the point for further goal setting. SOARing is eventually a *transformative* cyclical process that sends personal development planning (PDP) spiralling into future career performance appraisals and continuing professional development (CPD).

'The SOAR sessions have made a lot of changes in me. With the help of personal analysis and other online tests I was able to identify my MAP strengths, weaknesses and future goals. It helped me to align my development plan with my aspirations and analyse constraints in achieving those aspirations.'

MBA student's reflections at University of Bedfordshire, July 2010

I advocate SOAR as a pedagogy and process in any curriculum, but it has also proved beneficial for staff development at the University of Hertfordshire:

> 'From my point of view, SOAR provides an excellent framework for talking about career in a positive way. As well as running the workshop, I have used it in a coaching context to structure conversations about career and decision-making. The focus on Self is particularly useful as, although it might seem obvious that career decisions start with who a person is, it is not something that people are necessarily comfortable with. I use the Johari Window ... as it illustrates the need, not only to be self-aware, but also to be more open about skills and experience that might be relevant but not visible.'

Evaluation comments from participants in this workshop indicate a range of benefits:

> 'An excellent course, one of the most useful I've been on. I had a one-to-one with my manager the next day and a lot of opportunities came up thanks to this course.'

> 'Good to be encouraged (even if a pay rise/promotion is not possible!) to make the most of our jobs for personal satisfaction and increases our value to the university.'

> 'Came out feeling enthused and motivated to make the most of my current role and opportunities.'

> 'I should have done this course 20 years ago! :-).'

> 'Useful to look at skills used outside work which can be brought into the work environment for career progression.'

> 'I have reflected a lot on my career since the session – I think this particular course has left the biggest impression on me (all positive!).'
>
> Helen Charlwood, Human Resources Development Facilitator,
> University of Hertfordshire, 26 October 2012

▶ Is SOAR a transferable model?

SOAR has previously been comprehensively described (Kumar, 2008) so I merely pose the question here: what implications does this inside-out approach have for your own practices in employability development? Since I have received evaluations recently from other contexts where SOAR has transferred (apart from those already quoted), I will let the following examples speak for themselves:

> 'I have been very inspired by SOARing to success, and have used many elements and the concept behind it in the development of a new career approach ... to support career reflections early in the education in a way that student counsellors and the student themself can use. This has been a major influence in the development of e-portfolio, which is on its way to be implemented in the spring 2013. And we have developed a wide range of PDP tools for our daily practice based on elements from SOARing to success.'
>
> Louise Jørgensen, Career Counsellor, Roskilde University, Denmark

> 'My colleague and I are using the SOAR method in our bachelor of engineering program. Great way to develop personal and professional growth.'
>
> Ricardo Abdoel, Program Manager, Engineering, the Netherlands

I would like to thank Doug Cole, Helen Charlwood, Louise Jørgensen and Ricardo Abdoel for their uses of SOAR in different contexts and for responding to my request to share their evaluations with me via personal email communication.

32 Telling tales: the use of story to enhance employability

Beverly Leeds (NTF 2012)

Keywords: storytelling, stories, employability, blogs, blogging

Beverly Leeds is a Principal Lecturer at the University of Central Lancashire, and her research interests include storytelling to enhance employability, perceptions of time in e-learning and the use of technology to support work-based learners. She has project-managed a number of educational research projects that have produced widely-used Re-Usable Open Educational Resources (OERs).

One of the difficulties in enhancing employability skills is in providing students with a range of workplace experiences. Many degree programmes offer placement opportunities that provide students with such experiences, but not all students are able to participate and others may lack the confidence to apply. A lack of work-related experience may mean that students do not possess the skills to operate effectively in a work environment immediately upon graduation.

Learning about a subject discipline is not just about the subject itself but is also about the 'narratives' and 'sense-making' that are fundamental to it (Bruner, 1990). We use stories to assist us in this 'sense-making' and, even if these stories are about the experience of others, for some, they can be synonymous with experiencing the event in person (Ferguson et al., 1991). When we hear a story, we map it onto a framework that we already have which allows us to make sense of the story: an essential requirement for learning to occur (Laurillard, 2002). Stories are entertaining, easy to remember and above all believable, and therefore highly effective educational tools (Neuhauser, 1993). Providing students with experiences expressed as stories can assist in increasing their range of workplace experiences and develop their employability skills.

This essay explores the use of stories in providing work-related experiences and in enhancing employability skills for second-year undergraduate marketing students on a Professional Development module at the University of Central Lancashire (UCLan). The module concentrated on developing capability skills (Stephenson, 2001) and utilised the USEM 'employability model' (Yorke and Knight, 2002; Knight and Yorke, 2004) of four broad and interrelated components:

- Understanding subject knowledge
- Skilful practice
- Efficacy beliefs
- Meta-cognition

I explore how stories from experienced practitioners can provide students with a vicarious workplace experience, increasing their knowledge of workplace problems and issues whilst developing their employability skills. In addition, I look at the telling and sharing of students' own stories in the form of a blog, assisting with reflection and other learning skills.

Why stories?

Interest in storytelling for learning has grown partly because media-rich learning environments facilitate interaction and help bring stories to life (Jenkins, 2006), and because research indicates the effectiveness and value of storytelling in general (Rossiter, 2002). As stories deal with human or human-like experience, we tend to perceive them as an authentic and credible source of knowledge and, as they involve us in the actions and intentions of the characters, they necessitate active meaning-making. Practitioners prefer to use narrative explanations (Polkinghorne, 1988) and stories to explain experiences (Schön, 1993) rather than theoretical models and textbook examples. Using practitioner stories allowed our marketing students to view situations from different perspectives; a marketing practitioner story could demonstrate the consequences of real-world actions, explain meanings, and assist in preventing communication errors and consequent misunderstandings (Cox, 2001). By embedding the students in authentic, contextualised, real-world problems they were more engaged and able to transfer learning more effectively (Barnes, Christensen and Hansen, 1994). Practitioner stories demonstrated the organisational ethos and assisted students in knowing the boundaries of what is expected or permitted, by highlighting the rhetoric and reality about competencies required for employment in that workplace (McKenna, 1999).

▶ Case stories

A storytelling approach is not unusual; many learning instructional models use storytelling as the learning focus (Andrews, Hull and Donahue, 2009) but unusually we combined student stories with those from practitioners to prepare students for the complexity of workplace situations.

A series of 'case-stories', rather than case studies, were developed from practitioner stories in order to allow students to connect new knowledge with lived experience (Rossiter, 2002). Although less well known than a case study, a case-story is highly personal, has a shared outlook and is 'embedded in ecological systems of thought and the social world of activity' (Maslin-Ostrowski and Ackerman, 2004: 198). It is multidimensional and complex, featuring not only the story line and action, but also the scene and individual influences on the events, deliberately highlighting some aspects and ignoring others. Unlike well-structured case-study examples found in some textbooks, the case-stories were open-ended and lacked structure, having no predetermined solution criteria or parameters (Savery, 2006).

Thus case-stories were explicitly subjective, allowing ethical dilemmas to be raised, and designed to encourage students to recollect relevant experiences or other stories. They were by their very nature discriminatory and explanatory, but at the same time were evocative, comprehensible, and more easily recalled than a text or a formal lecture.

▶ Using stories

Six case-stories were developed as online resources recorded in audio format, supplemented with photographic images of the organisations. They included issues, events, personal reflection and past and future challenges at both micro and macro levels. Storytellers were encouraged to provide a context or situational reference point, identify who was involved, by what means, what took place, and for what purpose. As well as recognising issues and challenges for the organisations students were also expected to identify the nature of the organisation, its values and the personalities of its organisational members.

One case-story told by a local councillor, who was also the director of a social enterprise, Enviro Nappies, which facilitates the purchase of cotton nappies to low-income families. The story was littered with clues as to the nature of the organisation and its particular values, such as 'we are not interested in the latte-drinking mumsy networks' and 'our nappy nannies are all from low-income households and many are single mums'. The story also highlighted the many challenges the organisation faced and the different characters who worked for the organisation. Students accessed the case-stories through the university virtual learning environment before discussing the stories in small groups.

For the first four stories students were encouraged to explore their interpretation of the stories and then create a collective story about issues raised and suggest appropriate actions. Following these formative sessions, students were assessed on the remaining two case-stories by acting as consultants and presenting their recommendations. In order to develop employability skills as well as work-related experiences, students were given specific tasks to undertake, such as holding formal team meetings with an agenda and minutes, providing a project plan and presenting findings via a web-conference link. Resources to support these were provided online. To assist with reflection, students were asked to tell their own stories by blogging about their case-story experiences, and these blog entries formed part of their own assessed reflective story. They were encouraged to read and comment on other students' stories as well as highlight learning opportunities related to employability. This multiple storytelling and story-listening enabled them to share experiences and learn from each other's stories as well as from the case-stories.

▶ Evaluating stories

We evaluated the initiative through a short survey and the analysis of the students' blogs and their assessed reflective stories. Students felt connected to the organisations, viewing them as authentic work-related experiences which assisting in understanding wider workplace issues. Telling their own stories as part of a work-related community allowed them to be reflective practitioners and debate personal and contextual influences on problems and issues. The blogs provided the opportunity to learn from other students' experiences and to identify work-related learning opportunities such as networking and time management. Influences such as organisational culture, individual fears and goals, motivation, organisational and individual expectations, ethical and unethical practices, uncertainty, risks and benefits of particular choices and other factors such as the ability to function in the workplace were discussed and analysed. One blog entry highlighted a student's ignorance of minute taking when he confessed:

'I thought all we had to do was time how long each agenda item took – we just counted the minutes.'

Another demonstrated her prior knowledge of minute-taking from being the secretary of a village sports team:

> 'It's important to make sure someone is responsible for taking ownership of actions – once we had to cancel our presentation evening as no one had booked the room.'

The case-stories provided students with the ability to identify and develop workplace skills in different situations, with some of the students claiming they

> 'take more notice at work' and 'think about how others are feeling'.

Others referred to misaligned organisational values at her part-time work:

> 'we claim to be a caring organisation but management don't even care about their staff'.

One student felt that the case-stories allowed her to

> 'get inside someone's head' and 'apply my subject knowledge'.

Others considered the case-stories a chance to act as if they were working

> 'on a live project for a client' but were 'in a safe place'.

▶ Conclusions

Using case-stories as substitutes for engagement with real organisations allowed the students to experience a real situation in a safe classroom environment. The students' innate ability to follow a story provided them with a productive learning experience, forming part of their aptitude for thinking, explaining, understanding and remembering, and thereby contributing to employability skills. However, students also need to be reflective thinkers and be able to transfer learning from a story to another situation. The blogs served this purpose, allowing them to relate to the characters (other students) and plot (other experiences) within a specific work-related context.

The use of case-stories could be used by other subject disciplines to provide workplace experience by proxy. Stories from experienced managers would allow students to increase their knowledge of workplace problems and issues and develop appropriate behavioural tendencies relevant to work-place environments. Asking students to work on a case-story as a real client provides an opportunity to develop verbal and written communication skills. Working as a group also gives an opportunity to develop teamwork and leadership skills:

- sharing stories about experience assist students in recognising when they make progress
- hearing stories from others develops self-confidence and an awareness of appropriate professional behaviour

Case-stories enable the construction of more complex and interconnected knowledge by incorporating many human and circumstantial details which allow exploration of what people do in organisations, as well as what should or could be done. Story listening, as well as storytelling, can form a basis for learning how to explore organisational issues and problems in order to enhance and improve a student's employability prospects.

33 Authentic assessment and employability: a synergy?

Jane Thomas (NTF 2012)

Keywords: employability, assessment, authentic assessment, curriculum, work-based learning

> Jane Thomas is Deputy Head of Learning and Teaching and Professional Practice at the College of Human and Health Sciences, University of Swansea, Wales. Previously a nurse, she has worked across a range of programmes with responsibility for assessments, admissions, placements and quality and externally is an assessor for the UK Public Health Register. Her role as University Director of the Swansea Academy of Learning and Teaching (SALT) involves her in pedagogical practice from strategy to delivery, developing students' and teachers' full potential.

Assessment is a key and necessary element of the educational process, providing the means to quantify learning and the retention and application of knowledge. It is the aspect of learning which causes students the most anxiety and difficulty, so making it work in other ways can add value to the student experience. Designing assessment to enhance employability not only serves the educational need but also gives students career advantages.

Employability has become increasingly important for higher education recently; the introduction of fees, the economic downturn and ever-increasing student expectations all increase pressure to deliver graduates 'ready for the workplace'. A number of reports (Dearing, 1997; Leitch, 2006) have resulted in universities supporting, to varying degrees, the embedding of key skills in curricula, the notion of lifelong learning and transformative education.

Employability is seen as more than just getting a job (Harvey, 2003; Yorke, 2004), with less emphasis on the 'employ' aspect and more on 'ability'. It is essential that we differentiate between employability (capability) and employment (having a job) so that we promote the broader, valuable benefits of higher education rather than the purely instrumental ones enshrined in so many measures such as the DLHE (Destination of Leavers of Higher Education) survey. Similarly, degree classifications in themselves are not an indicator of employability, although it is increasingly common for employers to exclude applications on account of lower-range attainment thresholds.

Employability should be recognised as something developed by the graduate throughout their programme of study. While the prominence of employability as a driver in the educational process is well established, teachers and students benefit substantially from the orientation of teaching, learning and assessment towards it. As teachers in higher education we work to provide for learning in diverse and creative ways and to produce graduates with a body of knowledge, who can use research and apply their skills more widely. Knight and Yorke (2004) outline employability through the USEM model, the components of which include:

- ▶ Understanding (of the disciplinary subject)
- ▶ Skilful practices (including skills deployment)
- ▶ Efficacy beliefs and personal skills (including students' views of themselves)
- ▶ Meta-cognition (self-awareness and an ability to reflect upon learning)

The model turns on the consideration of the elements, the extent to which they are evident in the curriculum and application across disciplines. Understanding these elements and their interaction through curriculum analysis enables the contextualisation of employability in the curriculum, connecting employability to assessment in a way that benefits teachers, students and potential employers. In practice this gives students a clear rationale for their learning and recognition that good performance not only gives a good mark but can also help them to show their talents in the employment market. Assessment makes a fundamental and specific contribution to pedagogic engagement and should, therefore, feature strongly in employability strategies.

▶ Employability for public health

My experience of enhancing student employability through innovative curriculum design and assessment is in public health. Traditional assessment methods of essays and examinations were replaced with tasks linked directly to the skills required for public health practice, identified in consultation with employers, which included:

▶ production of research proposals
▶ literature review
▶ critical review of placement
▶ programme design

As an example, the design task requires students to (a) write a request, providing the brief for a specified programme/population and then (b) respond with an outline of the programme appropriate to specification outlined.

While this is a challenging assessment task, directly aligned to the programme design outcome (Biggs, 1996), it has proved very popular with students.

> 'the assessments were all different ... being assessed that way gave us a range of skills so useful in applying for jobs'.
> Recent graduate, MSc Public Health

Interestingly, students now choose to take examples of their assessed work to interviews to enable them to illustrate the skills they have relevant to the job.

Student response to the assessment strategy has been positive. For mature students particularly, these ways of assessing have more relevance and are less threatening, drawing as they do on a wider skill base. The students describe:

> 'being able to develop confidence in applying theory to practice and having our work and assessments mapped to professional competence indicators'.
> Current MSc student

In public health these are attractive attributes to employers beyond the recognition of obtaining a Masters degree in the subject.

> 'Having struggled with essays and exams in my first degree, I looked for a postgraduate course with more varied assignments. That is better for me but also they fit the kind of jobs I can apply for in public health.'
> Current applicant

▶ Authentic assessment

I am committed to designing assessment which addresses the world of work, enabling colleagues to appreciate that it must encompass both the similarities between the education and employment (structure, purpose) but also the differences (such as culture and reward). An enduring tension lies in the extent to which the attributes valued in education replicate those valued in the workplace. Reid and Fitzgerald (2010) propose 'authentic assessment', involving the student and developing personal and professional knowledge as fundamental to graduate employability.

Authentic assessment is based on using 'real' contexts, in scenario format or case-based examples, requiring the application of theoretical knowledge to practice. Examples can include clinical scenarios for health students, classroom contexts for student teachers, legal case studies for lawyers or field studies for scientific students. Gulikers et al. (2008) propose that authentic assessment is valid both in terms of construct and consequence. In assessment, 'construct validity' is whether an assessment measures what it should and 'consequential validity' relates to the impact or consequence for student learning. This may seem very straightforward in principle, but even a superficial review of commonly used assessment formats across disciplines reveals 'room for improvement' in one or both. It is incumbent on us to ensure that when we use authentic assessment we do so authentically.

The link between authentic assessment and employability requires students to do things which have relevance in the wider world, and particularly the workplace. That is more easily achieved in some disciplines than others (medieval problem-solving and battle strategy, for example, can be linked to current resource scenarios), but there is scope to use the assessment activity itself to demonstrate the application of knowledge, skills and attitudes congruent with professional working practice, teamwork, time scales and standards. The contribution of employers and professional bodies such as the General Medical Council, Nursing and Midwifery Council and the Solicitors Regulatory Authority to realistic and appropriate assessment should not be underestimated.

If students are encouraged to view their assessments as contributory to employability they will be more inclined to engage with, and invest in, the assessment process. That is certainly true in public health and is confirmed by colleagues in education, medicine and social work. However it is important to remember that assessments generally represent only a partial contribution to employability attributes, for example through placements and internships, articulation of graduate prospects, personal development planning, skills development and curriculum innovation/mapping.

► The view of employers

Work-based learning provides one route to building employability skills but is not a panacea. Informal feedback from employers in South Wales suggests that learning styles, modes of delivery and assessment styles do impact on the suitability of graduates for the world of work. The resultant application of theoretical knowledge to an area of practice or employment provides something of value, attractive to employers.

'We found it really useful having a Masters student with us as he looked at practice afresh and questioned what we did. He took a real interest in the data generated by the exercise initiatives and so we offered the opportunity to come back to us. That is good for him and his dissertation but also gives us constructive outcomes.'

Team Leader, Primary Healthcare Trust

'Having this student on placement has been particularly useful as we are experiencing an outbreak. He has made a difference to the team and so we have arranged for him to return on a rolling contract to continue the work.'

Public Health Manager

Since the Dearing Inquiry (1997) the potential value of exposure to placements has been recognised, but implementing placements for the wider student population is resource-intensive and availability is dependent on relationships with employers, suitable types of placement and pedagogic integrity. Structured, planned and effective placements make a clear contribution to the employability of students, not just in the short term but also in the longer term as well. The work-based learning approach has grown in terms of credibility and rigour in recent years. Many students looking for courses to prepare them for the world of work particularly seek out those with placements of using work-based learning.

'Although it was difficult to find a placement, when I did it turned out very well. I am back to the placement to do my dissertation on the intervention – not something I thought I could do.'

Full-time international student

'As a young sports science graduate, I chose to do this course to improve my chances of getting a job. Finding that the assessments are useful in the world of work have really added to my confidence and helped me get my job as a project worker.'

Full-time student

▶ Conclusion

Employability as an educational driver presents challenges in terms of how survey outcomes are linked to employability when they are subject to external variables. Graduates from professional programmes can be more likely to secure graduate-level employment whereas others may need time to build experience, a work profile, a portfolio of work as they go along before they attain that level of employment.

Yorke (2010) proposes that commitment to employability requires a readiness to reconsider and redesign curriculum, pedagogic approach and assessment. The time has come for educationalists to join these elements, drawing on pedagogic excellence and creativity to produce innovative and inspiring curricula. Students make course choices on the subjects taught and their curricular arrangement: that is what draws them in. Once studying, they have every reason to hope and expect that their teachers will have designed their assessment in such a way as to demonstrate the breadth and depth of their knowledge and how it can be used in the longer term.

34 Getting ready for action: student engagement in an employability project

Jamie Thompson (NTF 2007) *in association with Laura Bullerwell, Catherine Foster, Russell Jackson and Nichola Larkin (students)*

Keywords: *employability, self-authorship, relationships, collaboration, wellbeing, creativity*

> Jamie Thompson was a Probation Officer for nearly twenty years. He is now Principal Lecturer and Teaching Fellow in the Department of Social Work and Communities at Northumbria University. He believes that the student experience of higher education should be transformative and that universities need to articulate more clearly a focus on increased student self-awareness, personal and professional growth, relationships, collaboration and individual change. He has a particular interest in exploring ways to work creatively across disciplinary boundaries to engage learners and bring added value and meaning to our increasingly highly codified degree curricula.

Of course we want students to get good jobs through which they fulfil their aspirations and contribute to the world – but does employability really reflect the shapes and processes of people's lives and aspirations? Is it a suitable over-arching template for learning in higher education? As a teacher on a vocational programme (Social Work), I think less about employability and more about preparing students for lives of effective action and wellbeing. In a changing world characterised by conflict, inequality and environmental crises, under-pinned by a market economy that is perhaps unsustainable and morally bank-rupt, this notion of wellbeing is helpful. Subjective wellbeing is an idea that helps us to explore who we are and can be, not in terms of goods, services and the labour market but through our relationships, actions and behaviour.

▶ Relationships, resilience and wellbeing

There are some influences, dialogues and lines of thought that informed our employability project. Social work students want particular kinds of jobs and to be equipped to compete for and retain those jobs. However, in our experience of talking with students they also arrive at university wanting and expecting more. This preparedness for transformation and change proves fragile for many in the face of the reality of undergraduate experience. This was explored in the research report *Dispositions to Stay and Succeed* (Harding and Thompson, 2012), which identified two key findings. First, student academic success is significantly associated with critical curiosity and a disposition to make meaning from learning.[1] Second, academic staff and students associate success and satisfaction with the quality of relationships they experience (between students and with academic staff).

Relationships are central to what Baxter Magolda (1999) calls 'self-authorship'. Based on longitudinal research about narratives underpinning progression through school, university and employment, self-authorship is a level of personal development where we become able to think and act independently of external authority and beyond others' expectations. Baxter Magolda describes how individuals may never achieve self-authorship, or not until their late twenties or beyond. For her, formal education, including higher education, should take responsibility for accelerating this progress. Independent thinkers are needed and are also more likely to become personally fulfilled. To support this personal growth, learning experiences need to be built around three constituents of self-authorship:

▶ How do I know? (What do I know and what do I need to know?)
▶ Who am I? (Who do I want to be?)
▶ Relationships (What are they and how do they work in the world?)

Baxter Magolda offers a way of integrating the notion of relationships in a model of the higher education experience that embraces the traditional. Brown (2011) describes the importance of being prepared to make oneself vulnerable to develop and sustain relationships and personal growth. This implies a subtle version of personal resilience; the resilience to make oneself vulnerable as opposed to resilience as a set of protective behaviours creating a shield between the self and others. Interest in resilience in social workers has been a function of high attrition rates and sickness leave in the sector and the impact of the perceived negative public image of the profession in the UK. Two qualities that help us display this subtle version of resilience emerge from research (Collins, 2008; Kinman and Grant, 2011). The first is reflection;

to look back over what has happened to learn from experience and improve practice, to see difficulty as opportunity, is a catalyst for resilience. The second is emotional intelligence (Goleman, 1996) and in particular two connected components, self-awareness and empathy.

The final influence on our thinking is the idea of subjective wellbeing. Aked and Thompson (2011) offer five evidence-based themes for describing wellbeing that for us have high face-validity: activity, giving, connectedness, curiosity and learning.

Around a small case-study involving a craftwork collective of older women in Australia, Maidment and Macfarlane (2011) weave a powerful argument about the ways in which lives can be enhanced around these wellbeing themes through creative activity.

'How will our lives be measured – by ourselves and those whom we love and about whom we care? In terms of what we knew and understood? In terms of our academic qualifications or the size of our bank balance? No. We will measure ourselves and we will be measured and judged largely in terms of what we did – our actions. Can we act effectively without collaborating with others? Can we collaborate successfully without understanding, building and sustaining relationships? Can we make relationships without first understanding ourselves?'

Catherine, Jamie, Laura, Nichola and Russell (see Figure 34.1)

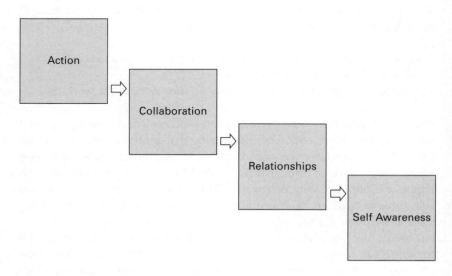

Figure 34.1 Contingencies

▶ So what did we do? ...

Relationships were formed and an enthused, eclectic group wanted to make something happen: social work students and staff; staff and students from the Department of Performing Arts; the artist-in-residence from a homeless charity, homeless people and refugees; victims of torture, officers from the counter-terrorism squad, bereaved parents of a young drug user, ex-drug users; and expert practitioners in autism, anger management, advocacy for children and domestic violence. We were expending energy but not funds. There was no fund. We agreed to hold an event in May – a month-long learning event with the theme of Insider and Outsider. Students would join with guests and hear about their lives and their experiences and reflect about themselves, the relationships they are forming and collaborations they see. The students would be invited to reflect their learning and their feelings in personal and creative ways. There would be prizes. At the end of the month we would celebrate together – make a performance and invite people to come and hear about what we had done. It would be a conference and we'd call it *Art as Action*.

So we did it. Most students turned up, and mostly tuned in and engaged – some became closely involved. The guests came, and it was often exciting and enjoyable and sometimes moving and emotional. And we celebrated. We held the performance and the conference and prizes were awarded for poems, photos, drawings, videos, a collage and a film presentation. All our collaborators loved it and the students gave us reams of feedback. We have been thinking and talking about this feedback and our experience of the month.

We reminded everyone to reflect about each session and take the opportunity to raise their self-awareness, explore personal and professional values and reflect about their identity as student social workers. Students had the opportunity to observe, experience and reflect on relationships with each other, with staff and with guests and to see how these relationships can become collaboration and action. Alongside this, the Insider/Outsider theme was effective in helping us think about the relationships between social workers and service users and how we are all sometimes Insiders and sometimes Outsiders. For some this was the most important part of the month; it helped people think about their personal and professional identity, who they are and who they want to be. All the guests, visitors and speakers provoked us to reflect on this relationship between those on the Inside and those on the Outside and how they can collaborate and act together.

Art as Action involved attempts by students to capture their experience of the month in creative ways. It takes courage to be creative. There were only ten contributions from some 80 students but they were experienced and appreciated by all. The majority of students recorded and submitted reflections and feelings about the month. Some worked with the artist-in-residence and helped organise the performance. It was a powerful event for many as a variety of insiders and outsiders made music, dance, film and theatre. Most of our guests from the month attended and some were very moved. At the end the audience joined the cast at the front and ate together. Finally we held the conference, where we tried to square our experiences with wider debates from other disciplines about the nature and ethics of art and of art as a collaborative, community activity through which we can be curious, learn, make connections, be active and give.

► What did we learn?

The feedback indicates four experiences:

- ► First, there was new knowledge. Students sought and found relevant content.
- ► Second, there were new ideas and fresh connections made – an expanding of perceptions and self-awareness.
- ► Third, there was the real world here in the less than real world of the university. Real people came and told their real stories here.
- ► Fourth, there was an emotional journey for many students. Feelings ran high and the stories of service users and carers and actors and singers and workers provoked anger, sympathy and personal and professional awareness.
- ► Finally, there was a dynamic to the month; new relationships and collaborations formed with Insiders and Outsiders, with fellow students and with academic staff.

Some students struggled to see the relevance to either their own preconceived idea of social work or to the degree curriculum. They talked about some parts of the month being more relevant than others. There was a related group who wanted to learn new things but who felt they hadn't. These content-focused students were few but there was a larger group, perhaps a quarter, who lacked enthusiasm, only came to selected parts of the month, didn't contribute, who didn't seem to care and whose feedback was desultory and bland. Some other students struggled with this reluctance to engage with the month and some tensions ensued.

It is clear that for a significant number of students the month was a transformative experience. However as we try learn, and move forward, it does seem there are difficulties attempting the spontaneous, organic or creative in a corporate institution like a university.

We are asked, 'if it's worth doing why can't it be integrated into the curriculum and assessed?' We have explored the idea of creating an environment rich with opportunities for students that sit outside the curriculum but there is resistance on a number of fronts. Is it appropriate to offer experiences that aren't available to everyone? How would the resources (the rooms, sundry costs) for such activity be accounted? How should it be accounted on staff workloads? Will it detract from the time and effort students apply to the formal curriculum? Can it be timetabled six months in advance?

'Are we more employable now? Yes, we understand those connections: self-awareness, relationships, collaboration, action; that curiosity, learning, connecting, activity and giving are good for work and wellbeing – but there is more. Our CVs are enriched and our responses to questions about what we did on our course have been transformed. (And by the way, we've submitted two abstracts for academic conferences this year as well as working with you on this chapter).'

Catherine, Laura, Nichola and Russell

Laura Bullerwell has a special interest working with young people and is a looked-after children's Advocate. She foresees a future developing a range of specialist skills that will be required to fulfil her passion to support families with complex lives.

Alongside university, Catherine Foster works with young people in care, domestic abuse victims and children with autism. Additionally, she has as interest in attachment and is currently writing an article on this subject. After graduation, Catherine wishes to work in the area of child protection.

Russell Jackson returned to full-time education after a 30-year gap and has embraced the learning process. He hopes to put his degree to practical use for a few years whilst not ruling out a further return to academia in the future.

Nichola Larkin returned to university at the age of 40 after raising two children. She combines her studies with working with looked-after children and with people with learning disabilities. She hopes to work in child protection and to continue to study.

At the time of writing all four students are nearing the end of the second year of the BSc (Hons) Social Work course at Northumbria University.

35 English language learning for international employability

Angela Goddard (NTF 2008) *in association with Alastair Henry*

Keywords: *English as a lingua franca, employability, digital dialogues, workplace communication, globalisation, third space*

Angela Goddard is a Professor of English Language, whose particular interest is language and creativity, particularly the creativity of everyday language users. Her work in the UK has involved every phase of education, including Chair of English Language A Levels for a UK national exam board and Editor of the Routledge *Intertext* series, which supports student research on a wide range of language topics.

The project detailed in this essay focuses on the idea of international English as an employability skill in current and future workplaces. The increasingly global nature of employment contexts, coupled with the rapid increase in numbers of users of English as a lingua franca, requires new skills of critical reflection on communication, including virtual networks. The English Language Learning for International Employability (ELLIE) project supports student engagement in authentic communication – *'digital dialogues'* – between international peers, while at the same time fostering student research on the new 'Englishes' currently evolving.

Historically, English as a lingua franca (ELF) described a context where English was a medium of communication but no one's first language (L1), but it has now broadened to include L1 users in the mix. With the more fluid notions of identity at play in a networked world, many different types of English users are in interactions beyond spatially defined communities, and the ELLIE project helps learners to rethink notions of culture and affiliation, crucial concepts within workplace communication. The growth of ELF communication has particular implications for L1 English users: new types of

English challenge ideas about language 'ownership', problematising L1 speaker norms and prescriptive notions of correctness. If L1 users are to be effective workplace communicators, they need the language-awareness skills that the ELLIE project demonstrably develops.

▶ Background

Changes in the role and status of English in the world have profound implications for all users of the language, regardless of whether they are native speakers (L1 users) or users of English as an additional language (EAL users). The ELLIE project represents a cluster of teaching/learning and research activities, which bring together different communities of English users, to the benefit of all involved.

The idea of large-scale varieties of English in use beyond L1 communities has been explored for some time in the World Englishes field (see Jenkins, 2009b); the idea that English can have a lingua franca role in different parts of the world, particularly within business communities, has also been articulated to some extent (Bargiela-Chiappini and Harris, 1997). However, as Saraceni (2008) notes, processes of globalisation, including the use of English in new communication contexts, is accelerating English towards the status of a *global* lingua franca.

The global status of English means that there are now many more EAL users of English than there are native speakers. Graddol (2006) suggests that this process is accelerating so quickly that we will soon see the end of 'English as a foreign language' altogether. But this does not mean that any one particular type of English will be used all around the globe. Although World Englishes scholarship has been successful in legitimising the idea of large-scale regional varieties of English as used in specific parts of the world (such as south-east Asia), the concept of a global lingua franca is not tied to particular regions or to particular Englishes. Current and future lingua franca interactions in English – regardless of whether they are online or face-to-face, and whether they involve native speakers or not – rely on participants' moment-to-moment ability to achieve levels of intersubjectivity:

> Because of the diversity at the heart of this communicative medium, LFE [Lingua Franca English] is intersubjectively constructed in each specific context of interaction. The form of this English is negotiated by each set of speakers for their purposes ... Therefore, it is difficult to describe this language a priori.
>
> (Canagarajah, 2007: 925)

▶ The challenges

A specific part of the ELLIE project has been concerned with understanding the perspective of EAL users within Sweden and the Netherlands, two countries seen as part of an *'expanding circle'* (Kachru, 1985) of English use. This term describes those communities where English has historically not been part of the social fabric of the culture. Our research on university-level student populations in northern Europe and Scandinavia has illustrated not only how central being a speaker of English is to students' idea of themselves as future employees, but also how much English use is already a part of their social, academic and working lives, all of which are heavily mediated by new technologies (see Goddard et al., 2013).

While these new 'expanding circle' populations of English users can add English to their repertoire of graduate employability skills, UK graduates typically have little expertise in foreign languages to offer, a deficit which has well-attested negative effects both personally and nationally (Reisz, 2010). But, perhaps more importantly, the assumption that they will be straightforwardly advantaged by the fact that *'the world speaks English'* is misjudged, since lingua franca English is not the same thing as British English or American English. If they are to achieve levels of intersubjectivity in lingua franca English exchanges in their future workplaces, students from L1 English communities have to learn to step outside their own particular variety of English and recognise that they neither 'own' English nor have the right to regulate notions of correctness. In short, they have to develop intercultural communication skills.

▶ ELLIE engagements

Although it might be assumed that language learning necessarily involves the study of intercultural communication processes, according to Kramsch (2006), that is far from the case. She sees the mainstream history and current state of language teaching (including English) as one where language itself is typically not seen as a cultural construct at all:

> Language continues to be taught as a fixed system of formal structures and universal speech functions, a neutral conduit for the transmission of cultural knowledge … In practice, teachers [do not] teach language as culture.

> (Kramsch, 2006)

Kramsch and Whiteside (2008) use the cultural theorist Homi Bhaba's (1992) notion of a conceptual 'third space' in their call for the exploration of language as a human construct. They urge teachers to help students see round the edges of language, calling this ability *'symbolic competence'* rather than the more instrumental *'communicative competence'*, which focuses on the practical transactions of the here-and-now.

The ELLIE project has created its own version of a 'third space' in order to do exactly what Kramsch and Whiteside call for. In a core learning and teaching aspect of the project, tutors in different universities across Europe, the UK and the USA have worked collaboratively on a shared virtual site to set up digital dialogues between student groups. From year to year, a typical cohort of participants has numbered roughly 150, drawn from programmes where issues of language and culture are of central concern (for example, English, Linguistics, Communication Studies, International Relations, European Studies, Social Science). Participants are allocated to smaller international groups in order to make conversations manageable. Interactions typically run over 6 weeks, with another 6 weeks for reflection and analysis.

Each week a set topic is discussed in an online forum, involving topics that are broad and accessible at different levels of expertise: for example, everyday routines and rituals, naming conventions, national stereotypes, media representations, language varieties and attitudes, humour and taboo, and so on. Students are supported as co-researchers and are free to analyse a topic area in its own right, but are pointed particularly towards how communication worked (or not). In all the partner universities, the project functions not as an add-on to mainstream study, but as an embedded part of programmes. Forum posts in any one year can total 3000.

A key aim in setting up the digital dialogues is to enable learners to step outside their own immediate 'spaces', in both a physical and a cognitive sense. Tutors problematise the idea of language as a neutral conduit by enabling students to 'fix' language for long enough to study negotiations of meaning and ask each other questions about their intentions, assumptions and understandings. A crucial factor in enabling language choices to become visible for study is the availability of some accessible communication tools. ELLIE participants have used various VLE platforms, including, most recently, Moodle discussion forums. In 2010, voice tools were added to the forums so that writers could record sound clips and add these to a post; participants could also upload images and video.

▶ ELLIE outcomes

Digital interactions between English-speaking peers don't just have the potential to create a 'third space' in the form of a global classroom. For each different community, there are benefits that relate to particular needs within the employability skillset. For all participants, there are opportunities for authentic communication, language that is distinctively different from text-book simulations, and also different from theoretical readings on international English. For L2 learners, there is valuable exposure to contemporary L1 English, as well as the confidence-boosting perception that native speakers can make mistakes. For L1 speakers, there is an opportunity to experience new styles of international English, and to explore communication as cultural negotiation, a process of ongoing perspective-setting and -taking.

For all participants, digital dialogues can provide a form of 'carbon-free internationalisation' (Goddard, 2007) at a time when physical relocation for Erasmus-type exchanges is not an affordable option for many. But interestingly, the dialogues have on several occasions led to new friendships and visits, and to further study in home or partner institutions. For example, Gilroy (2010), a participant in 2005–6, obtained PhD scholarship funding to research the complex identity-construction required by learners who are being assessed within such VLEs.

Finally, the online nature of the communication opens up new research questions about the 'hybrid' forms of English that characterise digital environments – the very environments that are increasingly at the centre of workplace interactions (see Goddard, 2011).

Goddard et al. (2013) offer more extensive coverage of the digital dialogues than can be included here. However, it is important to suggest what it means to strive for a 'third space' in communication, so some samples are given below, from the 2005 and 2010 cohorts:

(2005) UK student:

'I am originally from Wirral … the little piece of land between Liverpool and Wales.'

Part of the student's introduction of himself to his virtual group. He takes a kind of bird's-eye view of his location, a communicative strategy that fit the constraints of the tools available, which relied heavily on written language. In 2010, students often 'showed' instead of 'told', using a Google map tool and homemade videos to offer guided tours of their locations at ground level.

(2005) A UK student's assignment title:

'The face I gave myself in a faceless environment'

This participant analysed her own presentation of herself throughout the dialogues, which was (in her words) as 'a lass from Barnsley'. She realised that this had made little sense to her interlocutors and offered them her analysis, as a reflective commentary on what she had done.

(2005) A participant studying in Sweden:

'I am originally from Togo (West Africa) where French is spoken as the official language. It means somewhere I'm very fluent in French like you are in English.'

This is an elegant comment on the politics of language choices. The student wants others to recognise that identities are powerfully constrained by the medium of communication.

(2010) A UK student reflects on the different Englishes that have been used:

'I feel that English is starting to belong to everybody; everyone I have seen post here on Moodle has used it comfortably and made it their own.'

(2010) An American student analyses her experience of the web tools:

'You could go wild with videos and sounds and everything. Show you are very engaged to cultures and interested in one another ... I can see how important this could be in the business world.'

(2010) A Dutch student describes his development:

'I experienced the online sessions as positive. You can learn from each other, how "the other" culture is. So, this online sessions maked [*sic*] for me my mind open.'

▶ Conclusion

More research is currently under way on workplace identities and the use of English as a lingua franca. In the form of a longitudinal project, the ELLIE team is currently following the progress of students as they move from formal education through work placements and into employment. We have established a forum for our research and hope to involve more partners as we continue to trace the story of new Englishes (and their speakers) at work.

Alastair Henry teaches English and language education at University West in Trollhättan, Sweden. The author of a number of upper secondary and university textbooks, in his research he has examined the impact that students' out-of-school encounters with English have on classroom motivation, as well as the effects of global English on motivation to learn foreign languages.

36 Engaging with and owning the enterprise agenda

Pauline Kneale (NTF 2002)

Keywords: enterprise, entrepreneurship, intrapreneurship, student role models

Pauline Kneale is Professor of Pedagogy and Enterprise and Pro Vice-Chancellor of Teaching and Learning at Plymouth University. Previously she was Professor of Applied Hydrology with Learning and Teaching in Geography at the University of Leeds and Director of the White Rose CETL for Enterprise 2005–10. The CETL (Centre for Excellence in Teaching and Learning) was a partnership between the Universities of Leeds, Sheffield and York.

The White Rose CETL Enterprise at Leeds (WRCETLE) aimed to engage staff and students in all Schools in enterprising learning, to enhance students' enterprise skills and to support individual student entrepreneurs (Kneale, 2009a, 2009b).

The drive for enterprise learning was supported by the Entrepreneurship Intentions Survey (Ward, Robertson and Holden, 2008), which was repeated annually in Yorkshire universities and colleges from 2002 to 2007, with the result that 35 per cent of students indicated that they definitely or probably intended to be self-employed. The majority expected to set up two to five years after graduating, with those aged 22–35 more inclined to be entrepreneurial, 41 per cent as compared to 31 per cent of 18–21-year-olds. Approximately 4 per cent were engaged in trading while at university – approximately 8000 graduates each year in the region – some of whom became superb, accessible role models.

Enterprise is challenging to integrate in higher education because the term has a variety of nuanced definitions in the disciplines. Entrepreneurship may be perceived as an individual lifestyle or career choice unrelated to degree curricula, and there can be resistance to including curricular activities at the expense of traditional discipline content. Moreover, self-employment does not appeal to all.

There is under-representation of entrepreneurship among the under-25s in the UK, and many initiatives to develop enterprise awareness, such as 'Start Up Britain' (BIS, 2013). Young Enterprise (2012) introduces British school students to business start-up concepts through running small enterprises, usually for charitable purposes. In focus groups and university-wide questionnaires many students were clear that they had considered running their own business and decided against it:

'because I really enjoy being with people, I would much rather work in a large team'

'the areas that interest me need science and people and lots of expertise, that's the sort of world I want to work in'.

Enterprise is part of the student skills agenda. Encouraging better communication, leadership, creativity, confidence, negotiation and networking skills are beneficial whether graduates become intrapreneurial or entrepreneurial in the future.

This essay draws on reflections and the evaluations of the WRCETLE, students involved in enterprise activities and academic staff, and in particular on the issues and themes arising from interviews and focus groups with 34 student entrepreneurs who established their businesses before and during university.

Supporting development

The WRCETLE aimed for cross-campus impact through curricular and extracurricular activities funding active learning- or problem-based learning projects, with limited 'lecture' content, and sought longevity through becoming embedded in the curriculum (Kneale, 2009b, Clarke and Underwood, 2011). Leadership skills, intrapreneurship and business creation were key themes. Projects were supported in five styles:

1 Funding for well-framed bids from experienced staff.
2 Assigning a WRCETLE fellow to work with an individual for a short period to frame a project, module or extracurricular activities. This was particularly useful where the discipline partner was new to enterprise thinking and pedagogies.
3 Co-creation of materials where activities, sessions or modules were co-developed, or entirely developed by WRCETLE staff, co-taught initially by

WRCETLE and departmental staff, and thereafter by the Department or School.
4 Development of sessions or modules taught entirely by WRCETLE staff available to all university students as options or for specific programmes.
5 Workshops and activities created for and with students working independently in our micro-incubator and their own businesses.

Over 80 individual projects – single two-hour session interventions to full modules – were undertaken in styles 1–3, and 9 modules were created in style 4. The directly employed WRCETLE teaching fellows added considerable value in providing negotiated support for individual projects, enabling mature bid development and facilitating rapid dissemination of ideas and opportunities across campus.

A style 4 module for international postgraduate dental students focused on setting up a dental practice in their home country. Group work allowed students from the United Arab Emirates, Greece, Ireland, Singapore and elsewhere to understand business start-up, including acquiring and fitting out premises, employing and training staff, marketing and legal and financial matters. Students benefited from sharing concerns and researching the practical aspects of getting started, creating their own portfolio of support materials.

Where business start-up was not of immediate discipline relevance, we focused on professional and intrapreneurship (Pinchot and Pellman, 1999) skills to encourage development of enterprising workplace-relevant behaviours: communication, creativity, confidence, negotiation and networking. Using discipline-relevant contexts was a 'win–win' scenario. This approach enabled new modules and podules to be integrated into the curriculum of 25 Schools, including Law, Design, Environment, Classics, Chinese, Midwifery, Medicine and Education. Second-year historians, for example, gained publication, web and group-work experience alongside their research.

Working with colleagues from many disciplines reinforced my understanding that to be an effective advocate for curricula interventions requires:

▶ enthusiasm
▶ perseverance
▶ an appreciation of the discourse of the discipline
▶ disciplinary approaches to curriculum delivery
▶ appropriately nuanced examples.

Researching the role of enterprise in language degrees emphasised that point (Kneale and Sim, 2007), as did working with colleagues on projects to embed enterprise teaching locally and internationally; for medical and health learning (South Africa) and computer sciences (Ethiopia).

It became evident that 10–12 years of sustained funding for enterprise teaching had allowed some colleagues to 'develop a self-perpetuating virtuous circle where enterprise teaching improves my teaching, and my research'. Staff started with small-scale curriculum interventions that developed their confidence to create modules. For example, initial input to the 'Miscarriages of Justice' module led to the student-run Innocence Project providing *pro bono* advice to prisoners, the Leeds Student Legal Advice Clinic, and later to forensic-investigation web-based interdisciplinary role-play exercises. Here teaching initiatives led to further teaching and research grants and an international secondment. A tutor response:

'good for them good for us, good for the university, good for employers'.

Whilst research-led teaching is commonly discussed, in Law and other subjects we saw teaching-led research.

▶ Students as role models

WRCETLE supported enterprising students through open networking opportunities, workshops, modules and open access micro-incubator spaces with some office equipment. These became forums for students to make connections and to support each other in discussing day-to-day business problems. Students running their own businesses became role models through case studies and presentations. Their recent experiences in starting their businesses proved to be very accessible and engaging in class and one-to-one sessions. Students were genuinely intrigued by having fellow students as class exemplars.

'The reality of hearing from someone of your own age and with similar family and financial positions was fantastic.'

Six clusters of student-run enterprises emerged:

- ▶ hobby-based: photography, sport
- ▶ skills-based: Chinese massage, graphic and web design
- ▶ web-based: online translation, classic car sales, travel support
- ▶ import and distribution-based: widgets, specialist sports equipment
- ▶ retail: ice cream, catering, sandwich and juice bars, fitted suits

Students in the sixth, charity-oriented cluster typically resisted enterprise and entrepreneurship labels. Enactus (2013) activities proved to be a useful umbrella. Students used enterprise skills acquired through our sessions in voluntary local community settings, including teaching enterprise skills in schools.

Fewer than 10 per cent of the students created businesses related to their academic degree. Exceptions included graphic design businesses, students' art sales, and one of the online translation companies. Another online translation company was created by student in Management and Computing who employed language students.

For students in engineering and biological sciences a degree-related business was seen as impossible:

'You need professors with the laboratories and researchers and equipment.'

These students typically ran hobby and catering enterprises. Textile students felt success involved '*inventing the next Lycra*', and were very surprised by maths graduates running a bespoke tailoring business.

Our students commented very positively on the skillsets acquired through their degrees. They highlighted the relevance of research, analysis, IT, report writing, discussion and presentation skills for their degree and business.

'complete my degree and then really invest in the business'

'OK, I could drop out of university but that's just not what I want, I have the time to do both.'

Networking opportunities were particularly valued. The majority established businesses in partnerships, seeing the benefits of sharing ideas, setting and meeting agreed targets and the benefits to self-confidence of two or more brains:

'You have to get up when there's two of you.'

Students employed students:

'getting the right people is vital. I'm really picky about who I work with and I've got really high expectations and I want to work with talented people'.

Both men and women considered bringing more people on board or outsourcing tasks. While men were more likely to consider employing someone for a short period to complete a specific task:

'I didn't have time to develop the website and do my degree so I asked … to do that.'

'I gave him a fixed price and that worked OK'.

Women tended to look for long-term partners with complementary business skills.

For some students expansion could wait:

'I could be expanding the [business] now but I want to get my degree and I don't have time to be taking on someone new and leaving them to do most of the work. So I am waiting until the summer when my degree is finished before getting more people in the team.'

Students did not expect to find support for their business ideas at university and were generally working on their business ideas in parallel with their degrees. Some students ensured tutors were unaware of their business activities:

'they won't take me seriously as a … student, and it might stop me getting a first, and I want to do both'.

Many student conversations started with:

'I think I would like to come to [WRCETLE] events, but only if it's totally confidential.'

While always respecting confidentiality, these requests presented some barriers to sharing and celebrating some successes.

We saw some, typically men, in multiple or preparation businesses. These were designed to give '*me experience in …*'. Starting a more ambitious business was being postponed until after graduation.

'It would take too much time now and I know it would want all my attention'.

'I'm running this business for the next two years so that I get the experience, then I will close it down, or get someone else to run it for me, so that I can do what I really want. This is good experience now, and … fun, … but it won't get me the income I'm wanting.'

Our female entrepreneurs generally focused on planning or running one business, and some deferred start-up until after graduation.

▶ Conclusions

One WRCETLE aim was to encourage and support students who were not considering self-employment. Many students were equivocal, recognising tensions in their thinking about future careers. Everyone found the student case studies encouraging, but the reality of the time investment, potentially limited income and self-discipline challenged some. Others found the materials very helpful in reinforcing ideas and opening up new opportunities.

Small-scale businesses:

'are achievable. You don't have to get big funds and employ 30 people to be successful'.

Different concepts of success, and the way in which the entrepreneurs expressed their appreciation of '*being their own boss*' and

'managing their own time was ... mega news in my head, although I want to make good money and all, ... it made me really think about what I want to do and it's going to be ... hard'.

An overarching theme from the students was passion, thinking and rethinking. The passion to pursue personal dreams:

'We'll see what the future brings, but for now the best thing is just not dreading Monday mornings any more.'

The modules and case-studies made an impact:

'I hadn't thought about my career in this way. I was thinking that after university I would get a job ... this case-study showed how I could be finding more from it than the money.'

The WRCETLE experience mirrored our theoretical understanding that while many enterprise issues are the same for men and women, female students tend to start later on 'safer' projects, to look strongly to personal networks for support, and to focus exclusively on making one business a success

(Carter, Marlow and Henry, 2009; Wagner, 2007). The outcomes support the notion that we need many different avenues to support the enterprise agenda, to be sensitive to discipline nuances, and recognise that there are many, many pathways.

Conclusion: Sustaining excellence

Tim Bilham (NTF 2007)

As I write this concluding section, looking out upon the North Cornish coast, I am contemplating the nature of sustainability and of excellence in learning and teaching.

Sustaining our environment – its ecology, its resources, its diversity – seems to me to be also about sustaining its excellence and at a fundamental level that requires people ... and people with knowledge, vision, shared values of social and intergenerational justice, immense communication skills, courage, resilience and persistence.

Sustaining excellence in teaching and learning in our universities is about maintaining the highest levels of experience and outcomes for our students. There are also some critical prerequisites: vision, leadership, communication, sharing of practice, preparedness to take risks and a consistent focus upon the learner.

And it, too, is about people: appointing high-quality staff, nurturing them, developing them, maintaining their motivation and seeing in turbulent environments opportunities for innovation, creativity and change. It is about engaging and inspiring students and opening up new opportunities for them. It is also about culture and processes, and if there were to be only one change in our universities, the proper recognition of teaching and teachers would do more to secure and sustain excellence in learning than any other single initiative.

Of course the notion of excellence is problematic and contested, and many organisations, including the UK Higher Education Academy, continue to seek to capture an adequate understanding of it through HEA initiatives such as the literature review 'What constitutes teacher excellence in higher education?',[1] the Recognising Teaching Excellence (ReTE) change programme[2] and the UK Professional Standards Framework (UKPSF).[3]

It is beyond our scope to even try to define it here, but however excellence may eventually come to be considered I hope we have captured, through the essays in this book, some elements, examples and characteristics of excellence that you can deploy, adapt and improve upon in your own teaching and in the support of your students. If you do, please find ways of sharing them too. By doing so you will help sustain the levels that the authors of this book have achieved and continue to improve upon.

And what of the future? Well, the fact that half of the essays in this book come from National Teaching Fellowships awarded in the last three years must give us great confidence and reassurance that whilst schemes like the NTFS exist, and university teachers are inspired to follow in the footsteps of others, excellence in learning and teaching and in the student experience can be not only sustained but enhanced.

In a book that gives considerable voice to our students, it is surely appropriate to give the final word to a student, indeed one who has researched the very field of teacher excellence in higher education for her doctorate, and who as a part-time, mature, working student, perhaps is representative of a changing demographic of our future learners.

Having been denied early educational opportunities, Heather Sparrow graduated in the UK and now works in Australia, where she undertook a professional doctorate rather than a traditional Ph.D. Thus she is also representative of a student from our international community, for surely it must be through working across boundaries, across cultures, across disciplines, and across networks and communities that we will achieve greater understanding and excellence.

I have not met Heather, but I have met many students like her. In the introduction to her doctoral study of teacher excellence (Sparrow, 2013) Heather says:

'At a (school) career guidance meeting, I was asked by a senior staff member what I was planning to do: "I'm thinking of going to university", I said. There was a slight hesitation, then a cold, hard voice replied, "People like you don't go to university." Since that time, I have encountered many inspirational teachers. I have worked alongside the very best of colleagues who have collaborated with me, sharing enthusiasm, expertise, and thinking. I have enjoyed learning alongside many students, who consistently challenged me to try new things and see the world in different ways. I have wonderful friends, who have put out their hands to help me up and push me along. And I have been supported by a family who have been unstinting in their encouragement and practical help. I acknowledge you all. You make it possible for "people like me", not only to go, but to succeed at university.'

For all of our students we help shape their lives.

References

Aalborg University (2010), *Principles of Problem and Project Based Learning*. Available at http://www.pbl.aau.dk/digitalAssets/33/33124_pbl_aalborg_modellen.pdf (accessed 26 April 2013)

Aaronson, L. (2008), The 'Novel Approach': popular fiction as a teaching tool in undergraduate microbiology courses, *Focus on Microbiology Education* 15: 2–4

Ainscow, M., Booth, T. and Dyson, A. (2004), Understanding and developing inclusive practices in schools: a collaborative action research network, *International Journal of Inclusive Education*, 8(2): 125–139

Aked, J. and Thompson, S. (2011), *Five Ways to Wellbeing*, New Economics Foundation. Available at http://www.neweconomics.org/publications/entry/five-ways-to-wellbeing (accessed December 2012)

Alaneme, E. (2011), Nigeria: Universities now 117, *Daily Champion*, 8 March 2011. Available to subscribers at http://allafrica.com/stories/201103080664.html (accessed 17 May 2013)

Albanese, M. (1999), Rating educational quality: factors in the erosion of professional standards, *Academic Medicine*, 74(6): 652–658

Ali, N., Ahmed, L. and Rose, S. (2012), 'Undergraduate psychology students' perception of and engagement with feedback across the three years of study', in Z.M. Charlesworth, E. Cools and C. Evans (eds), *Individual Differences*, Proceedings of the 17th Annual Conference of the Education, Learning, Styles and Individual differences Network (ELSIN), Cardiff, Wales: University of Glamorgan, pp. 19–28

Aliaga, M., Cobb, G., Cuff, C., Garfield, J., Gould, R., Lock, R., Moore, T., Rossman, A., Stephenson, B., Utts, J., Velleman, P. and Witmer, J. (2005), Gaise college report, *American Statistical Association*. Available at http://www.amstat.org/education/gaise/ (accessed 7 March 2013)

Alston, K. (2001), Re/thinking critical thinking: the seductions of everyday life, *Studies in Philosophy and Education* 20: 27–40

Anderson, T. (2005) 'Distance learning – social software's killer app?' *ODLAA 2005 Conference*. Available at: http://tinyurl.com/9tytsx (accessed 29 March 2009)

Andrews, D. H., Hull, T.D. and Donahue, J. A. (2009), Storytelling as an instructional method: Descriptions and research questions, *Interdisciplinary Journal of Problem-based Learning*, 3(2): 6–23

Angeli, C. and Valanides, N. (2008), Instructional effects on critical thinking: performance on ill-defined issues, *Learning and Instruction*, 19: 322–334

Appadurai, A. (1997), *Modernity at Large: Cultural dimensions of globalisation*, Minneapolis: University of Minnesota Press

Armellini, A. (2012), *Carpe Diem: The 7Cs of design and delivery*, Beyond Distance Research Alliance blog

Armstrong, D. (2005), Reinventing inclusion: New Labour and the cultural politics of special education, *Oxford Review of Education*, 31(1): 135–151

Atkinson, T. and Claxton, G. (2000), *The Intuitive Practitioner: On the value of not always knowing what one is doing*, Maidenhead: Open University Press

Atlay, M., Gaitán, A. and Kumar, A. (2008), 'Stimulating learning–Creating CRe8', in C.

References **265**

Nygaard and C. Holtham (eds), *Understanding learning-centred higher education,* Frederiksberg, Denmark: Copenhagen Business School, 231–250

Bahou, L. (2011), Rethinking the challenges and possibilities of student voice and agency, *Educate,* 2–14

Bakhshi, S., Harrington, K. and O'Neill, P. (2009), Psychology students' experiences of peer mentoring at the London Metropolitan University Writing Centre, *Psychology Learning and Teaching,* 8(1), 6–13

Balsamo, A. (2011), *Designing Culture: The technological imagination at work,* Durham, NC: Duke University Press

Bandura, A. (1986), *Social Foundations of Thought and Action: A social cognitive theory,* Englewood Cliffs, NJ: Prentice-Hall

Bargiela-Chiappini, F. and Harris, S. (eds) (1997), *The Languages of Business: An international perspective,* Edinburgh: Edinburgh University Press

Barnes, L. B., Christensen, C. R. and Hansen, A. J. (1994), *Teaching and the Case Method: Text, cases, and readings,* Boston: Harvard Business School Press

Barnett, H. (2012), *Broad Vision: Inspired by … images from science,* London: University of Westminster

Barnett, H. and Lange, S. (2013, forthcoming), *Fluid Networks and Emergent Learning: An interdisciplinary case study,* Mutamorphosis conference proceedings, CIANT, Prague

Barnett, H. and Smith, J. (2011), *Broad Vision: The art and science of looking,* London: University of Westminster

Barnett, R. (1992), *Improving Higher Education: Total quality care,* Maidenhead: Open University Press

Barnett, R. (1997), *Higher Education: A critical business,* Buckingham: Society for Research into Higher Education and the Open University

Barnett, R. (2012), *The Future University: Ideas and possibilities,* New York and London: Routledge

Barnett, R. and Di Napoli R. (eds) (2008), *Changing Identities in Higher Education: Voicing perspectives,* London: Routledge

Barrie, S. (2006), Understanding what we mean by the generic attributes of graduates, *Higher Education,* 51: 215–241

Barry, N. and Hallam, S. (2002), 'Science and psychology of music performance', in R. Parncutt and G.E. McPherson (eds), *Instrumental Teaching: A practical guide to better teaching and learning,* London: Oxford University Press, Ch. 10

Barthes, R. (1972), *Mythologies,* trans Annette Lavers, New York: Hill & Wang

Basaza, G. N., Milman, N. B. and Wright, C. R. (2010), The challenges of implementing distance education in Uganda: A case study, *International Review of Research in Open and Distance Learning,* 11(2), 85–91

Bauman, Z. (2005), 'The liquid-modern challenges to education', in S. Robinson and C. Katulushi (eds) *Values in Higher Education,* Leeds: Aureus/University of Leeds: 36–50

Baxter, J. (2011), *Public Sector Professional Identities: A review of the literature,* Maidenhead: Open University Press

Baxter Magolda, M. B. (1999), *Creating Contexts for Learning and Self-Authorship: Constructive-developmental pedagogy* (1st edn), Nashville, TN: Vanderbilt University Press

Baxter Magolda, M. B. (2002), *Knowing and Reasoning in College,* San Francisco: Jossey-Bass

Becher, T. (1994), The significance of disciplinary differences, *Studies in Higher Education,* 19: 151–161

Beetham, H. (2007), 'An approach to learning activity design', in H. Beetham and R. Sharpe (eds), *Rethinking Pedagogy for a Digital Age: Designing and delivering e-learning,* London: Routledge: 26–40

Belbin Team Role Summary Descriptions (2012). Available at http://www.belbin.com/content/page/5002/BELBIN(uk)-2012–TeamRoleSummaryDescriptions.pdf (accessed 26 April 2013)

Benson, J. (1989), Structural components of statistical test anxiety in adults: An exploratory model, *Journal of Experimental Education*, 57: 247–261

Berk, R. A. (2000), Does humor in course tests reduce anxiety and improve performance? *College Teaching*, 48: 151–158

Berk, R. A. (2003), *Professors Are from Mars®, Students Are from Snickers®*, Sterling, VA: Stylus

Berk, R. A. (2007), Humor as an instructional defibrillator, *Journal of Health Administration Education*, 24(2): 97–116

Berk, R. A. and Nanda, J. P. (2006), A randomized trial of humor effects on test anxiety and test performance, *HUMOR: International Journal of Humor Research*, 19: 425–454

Bhabha, H. (1992), 'Post-colonial authority and post-modern guilt', in L. Grossberg, C. Nelson and P. Treichler (eds), *Cultural Studies*, London: Routledge

Biggs, J. (1996), Enhancing teaching through constructive alignment, *Higher Education*, 32(3): 347–364

Biggs, J. (2003), *Teaching for Quality Learning at University*, Buckingham: Open University Press

Biggs, J. and Tang, C. (2007), *Teaching for Quality Learning at University*, Maidenhead: Open University Press and McGraw Hill

BIS (2013), Department for Business Innovation and Skills in HE. Available at https://www.gov.uk/starting-up-a-business (accessed 1 May 2013)

Black, P. and Wiliam, D. (1998), Assessment and classroom learning, *Assessment in Education: Principles, Policy and Practice*, 5(1): 7–74

Bland, D. and Atweh, B. (2007), Students as researchers: Engaging students' voices in PAR, *Educational Action Research*, 15(3): 337–349

Bloom, B. S. (1956), *Taxonomy of Educational Objectives Handbook of Cognitive Domain*, New York: McKay

Bolton, G. (2010), *Reflective Practice,* London: SAGE

Boud, D. and Molloy, E. (eds) (2012), *Feedback in Higher and Professional Education: Understanding it and doing it well,* London: Routledge

Bovill, C. and Bulley, C. (2011), 'A model of active student participation in curriculum design: Exploring desirability and possibility', in C. Rust, *Improving Student Learning (18). Global theories and local practices: Institutional, disciplinary and cultural variations,* Oxford: Oxford Centre for Staff and Educational Development, 176–188

Bovill, C., Cook-Sather, A. and Felten, P. (2011), Students as co-creators of teaching approaches, course design, and curricula: Implications for academic developers, *International Journal for Academic Development*, 16(2): 133–145

Bovill, C., Morss, K., and Bulley, C. (2008), *Curriculum Design for the First Year, Quality Enhancement Themes: The first-year experience,* Glasgow, Scotland: QAA (Scotland)

boyd, D. (2009), *When Teachers and Students Connect Outside School.* Available at http://www.zephoria.org/thoughts/archives/2009/05/27/when_teachers_a.html (accessed 21 April 2013)

boyd, D. (2010), 'Social network sites as networked publics: Affordances, dynamics, and implications', In Z. Zizi Papacharissi (ed.), *Networked Self: Identity, community, and culture on social network sites*, pp. 39–58

Bragg, S. and Fielding, M. (2005), 'It's an equal thing … It's about achieving together: Student voices and the possibility of radical collegiality', in H. Street and J. Temperley (eds), *Improving Schools Through Collaborative Enquiry*, London: Continuum

Brennan, R. (2012), Experience alone is not experiential learning, *HEA/AM Marketing Education Digest*, 1(3)

Brockbank, A. and McGill, I. (2007), *Facilitating Reflective Learning in Higher Education* (2nd edn), Maidenhead: Society for Research into Higher Education and Open University Press

Brown, A. L. (1992), Design experiments: Theoretical and methodological challenges in creating complex interventions in classroom settings, *Journal of the Learning Sciences,* 2(2): 141–178

Brown, B. (2011), *The Power of Vulnerability* TED Talks. Available at http://www.ted.com/talks/brene_brown_on_vulnerability.html (accessed June 2012)

Brown, J. S. (2000), Growing up digital: How the web changes work, education, and the ways people learn, *Change,* 32(2): 11–20

Brown, V. A., Harris, J. A. and Russell, J. Y. (2010), *Tackling Wicked Problems: Through the transdisciplinary imagination,* London and Washington, DC: Earthscan

Bruner, J. (1990), *Acts of Meaning,* Cambridge, MA: Harvard University Press

Bryant, J., Crane, J. S., Comisky, P. W. and Zillmann, D. (1980), Relationship between college-teachers' use of humor in the classroom and students' evaluations of their teachers, *Journal of Educational Psychology,* 72(4): 511–519

Bryson, C. (2011), *Clarifying the Concept of Student Engagement: A fruitful approach to underpin policy and practice,* paper presented at the HEA Conference, Nottingham, England, 5–6 July

Bryson, C. (2013), 'Creating space for autonomy and student engagement through partnership and letting go', in T. D. Bilham (ed.), *For the Love of Learning: Innovations from outstanding university teachers,* Basingstoke: Palgrave Macmillan

Bryson, C. and Hand, L. (2007), The role of engagement in inspiring teaching and learning, *Innovations in Teaching and Education International,* 44(4): 349–362

Bryson, C. and Hardy, L. (2012), 'The nature of student engagement, what the students tell us', in I. Solomonides, A. Reid and P. Petocz (eds), *Engaging with Learning in Higher Education,* London: Libri

Burgess, R. (2007), *Measuring and Recording Student Achievement: Report of the Scoping Group,* London: Universities UK and SCOP

Burnett, R. (2011), *Transdisciplinarity: A new learning paradigm for the digital age?* Weblog posted to http://rburnett.ecuad.ca/main/2011/12/27/transdisciplinarity-a-new-learning-paradigm-for-the-digital.html

Butler, D. L. and Winne, P. H. (1995), Feedback and self-regulated learning: A theoretical synthesis, *Review of Educational Research,* 65(3): 245–281

Calman, K. C., Downie, R. S., Duthie, M. and Sweeney, B. (1988), Literature and medicine: A short course for medical students, *Medical Education,* 22: 265–269

Canagarajah, S. (2007), Lingua franca English, multilingual communities, and language acquisition, *Modern Language Journal,* 91: 923–39

CAOT (Canadian Association of Occupational Therapists) (2002), *Enabling Occupation: An occupational therapy perspective* (rev. edn), Ottawa, ON: CAOT Publications ACE

Carr, N. (2010), *The Shallows: What the internet is doing to our brains,* New York: Norton

Carter, S. L., Marlow, S. and Henry, C. (2009), Exploring the impact of gender upon women's business ownership, *International Small Business Journal,* 27(2): 139–47

Cassidy, S. and Eachus, P. (2000), Learning style, academic belief systems, self-report student proficiency and academic achievement in higher education, *Education Psychology: An International Journal of Experimental Psychology,* 20(3): 307–322

CELL (Centre of Excellence in Leadership of Learning) (2009), *Summary of Research on Project Based Learning.* CELL. Available at http://cell.uindy.edu/docs/PBL%20research%20summary.pdf (accessed 26 April 2013)

Chalmers, D. and Fuller, R. (1996), *Teaching for Learning at University,* London: Kogan Page

Chambers, D. W. (1993), Toward a competency-based curriculum, *Journal of Dental Education*, 57(11): 790–793

Chickering, A. W. and Gamson, Z. F. (1987), Seven principles for good practice in undergraduate education, AAHE Bulletin. Available at http://wwwtemp.lonestar.edu/multimedia/SevenPrinciples.pdf (accessed 26 April 2013)

Clarke, J. and Underwood, S. (2011), Learning based on 'entrepreneurial volunteering': Using enterprise education to explore social responsibility, *Industry and Higher Education*, 25(6): 461–467

Clarke, M. (2007), *Verbalising the Visual: Translating art and design into words*, Lausanne, Switzerland: AVA

Claxton, G. (2002), *Building learning power: Helping young people become better learners*, Bristol: TLO

Clughen, L. and Connell, M. (2012), Writing and resistance: Reflections on the practice of embedding writing in the curriculum, *Arts and Humanities in Higher Education*, 11, 333–345

Collins, S. (2008), Statutory social workers: Stress, job satisfaction, coping, social support and individual differences, *British Journal of Social Work*, 38: 1173–1193

Conners, F. A., McCown, S. M. and Roskos-Ewoldson, B. (1998), Unique challenges in teaching undergraduates statistics, *Teaching of Psychology*, 25(1): 40–42

Connolly, T. (ed.) (2011), *Leading Issues in Games-Based Learning Research*, Reading, England: Academic Publishing International

Conole, G. (2012), *The 7Cs of design and delivery*. Available at http://e4innovation.com/ (accessed 21 May 2013)

Conole, G. (2013a), *Designing for Learning in an Open World*, New York: Springer

Conole, G. (2013b), *Current Thinking on the 7Cs of Learning Design*. Blog post, available at http://e4innovation.com/?p=628 (accessed 21 May 2013)

Conole, G. and Dyke, M. (2004), What are the affordances of information and communication technologies? *ALT-J: Research in Learning Technology*, 12(2): 113–124

Cormier, D. (2008), Rhizomatic education: Community as curriculum, *Innovate Journal of Online Education*, 4(5)

Cox, K. (2001), Stories as case knowledge: Case knowledge as stories, *Medical Education*, 35: 862–866

Crick, R. D., Broadfoot, P. and Claxton, G. (2004), Developing an Effective Lifelong Learning Inventory: The ELLI Project, *Assessment in Education*, 11(3): 247–272

Crossley, J., Johnson, G., Booth, J. and Wade, W. (2011), Good questions, good answers: Construct alignment improves the performance of workplace-based assessment scales, *Medical Education*, 45(6): 560–569

Crossley, M. and Amos, M. (2011), SimZombie: A case-study in agent-based simulation construction, *Agent and Multi-Agent Systems: Technologies and Applications, Lecture Notes in Artificial Intelligence (LNAI)*, 6682: 514–523

Cunliffe-Charlesworth, H. (2008), Writing is harder compared to designing: Encouraging academic writing in designers and artists, *Writing Purposefully in Art and Design: Case Study*. Available at http://www.writing-pad.ac.uk/index.php?path=photos/21_Resources/05 (accessed 21 May 2013)

Curtis, W., Goodson, A., McDonnell, J., Shield, S. and Wyness, R. (2012), Learning together and expanding horizons: Reflections on a student–lecturer collaborative enquiry, *Enhancing Learning in the Social Sciences*, 4(3)

Daniel, J. (2010), Ethiopia lifts ban on distance education, *Commonwealth of Learning Blog*, 27 October. Available at http://www.col.org/blog/Lists/Posts/Post.aspx?ID=67 (accessed 29 November 2012)

Davidson, C. (2011), *Now You See It: How the brain science of attention will transform the way we live, work and learn*, London: Viking

Dearing, R. (1997), *Higher Education in the Learning Society*, Leeds: National Committee of Inquiry into Higher Education. Available at http://www.leeds.ac.uk/educol/ncihe/ (accessed 22 November 2012)

DeCesare, M. (2007), 'Statistics anxiety' among sociology majors: A first diagnosis and some treatment options, *Teaching Sociology*, 35(4): 360–367

de Freitas, S. (2006), *Learning in Immersive Worlds: A review of game-based learning*, paper prepared for the JISC e-learning programme 2006. Available at http://www.jisc.ac.uk/media/documents/programmes/elearninginnovation/gamingreport_v3.pdf (accessed 26 April 2013)

DfE (Department for Education) (2012), *Teachers' Standards Effective from 1 September 2012*. Available at http://www.education.gov.uk (accessed 6 December 2012)

DfEE (Department for Education and Employment) (1999), *Learning to Succeed – A new framework for post-16 learning*, London: DfEE

DfES (Department for Education and Skills) (2001), *The Code of Practice for Special Educational Needs*, London: DfES

Dillenbourg, P. (1999), 'What do you mean by collaborative learning?', in P. Dillenbourg (ed.), *Collaborative-learning: Cognitive and computational approaches*, Oxford: Elsevier: 1–19

Dillenbourg, P. (2002), *Over-Scripting CSCL: The risks of blending collaborative learning with instructional design*, Lausanne, Switzerland: Swiss Federal Institute of Technology. Available at http://hal.archives-ouvertes.fr/docs/00/19/02/30/PDF/Dillenbourg-Pierre-2002.pdf (accessed 21 May 2013)

Dillon, G.L. (1981), *Constructing Texts: Elements of a theory of composition and style*, Bloomington: Indiana University Press

Dixon, M. (2006), Globalisation and International higher education: Contested positionings, *Journal of Studies in International Education*, 10: 319–333

Dolmans, D. H., Wolfhagen, I. H, Heineman, E. and Scherpbier, A. J. (2008), Factors adversely affecting student learning in the clinical learning environment: A student perspective, *Education for Health*, 21(3): 32

DRC (Disability Rights Commission) (2006), *Disability equality duty*, DRC. Available at http://www.dotheduty.org/ (accessed 14 March 2013)

Duch, B. J., Allen, D. E. and Groh, S. E. (eds) (2001), *The Power of Problem-Based Learning: A practical 'how to' for teaching undergraduate courses in any discipline*, Brighton: Falmer and KP

Dweck, C. (2000), *Self-Theories: The role in motivation, personality and development*, London: Psychology Press

Dymoke, S. (ed.) (2011), *Reflective Teaching and Learning in the Secondary School* (2nd edn), London: Sage

Edge, K. (2009), *Undergraduate Symposium* (handout), Cardiff School of Art and Design, Wales

Edmunds, M. (2009), *Review of the Student Learning Experience in Physics (2008)*, Hull: HEA Physical Sciences Centre. Available at http://www.heacademy.ac.uk/physsci/home/projects/subjectreviews/physics (accessed 3 December 2012)

Elander, J., Harrington, K., Norton, L., Robinson, H. and Reddy, P. (2006), Complex skills and academic writing: A review of evidence about the types of learning required to meet core assessment criteria, *Assessment and Evaluation in Higher Education*, 31, 71–90

Elander, J., Westrup, R., Calwell, T. F., Foxcroft, A., Norton, L., Crooks, S. and Wardley, K. (2011), 'Development and evaluation of student transition writing mentoring programmes', in C. Rust (ed.), *Proceedings of the 2010 Conference of the International Society for the Scholarship of Teaching and Learning and the 18th International Symposium of the Improving Student Learning Society*, Oxford: Oxford Centre for Staff and Learning Development: 63–77

Elliott, J. (2006), *Reflecting Where the Action Is* (World Library of Educationalists), London: Routledge

Enactus (2013), Available at http://www.enactusuk.org/news (accessed 1 March 2013)

Engeström, Y. (2006), 'Activity theory and expansive design', in S. Bagnara and G. Crampton-Smith (eds), *Theories and Practice of Interaction Design*, Hillsdale, NJ: Lawrence Erlbaum

Ennis, R. H. (1996), *Critical Thinking*, Englewood Cliffs, NJ: Prentice Hall

Epting, L. K., Zinn, T. E., Buskist, C. and Buskist, W. (2004), Student perspectives on the distinction between ideal and typical teachers, *Teaching of Psychology*, 31(3): 181–183

Erichsen, E. A. and Bolliger, D. U. (2011), Towards understanding international graduate student isolation in traditional and online environments, *Education Technology Research and Development, 59:* 309–326

Ericsson, K. A. (2004), Deliberate practice and the acquisition and maintenance of expert performance in medicine and related domains, *Academic Medicine*, 79(10): S70–S81

Ethiopian Embassy (2007), *Profile on Distance Education At All Levels*, Ethiopian Embassy Report 172. Available at http://www.ethiopianembassy.org/AboutEthiopia/InvestmentProjectProfiles/Services/Education/Distance_Education_At_All_Levels.pdf (accessed 3 December 2012)

Falchikov, N. (2005), *Improving Assessment through Student Involvement?: Practical solutions for aiding learning in higher and further education?*, London: Routledge

Fanghanel, J. (2012), *Being an Academic*, Abingdon, England: Routledge

Ferguson, W., Bareiss, R., Birnbaum, L. and Osgood, R. (1991), ASK systems: An approach to the realization of story-based teachers, *Journal of the Learning Sciences,* 2(1): 95–134

Field, A. P. (2010), 'Teaching statistics', in D. Upton and A. Trapp (eds), *Teaching Psychology in Higher Education*, Chichester, England: Wiley-Blackwell: 134–163

Field, A. P. (2013), *Discovering Statistics Using IBM SPSS Statistics: And sex and drugs and rock 'n' roll* (4th edn), London: Sage

Field, A. P. and Hole, G. J. (2003), *How to Design and Report Experiments*, London: Sage

Field, A. P., Miles, J. N. V. and Field, Z. C. (2012), *Discovering Statistics Using R: And sex and drugs and rock 'n' roll*, London: Sage

Fielding, M. (2001), Students as radical agents of change, *Journal of Educational Change*, 2(2): 123–141

Fielding, M. (2004), Transformative approaches to student voice: Theoretical underpinnings, recalcitrant realities, *British Educational Research Journal*, 30(2): 295–311

Fielding, M. (2012), Beyond student voice: Patterns of partnership and the demands of deep democracy, *Revista de Educación*, 359: 45–65

Firmin, M., Hwang, C-E., Copella, M. and Clark, S. (2004), Learned helplessness: The effect of failure on test-taking, *Education*, 124: 688

Fleming, N. D. (2001), *Teaching and Learning Styles*, VARK Strategies. Honolulu, Hawaii: Honolulu Community College

FME (Federal Ministry of Education) (2010), *Education Sector Development Program IV, 2010/11–2014/15*, FME, Federal Democratic Republic of Ethiopia. Available at http://planipolis.iiep.unesco.org/upload/Ethiopia/Ethiopia_ESDP_IV.pdf (accessed 3 December 2012)

Foden, G. (2010), *Turbulence,* London: Faber & Faber

Frame, P. and Burnett, J. (eds) (2008), *Using Auto/Biography in Learning and Teaching,* SEDA Paper 120, London: SEDA

Friedman, H. H., Friedman, L. W. and Amoo, T. (2002), Using humor in the introductory statistics course, *Journal of Statistics Education,* 10(3). Available at http://www.amstat.org/publications/jse/v2010n2003/friedman.html (accessed 18 February 2009)

Fromm, E. (1977), *To Have or to Be?* London: Jonathan Cape

Fuchs Ebaugh, H. R. (1988), *Becoming an Ex: The process of role exit,* Chicago and London, University of Chicago Press

Garner, R. L. (2006), Humor in pedagogy: How ha-ha can lead to aha! *College Teaching,* 54(1): 177–180

Gaver, W. W., Bowers, J., Boucher, A., Gellerson, H., Pennington, S., Schmidt, A., Steed, A., Villars, N. and Walker, B. (2004), *The Drift Table: Designing for ludic engagement,* in CHI'04, Design Expo, New York: ACM Press

GDC (General Dental Council) (2011), *General Dental Council: Preparing for practice,* London: GDC

Ghul, R. and Marsh, I. (2009), *Design and Evaluation of the Contexts of Participation Interactive Resource,* Higher Education Academy (Health Sciences and Practice) Mini-project Report. Available at http://www.heacademy.ac.uk/assets/documents/subjects/health/2009rghul.pdf (accessed 20 February 2013)

Ghul, R. and Marsh, I. (2013), Teaching participation in occupations to first-year occupational therapy students: An action research study, *British Journal of Occupational Therapy,* 76(2): 101–107

Gibbs, G. and Dunbar-Goddet, H. (2009), Characterising programme-level assessment environments that support learning, *Assessment and Evaluation in Higher Education,* 34(4): 481–489

Gibson, S. (2012), Narrative accounts of university education: Socio-cultural perspectives of students with disabilities, *Disability and Society,* 27(3): 353–369

Gibson, S. and Kendall L. (2010), Stories from school: Dyslexia and learners' voices on factors impacting on achievement, *Support for Learning,* 25(4): 187–93

Gilroy, H. (2010), When wor(l)ds collide: An analysis of student face and identity management in online assessed discussion forums. Paper presented at the 5th International Symposium on Politeness, Basel, Switzerland, 30 June–2 July

Ginsburg, S., Regehr, G. and Lingard, L. (2004), Basing the evaluation of professionalism on observable behaviors: A cautionary tale, *Academic Medicine,* 79(10): S1–S4

Glaser, E. M. (1941), *An Experiment in the Development of Critical Thinking,* New York: Teacher's College Press and Columbia University Press

Goddard, A. (2007), 'Carbon-free internationalisation', in J. Fielden (ed.) *Global Horizons for UK Universities,* London: Council for Industry and Higher Education, 38

Goddard, A. (2011), 'Type you soon!' A stylistic approach to language use in a virtual learning environment, *Language and Literature,* 20(3): 184–200

Goddard, A., Henry, A., Mondor, M. and van der Laaken, M. (2013), 'Have you ever been to England? You know, they speak really weird English there': Some implications of the growth of English as a global language for the teaching of English in the UK, *English in Education,* 47(1): 79–95

Goffee, R., and Jones, G. (2006), *Why Should Anyone be Led by You?,* Boston, MA: Harvard Business School Press

Goleman, D. (1996), *Emotional Intelligence,* London: Bloomsbury

Gordon, S. (2004), Understanding students' experiences of statistics in a service course, *Statistics Education Research Journal,* 3(1): 40–59

Graddol, D. (2006), *English Next: Why global English may mean the end of 'English as a foreign language',* British Council. Available at http://www.britishcouncil.org/learning-research-english-next.pdf (accessed 22 May 2013)

Grant, B. and Manathunga, C. (2011), Supervision and cultural difference: Rethinking institutional pedagogies, *Innovations in Education and Teaching International,* 48(4): 351–354

Gray, C. and Malins, J. (2004), *Visualizing research: A guide to the research process in art and design.* Farnham, England: Ashgate

Grenier, M. (2010), Moving to inclusion: A socio-cultural analysis of practice, *International Journal of Inclusive Education,* 14(4): 387–400

Gropius, W. (1919), *Bauhaus manifesto and program.* Available at http://bauhaus-online.de/en/atlas/das-bauhaus/idee/manifest (accessed 29 November 2012)

Gulikers, J. T. M., Kester, L., Kirschner, P. A. and Bastiaens, T. J. (2008), The effect of practical experience on perceptions of assessment authenticity, study approach, and learning outcome, *Learning and Instruction,* 18: 172–186

Haglund, M. E. M., aan het Rot, M., Cooper, N. S., Nestadt, P. S., Muller, D., Southwick, S. M. and Charney, D. S. (2009), Resilience in the third year of medical school: A prospective study of the associations between stressful events occurring during clinical rotations and student well-being, *Academic Medicine,* 84(2): 258–268

Hallam, S. (1995), Professional musicians' approaches to the learning and interpretation of music, *Psychology of Music,* 23: 111–128

Harding, J. and Thompson, J. (2012), *Dispositions to Stay and to Succeed: Final report of the 'What Works' research project,* Newcastle-upon-Tyne: Northumbria University

Harlow, L., Mulaik, S. and Steiger, J. (1997), *What If There Were No Significance Tests?* Hillsdale, NJ: Lawrence Erlbaum

Harrington, K., Norton, L., Elander, J., Lusher, J., Aiyegbayo, O., Pitt, E., Robinson, H. and Reddy, P. (2006), 'Using core assessment criteria to improve essay writing', in C. Bryan and K. Clegg (eds), *Innovative Assessment in Higher Education,* London: Routledge: 110–119

Hartley, P and Whitfield, R. (2011), Programme-focused assessment, *Educational Developments,* 12(4)

Harvey, L. (2003) *Transitions from Higher Education to Work; A briefing paper.* Available at http://bit.ly/oeCgqW (accessed 22 November 2012)

HEA (Higher Education Academy) (2010), *Research and Evidence Base for Student Engagement,* York, England: HEA. Available at http://www.heacademy.ac.uk/ourwork/universitiesandcolleges/alldisplay?type=resources&newid=ourwork/studentengagement/Research_and_evidence_base_for_student_engagement&site=york (accessed 9 December 2012)

HEA (Higher Education Academy) (2011a), *Exploring Transitions to Higher Education for Students with Identified Disabilities,* HEA ESCalate. Available at http://escalate.ac.uk/7144 (accessed 24 June 2013)

HEA (Higher Education Academy) (2011b), *Teaching International Students Project,* York, England: HEA. Available at http://www.heacademy.ac.uk/assets/documents/internationalisation/Introduction_to_project.pdf (accessed 24 June 2013)

Healey, M. and Jenkins, A. (2009), *Developing Undergraduate Research and Inquiry,* York: Higher Education Academy. Available at http://www.heacademy.ac.uk/assets/York/documents/resources/publications/DevelopingUndergraduate_Final.pdf (accessed 21 May 2013)

HEAT (2012), *Health Education and Training Modules for Ethiopian Health Extension Workers.* Available to download as open educational resources at http://www.open.ac.uk/africa/heat (accessed 8 December 2012)

Hefferman, M. (2011), *Wilful Blindness: Why we ignore the obvious at our peril,* London: Simon & Schuster

Higgins, R., Hartley, P. and Skelton A. (2002), The conscientious consumer:

Reconsidering the role of assessment feedback in student learning, *Studies in Higher Education*, 27(1): 53–64

Holmes, L. (2001), Reconsidering graduate Eemployability: The 'graduate identity' approach, *Quality in Higher Education*, 7(2): 111–119

Holt, J. (1982), *How Children Fail*, Harmondsworth: Penguin

Honey, P. and Mumford, A. (1982), *Manual of Learning Styles*, London: P. Honey

Huxley, A. (1960), *Preface* to his *Collected Essays*, London: Chatto & Windus, 1960

Illich, I. (1971), *Deschooling Society*, New York: Harper & Row

Ioannidis, J. P. A. (2005), Why most published research findings are false, *PLoS Medicine*, 2(8): e124

Jacklin, A. and Robinson, C. (2007), What is meant by support in higher education? *Journal of Research in Special Educational Needs*, 7(2): 114–123

James, A. and Chapman, Y. (2009), Preceptors and patients – The power of two: Nursing student experiences on their first acute clinical placement, *Contemporary Nurse*, 34(1), 34–47

Jankowska, M. (2011), A reflection on adaptability, achievement motivation and success of Central and Eastern European students in one English university, *Compare*, 41(6): 801– 818

Jenkins, H. (2006), *Convergence culture: Where old and new media collide*, New York: NYU Press

Jenkins, H. (2009a), *Confronting the Challenges of Participatory Culture: Media education for the 21st century*, Boston, MA: MIT Press

Jenkins, H., Clinton, K., Purushotma, R., Robinson, A. J. and Weigel, M. (2006), *Confronting the Challenges of Participatory Culture: Media Education for the 21st Century*, Chicago: MacArthur Foundation Publication, 1(1): 1–59

Jenkins, J. (2009b), *World Englishes*, London: Routledge

Jessen, A. and Elander, J. (2009), Development and evaluation of an intervention to improve further education students' understanding of higher education assessment criteria: Three studies, *Journal of Further and Higher Education*, 33: 359–380

Jessop, T., El Hakim, Y. and Gibbs, G. (2011), TESTA: Research inspiring change. *Educational Developments,* 12(4): 12–16

Jessop, T., McNab, N. and Gubby, L. (2012), Mind the gap: An analysis of how quality assurance procedures influence programme assessment patterns, *Active Learning in Higher Education.* 13(3): 143–154

Johansen, B. (2009), *Leaders Make the Future: Ten new leadership skills for an uncertain world,* San Francisco: Berrett-Koehler

Johnson, S. (2001), *Emergence*, London: Penguin

Johnson, S. (2010), *Where Good Ideas Come From: The seven patterns of innovation*, London: Penguin

John-Steiner, V., Weber, R. and Minnis, M. (1998), The challenge of studying collaboration, *American Educational Research Journal*, 35(4): 773–783

Jones, E. (ed.) (2010), *Internationalisation and the Student Voice: Higher education perspectives*, London: Routledge

Jones, E. and Killick, D. (2007), 'Internationalisation of the curriculum', in E. Jones and S. Brown (eds), *Internationalising Higher Education*, London: Routledge: 109–119

Jones-Devitt, S. and Smith, L. (2007), *Critical Thinking in Health and Social Care*, London: Sage

Kachru, B. (1985), 'Standards, codification and sociolinguistic realism: The English language in the outer circle', in R. Quirk and H. Widdowson (eds), *English in the World: Teaching and learning the language and literatures*, Cambridge: Cambridge University Press

Kamel Boulos, M.N. and Wheeler, S. (2007), The emerging Web 2.0 social software: An enabling suite of sociable technologies in health and health care education, *Health Information and Libraries Journal*, 24(1): 2–23

Kaplan, R. M. and Pascoe, G. C. (1977), Humorous lectures and humorous examples – some effects upon comprehension and retention, *Journal of Educational Psychology*, 69(1): 61–65

Kay, J., Dunne, E. and Hutchinson, J. (2010), *Rethinking the Values of Higher Education – Students as change agents?*, Gloucester, England: Quality Assurance Agency for Higher Education

Keegan, H. and Bell, F. (2011), YouTube as a Repository: The creative practice of students as producers of open educational resources, *European Journal of Open, Distance and E-Learning (EURODL), Special Issue*: 10. Available at http://www.eurodl.org/?p=special&sp=articles&article=456

Keen, A. (2008), *The Cult of the Amateur: How blogs, Myspace, YouTube, and the rest of today's user-generated media are destroying our economy, our culture, and our values* (reprint edn), New York: Doubleday

Keller, F. S. (1968), Good-bye, teacher ..., *Journal of Applied Behaviour Analysis, 79*

Kember, D. (1997), A reconceptualisation of the research into university academics' conceptions of teaching, *Learning and Instruction*, 7(3): 255–275

Killick, D. (2006), *Cross-Cultural Capability and Global Perspectives*, Guidelines for Curriculum Review, Leeds, England: Leeds Metropolitan University

Killick, D. (2007), 'Internationalisation and engagement with the wider community', in E. Jones and S. Brown (eds), *Internationalising Higher Education*, London, Routledge: 135–153

Killick, D. (ed.) (2011), *Embedding a Global Outlook as a Graduate Attribute at Leeds Metropolitan University*, Leeds: Leeds Metropolitan University

Killick, D. (2012), Seeing-ourselves-in-the-world: Developing global citizenship through international mobility and campus community, *Journal of Studies in International Education*, 16(4): 372–389

Kilpatrick, S., Barrett, M. and Jones, T. (2003), *Defining Learning Communities*, Discussion Paper D1/2003, CRLRA Discussion Paper Series, University of Tasmania, Australia. Available at http://www.crlra.utas.edu.au/files/discussion/2003/D1–2003.pdf (accessed 21 May 2013)

Kinman, G. and Grant, L. (2011), Exploring stress resilience in trainee social workers: The role of emotional and social competencies, *British Journal of Social Work*, 41: 261–275

Klein, D. M., Bryant, J. and Zillmann, D. (1982), Relationship between humor in introductory textbooks and students' evaluations of the texts' appeal and effectiveness, *Psychological Reports*, 50(1): 235–241

Kneale, P. E. (2009a), 'Insights into the activities and motivations of women students creating businesses', in M. R. Markovic and I. S. Kyaruzi (eds), *Female Entrepreneurship and Local Economic Growth*, Denver, CO: Outskirts Press: 47–65

Kneale, P. E. (2009b), Raising student awareness of enterprise skills: Accredited and non-accredited routes, *Planet*, Special Edition, 21: 39–42

Kneale, P. E. and Sim, P. (2007), *Enterprise and Languages Final Report*, Higher Education Academy Languages and Linguistics Subject Centre. Available at www.routesintolanguages.ac.uk/enterprise (accessed 1 March 2013)

Knight, J. and de Wit, H. (1995), 'Strategies for internationalisation of higher education: Historical and conceptual perspectives', in H. de Wit (ed.), *Strategies for Internationalisation of Higher Education*, Amsterdam, Netherlands: EAIE, Ch. 1

Knight, P. T. and Yorke, M. (2004), *Learning, Curriculum and Employability in Higher Education*, London: RoutledgeFalmer

Knowles, M. (1985), *Andragogy in Action,* San Francisco: Jossey Bass

Koiston, S., Goodall, H. and Hughes, O. (2011), Taking on big, real world projects – what do we really learn?, *Third Annual ESCalate Student Conference,* Liverpool Hope University

Kolb, D. A. (1976), *The Learning Style Inventory: Technical manual,* Boston, MA: McBer

Kolb, D.A. (1984), *Experiential Learning: Experience as the source of learning and development,* Englewood Cliffs, NJ: Prentice-Hall

Kop, R. and Hill, A. (2008), Connectivism: Learning theory of the future or vestige of the past?, *International Review of Research in Open and Distance Learning,* 9(3)

Kotsopoulous, D. (2010), When collaborative is not collaborative: Supporting student learning through self-surveillance, *International Journal of Educational Research,* 49: 129–140

Kramsch, C. (2006), From communicative competence to symbolic competence, *Modern Language Journal,* 90: 246–252

Kramsch, C. and Whiteside, A. (2008), Towards a theory of symbolic competence, *Applied Linguistics,* 29(4): 654–671

Krause, K. Hartley, R. James, R. and McInnis, C. (2005), *The First-Year Experience in Australian Universities: findings from a decade of national studies,* Canberra, Australia: DEST

Kubler-Ross, E. (1970), *On Death and Dying,* London: Tavistock

Kuh, G. (2008), *High impact practices: What they are, who has access to them and why they matter,* Washington, DC: AACU

Kulik, A., Kulik, C-L. and Carmichael, K. (1974), The Keller Plan in science teaching, *Science,* 183(4123): 379–383

Kumar, A. (2008), *Personal, Academic and Career Development in Higher Education–SOARing to Success,* London and New York: Routledge and Taylor & Francis. Companion website: http://www.routledge.com/professional/978041542360–1/ (accessed 10 December 2012)

Kumar, A. (2012), SOARing for Employability – Can this serve as a transferable pedagogy and process for developing 'global graduates'?, Proceedings of the 7th QS-APPLE Conference, Manila, Philippines, November 2011: 4–15. Available at http://www.qsapple.org/downloads/7th_qsapple_proceedings.pdf (accessed 10 December 2012)

Lange, S. and Dinsmore, J. (2012), *Collaborative Discovery across Disciplinary Divides: Promoting interdisciplinary learning via student-led extracurricular art/science research and practice,* Networks Magazine, 18. Available at http://arts.brighton.ac.uk/projects/networks/issue-18–july-2012/collaborative-discovery-across-disciplinary-divides-promoting-interdisciplinary-learning-via-student-led-extracurricular-artscience-research-and-practice (accessed 12 December 2012)

Laurillard, D. M. (1993), *Rethinking University Teaching: A conversational framework for the effective use of learning technologies,* London: Routledge

Laurillard, D. M. (2002), *Rethinking University Teaching: A conversational framework for the effective use of learning technologies* (2nd edn), London: Routledge.

Lea, M. and Street, B. (1998), Student writing in higher education: An academic literacies approach, *Studies in Higher Education,* 23: 157–72

Leask, B. (2010), 'Beside me is an empty chair: The student experience of internationalisation', in E. Jones (ed.), *Internationalisation and the Student Voice,* New York and London: Routledge

Leathwood, C. (2006), Gender, equity and the discourse of the independent learner in higher education, *Higher Education,* 52: 611–633

Leitch, S. (2006), *Prosperity for all in the Global Economy: World class skills,* Department of

Employment and Learning. Available at http://www.delni.gov.uk (accessed 22 November 2012)

Lesser, L. M. (2001), Musical Means: Using songs in teaching statistics, *Teaching Statistics*, 23(3): 81–85

Lesser, L. M. and Glickman, M. E. (2009), Using magic in the teaching of probability and statistics, *Model Assisted Statistics and Applications*, (4): 265–274

Lesser, L. M. and Pearl, D. K. (2008), Functional fun in statistics teaching: Resources, research and recommendations, *Journal of Statistics Education*, 16(3). Available at http://www.amstat.org/publications/jse/v2016n2003/lesser.html (accessed 22 June 2009)

Lillis, T. (2001), *Student Writing: Access, regulation, desire*, London: Routledge

Little, S. (2011) *Staff–student Partnerships in Higher Education*, London: Continuum

Lomax, R. G. and Moosavi, S. A. (2002), Using humor to teach statistics: Must they be orthogonal? *Understanding Statistics*, 1(2): 113–130

Lowe, H. and Cook, A. (2003), Mind the gap: Are students prepared for higher education?, *Journal of Further and Higher Education*, 27(1): 53–76

Madriaga, M. (2007), Enduring disablism: Students with dyslexia and their pathways into UK higher education and beyond, *Disability and Society*, 22(4): 399–412

Maidment, J. and Macfarlane, S. (2011), Older women and craft: Extending educational horizons in considering wellbeing, *Social Work Education*, 3(6): 700–711

Mann, S. (2001), Alternative perspectives on the student experience: Alienation and engagement, *Studies in Higher Education*, 26(1): 7–19

Mansell, W. (2007), *Education by Numbers: The tyranny of testing*, London: Politico's

Maslin-Ostrowski, P. and Ackerman, R. (2004), 'Case story', in M. W. Galbraith (ed.), *Adult Learning Methods: A guide for effective instruction*, Malabar, FL: Krieger

Mason, M. (ed.) (2008), *Complexity Theory and the Philosophy of Education*, Oxford: Wiley-Blackwell

Mazur, E. (1997), *Peer Instruction: A user's manual*, Englewood Cliffs, NJ: Prentice Hall

McClarty, K. L., Orr, A., Frey, P.M., Dolan, R. P., Vassileva, V. and McVay, A. (2012), *A Literature Review of Gaming in Education*, Pearson Research Report. Available at http://www.pearsonassessments.com/hai/Images/tmrs/Lit_Review_of_Gaming_in_Education.pdf (accessed 26 April 2013)

McCloskey, D. and Ziliak, S. (2008), *The Cult of Statistical Significance: How the standard error costs us jobs, justice, and lives*, Ann Arbor: University of Michigan Press

McCulloch, A. (2009), The student as co-producer: Learning from public administration about the student–university relationship, *Studies in Higher Education*, 34(2): 171–183

McKenna, S. (1999), Storytelling and 'real' management competence, *Journal of Workplace Learning*, 11(3): 95–104

McKenzie, A., Bourn, D., Evans, S., Brown, M., Shiel, C., Bunney, A., Collins, G., Wade, R., Parker, J. and Annette, J. (2009), *Global Perspectives in Higher Education*, London: Development Education Association

McPeck, H. (1990), *Teaching Critical Thinking: Dialogue and dialectic*. New York: Routledge

Melzack, R. and Wall, P. D. (1965), Pain mechanisms: A new theory, *Science*, 19, 150(699): 971–979

Meyer, J. H. F. and Land, R. (2003), 'Threshold Concepts and Troublesome Knowledge: Linkages to ways of thinking and practising', in C. Rust (ed.), *Improving Student Learning: Theory and practice ten years on*, Oxford: OCSLD

Meyer, J. H. F. and Land, R. (eds) (2006), *Overcoming Barriers to Student Understanding: Threshold concepts and troublesome knowledge*, London and New York: Routledge and Taylor & Francis

Meyer, S. (2006), *Twilight*, London: Atom Books

Mezirow, J. (1997), 'Transformative Learning: Theory into practice', in P. Cranton (ed.), *Transformative Learning in Action: Insights from practice*, San Francisco: Jossey-Bass

Mezirow, J. and Associates (eds) (2000), *Learning as Transformation: Critical perspectives on a theory in progress*, San Francisco: Jossey-Bass

Mohanty, C. (2003), *Feminism Without Borders: Decolonising theory, practicing solidarity*, London and Durham, NC: Duke University Press

Mortimore, T. (2013), Dyslexia in higher education: Creating a fully inclusive institution, *Journal of Research in Special Educational Needs*, 13(1): 38–47

Mortimore, T. and Crozier, W. (2006), Dyslexia and difficulties with study skills in higher education, *Studies in Higher Education*, 31(2): 235–251

NUS (National Union of Students) (2009), *Assessment Purposes and Practices*, NUS briefing paper

Neary, M. (2011), *Student as Producer: Student engagement and the idea of the University*, paper presented at Student Engagement Conference, Galway University, 9–10 June

Neuhauser, P. C. (1993), *Corporate Legends and Lore: The power of storytelling as a management tool*, New York: McGraw-Hill

Neumann, D. L. Hood, M. and Neumann, M. M. (2002), Statistics? You must be joking: The application and evaluation of humor when teaching statistics, *Journal of Statistics Education*, 17(2). Available at http://www.amstat.org/publications/jse/v2017n2012/neumann.html (accessed 25 March 2013)

Nicol, D. J. and Macfarlane-Dick, D. (2006), Formative assessment and self-regulated learning: A model and seven principles of good feedback practice, *Studies in Higher Education*, 31(2): 199–218

Norcini, J. J., Arnold, G. K. and Kimball, H. R. (1995), The Mini-CEX (clinical evaluation exercise): a preliminary investigation, *Annals of Internal Medicine*, 123(10): 795–799

Norton, L. (2004), Using assessment criteria as learning criteria: A case study in psychology, *Assessment and Evaluation in Higher Education*, 29, 687–702

Norton, L., Harrington, K., Elander, J., Sinfield, S. Lusher, J., Reddy, P., Aiyegbayo, O. and Pitt, E. (2005), 'Supporting students to improve their essay writing through assessment criteria focused workshops', in C. Rust (ed.), *Improving Student Learning: Diversity and inclusivity*, proceedings of the 2004 12th International Symposium, Oxford: Oxford Centre for Staff and Learning Development: 159–174

Norton, L., Keenan, P., Williams, K., Elander, J. and McDonough, G. (2009a), *Helping Students Make the Transition from A-level to Degree-Level Writing: A staged action research approach*, Paper presented at the British Educational Research Association Annual Conference, University of Manchester, 2–5 September 2009. Published in Education-Line, available at http://www.leeds.ac.uk/educol/documents/184216.doc (accessed 6 December 2012)

Norton, L. and Pitt, E., with Harrington, K., Elander, J. and Reddy, P. (2009b), *Writing Essays at University: A guide for students by students*, London Metropolitan University: Write Now Centre for Excellence in Teaching and Learning. Available at http://www.writenow.ac.uk/assessmentplus/ (accessed 3 December 2012)

Norton, L. S. (1990), Essay writing: What really counts? *Higher Education*, 20: 411–442

Norton, L. S., Dickins, T. E. and McLaughlin Cook, A. N. (1996), Rules of the game in essay writing, *Psychology Teaching Review*, 5: 1–14

Novak, G. M., Patterson, E. T., Gavrin, A. D., and Christian, W. (1999), *Just-In-Time Teaching: Blending active learning with web technology*, Englewood Cliffs, NJ: Prentice Hall

O'Grady, G., Yew, E., Goh, K.P.L. and Schmidt, H. (eds) (2012), *One-Day, One-Problem: An approach to problem-based learning*, New York: Springer. See also G. O'Grady and W. A. M. Alwis (2002), 'One day, one problem at Republic Polytechnic', paper presented at the 4th Asia-Pacific conference on PBL. Available at http://www.myrp.sg/ced/research/papers/one_day_one_problem_at_rp.pdf (accessed 3 December 2012)

Olakulehin, F. K. (2008), Open and distance education as a strategy for human capital development in Nigeria, *Open Learning,* 23(2): 123–130

Olssen, M. and Peters, M. (2005), Neoliberalism, higher education and the knowledge economy: From the free market to knowledge capitalism, *Journal of Educational Policy,* 20(3), 313–45

O'Neill, G. and McMahon, S. (2012), Giving student groups a stronger voice: Suing participatory research and action (PRA) to initiate change to the curriculum, *Innovations in Education and Teaching International,* 49(2): 161–171

O'Neill, P., Harrington, K. and Bakhshi, S. (2009), Training peer tutors in writing: A pragmatic, research-based approach, *Zeitschrift Schreiben (European Journal of Writing).* Available at http://www.zeitschrift-schreiben.eu/cgi-bin/joolma/index.php?option=com_content&task=view&id=75&Itemid=32 (accessed 6 December 2012)

O'Neill, S. (2011), Open your mind to interdisciplinary research, *New Scientist,* 16 February. Available at http://www.newscientist.com/article/mg20928002.100–open-your-mind-to-interdisciplinary-research.html?full=true (accessed 3 December 2012)

Onwuegbuzie, A. J. and Wilson, V. A. (2003), Statistics anxiety: Nature, etiology, antecedents, effects, and treatments – a comprehensive review of the literature, *Teaching in Higher Education,* 8(2): 195–209

Orr, S., Blythman, M. and Mullin, J. (2006), Designing Your Writing/Writing Your Design: Art and Design students talk about the process of writing and the process of design, *Across the Disciplines: Journal of Interdisciplinary Perspectives on Language, Learning and Academic Writing.* Available at http://wac.colostate.edu/atd/visual/orr_blythman_mullin.cfm (accessed 21 May 2013)

Ovens, P. (2000), Becoming scientific and becoming professional: Towards moderating rationalism in the initial teacher education curriculum, *Curriculum Journal,* 11(2): 177–197

Ovens, P. (2003), 'Using a Patchwork Texts approach to develop a critical understanding of science'. In *The Patchwork Text: A radical reassessment of coursework assignments,* Special Issue, *Innovations in Education and Training International,* 40 (2)

Ovens, P., Wells, F., Wallis, P. and Hawkins, C. (2011), *Developing Inquiry for Learning: Reflecting collaborative ways to learn to learn in Higher Education,* London: Routledge

Pascarella, E. and Terenzini, P. (2005), *How College Affects Students,* San Francisco: Jossey Bass

Paul, R. (2004), *The state of critical thinking today: The need for a substantive concept of critical thinking.* Available at http://www.criticalthinking.org/pages/the-state-of-critical-thinking-today/523 (accessed 29 November 2012)

Paxton, P. (2006), Dollars and sense: Convincing students that they can learn and want to learn statistics, *Teaching Sociology,* 34(1): 65–70

Perkins, D. (2006), 'Constructivism and troublesome knowledge', in J. H. F. Meyer and R. Land (eds), *Overcoming Barriers to Student Understanding: Threshold concepts and troublesome knowledge,* London: Routledge: 33–47

Perry, W. (1976), *Open University: A personal account by the first Vice-Chancellor,* Milton Keynes: Open University Press

Perry, W. (1999), *Forms of Intellectual and Ethical Development in the College Years: A scheme,* New York: Harcourt Brace

Petrie, K. (2006), *Glass and Print,* London: A&C Black and Philadelphia: University of Pennsylvania Press

Petrie, K. (2007), Parallels and connections: Emerging trends in ceramics and glass design research, *International Association of Societies of Design Research Conference proceedings.* Available at http://www.sd.polyu.edu.hk/iasdr/

Petrie, K. (2011a), *Ceramic Transfer Printing,* London: A&C Black and Columbus, OH: American Ceramic Circle

Petrie, K. (2011b), Creative glass research: Case studies from art and design. *Glass Technology–European Journal of Glass Science and Technology Part A* 52(1), 1–10

Petrie, K. and Sarmiento, J. (2010), Enhancing student experience: Two case studies for integrating, energizing and challenging students in art and design, *International Journal of Learning*, 16(12)

Pinchot, G. and Pellman, R. (1999), *Intrapreneuring in Action: A handbook for business innovation*, San Francisco: Berrett-Koehler

Polkinghorne, D. (1988), *Narrative Knowing and the Human Sciences*, Albany: State University of New York Press

Prescott, L. E., Norcini, J. J., McKinlay, P. and Rennie, J. S. (2002), Facing the challenges of competency-based assessment of postgraduate dental training: Longitudinal Evaluation of Performance (LEP), *Medical Education*, 36(1): 92–97

Price, M., Rust, C., O'Donovan, B., Handley, K. with Bryant, R. (2012), *Assessment Literacy: The foundation for improving student learning*, Oxford: ASKe (Centre for Excellence in Teaching and Learning)

Pring, R. (2004), *Philosophy of Educational Research*, London: Continuum

Pyrczak, F. (2009), *Statistics with a Sense of Humor* (2nd edn), Los Angeles, CA: Pyrczak

QAA (Quality Assurance Agency for Higher Education) (2000), *Code of Practice for the Assurance of Academic Quality and Standards in Higher Education, Section 6: Assessment of students*, Gloucester: QAA

QAA (Quality Assurance Agency for Higher Education) (2007), *Psychology*, QAA. Available at http://www.qaa.ac.uk/academicinfrastructure/benchmark/statements/Psychology07.pdf (accessed 23 June 2009)

Raine, D. and Symons, S. (2012), Problem-based learning: Undergraduate physics by research, *Contemporary Physics*, 53(1): 39–51

Raine, D. J., Barker, T., Abel, P. and Symons, S.L. (2010), A problem-based learning approach to mathematics support?, in C. M. Marr and M. J. Grove (eds), *Responding To The Mathematics Problem: The implementation of institutional support mechanisms*, Maths, Stats & OR Network 2010. Available at http://www.mathcentre.ac.uk/resources/uploaded/mathssupportvolumefinal.pdf (accessed 27 October 2012)

Reavey, D. (1997), 'A Masters programme that matters to the New South Africa', in P. Knight (ed.), *Masterclass: Curriculum, learning and teaching at Masters level*, London: Cassell

Reavey, D. (2011), Wanted! Agents of change!, *ESCalate New*, Spring: 7–8

Reavey, D. (2013), *Wanted! Agents of change! What the literature says about the choices we made*. Available at: www.chi.ac.uk

Rees, C. E. and Knight, L. V. (2007), The trouble with assessing students' professionalism: Theoretical insights from sociocognitive psychology, *Academic Medicine*, 82(1): 46–50

Reid, C. and Fitzgerald, P. (2010), 'Assessment and Employability', in M. Hammick and C. Reid, *Contemporary Issues in Assessment in Health Sciences and Practice Education* (2010), Occasional paper 11, York: Higher Education Academy, Ch. 4

Reisz, M. (2010), 'Sorry, non comprende, I'm British', *Times Higher Education*, 21–27 October

Revans, R. W. (1982), *The Origins and Growth of Action Learning*, Bromley, England: Chartwell Bratt

Reynolds, M. and Vince, R. (eds) (2004), *Organizing Reflection*, Farnham: Ashgate

Rheingold, H. and Weeks, A. (2012), *Net Smart: How to Thrive Online*, Cambridge, MA: MIT Press

Ritchie, L. and Williamon, A. (2011a), Measuring distinct types of musical self-efficacy, *Psychology of Music*, 38: 328–344

Ritchie, L. and Williamon, A. (2011b), Self-efficacy for musical learning in primary school children, *Journal of Research in Music Education*, 59: 146–161

Ritchie, L. and Williamon, A. (2012), Self-efficacy as a predictor of Musical Performance Quality, *Psychology of Aesthetics, Creativity, and Arts*, 6(4): 334–340

Ritchie, L. and Williamon, A. (2013), Measuring musical self-regulation: Linking processes, skills, and beliefs, *Journal of Education and Training Studies*, 1: 106–117

Rogers, C. (1994), *Freedom to Learn*, Columbus, OH: Merrill

Rogers, C. (1996), *Teaching adults*, (2nd edn), Buckingham: Open University Press

Rogoff, B. (1990), *Apprenticeship in thinking*, Oxford: Oxford University Press

Root, R. and Thorne, T. (2001), Community-based projects in applied statistics, *American Statistician*, 55: 326–331

Rossiter, M.D. (2002), Narrative and stories in adult teaching and learning, *ERIC Digest*. Available at http://www.ericdigests.org/2003–4/adult-teaching.html (accessed 16 November 2012)

Rotter, J. B. (1966), Generalized expectancies for internal versus external control of reinforcement, *Psychological Monographs*, 80: 1–28

Rumelhart, D. E. and Norman, D. A. (1981), 'Accretion, tuning and restructuring: Three models of learning', in J. W. Cotton and R. Klatzky (eds), *Semantic factors in cognition*, Hillsdale, NJ: Lawrence Erlbaum: 37–60

Rust, C., Price, M. and O'Donovan, B. (2003), Improving students' learning by developing their understanding of assessment criteria and processes, *Assessment and Evaluation in Higher Education*, 28: 147–164

Saraceni, M. (2008), English as a lingua franca: Between form and function, *English Today* 94, 24(2): 20–26

Savery, J. R. (2006), Overview of problem-based learning: Definitions and distinctions, *Interdisciplinary Journal of Problem-based Learning*, 1(1): 9–20

Savickas, M. L. and Porfeli, E. J. (2012), Career Adapt-Abilities Scale: Construction, reliability, and measurement equivalence across 13 countries, *Journal of Vocational Behavior*, 80(3): 661–673

Savicki, V. (ed.) (2008), *Developing Intercultural Competence and Transformation: Theory, research and application in international education*, Sterling, VA: Stylus

Schacht, S. P. and Stewart, B. J. (1990), What's funny about statistics – a technique for reducing student anxiety, *Teaching Sociology*, 18(1): 52–56

Schön, D. (1987), *Educating the Reflective Practitioner*, San Francisco: Jossey-Bass

Schön, D. A. (1993), *The Reflective Practitioner: How professionals think in action*, New York: Basic Books

Schunk, D. (1991), Self-efficacy and academic motivation, *Educational Psychologist*, 26: 207–231

Schutz, P. A., Drogosz, L. M., White, V. E. and DiStefano, C. (1998), Prior knowledge, attitude, and strategy use in an introduction to statistics course, *Learning and Individual Differences*, 10(4): 291–308

Seabrook, M. A. (2003), Medical teachers' concerns about the clinical teaching context, *Medical Education*, 37(3): 213–222

Seale, J. (2010), Doing student voice work in higher education: An exploration of the value of participatory methods, *British Educational Research Journal*, 36(6): 995–1015

Seimens, G. (2005) *Connectivism as Network Creation*. Available at http://www.elearnspace.org/Articles/networks.htm (accessed 21 April 2013)

Selander, S. (2008), Designs for learning and ludic engagement, *Digital Creativity*, 19(3): 145–152

Somekh, B. (2006), *Action Research: A methodology for change and development*, Maidenhead: Open University Press

Sparrow, H. (2013), Teaching excellence: an illusive goal in higher education teaching and learning, *Theses: Doctorates and Masters*. Paper 582. http://ro.ecu.edu.au/theses/582 (accessed 6 September 2013).

Spiro, J. (2010a), 'Crossing the bridge from appreciative reading to reflective writer: The assessment of creative process', in A. Paran and L. Sercu (eds), *Testing the Untestable in Language Education,* Clevedon: Multilingual Matters: 165–190

Spiro, J. (2010b), 'Acting and Interacting: Teacher narratives and the building of global community', in V. Yuzer and G. Kurnbacak (eds), *Transformative Learning and Online Education: Aesthetics, dimensions and concepts,* Hershey, PA: IGI Global: 97–110

Spiro, J. (2011), Guided interaction as intercultural learning: Designing internationalisation into a mixed delivery teacher education programme, *Higher Education Research and Development,* 30(5): 635–646

Spiro, J., Henderson, J. and Clifford, V. (2012), Independent learning crossing cultures: Learning cultures and shifting meanings, *Compare,* 42(2)

Spurrier, J. (2001), A capstone course for undergraduate statistics majors, *Journal of Statistics Education,* 9:1

Stahl, S. A. (2002), 'Different strokes for different folks?', in L. Abbeduto (ed.), *Taking Sides: Clashing on controversial issues in educational psychology,* Guilford, CT: McGraw-Hill: 98–107

Stenhouse, L. (1975), *An Introduction to Curriculum Research and Development,* London: Heinemann Education

Stephenson, J. (2001), 'Ensuring a holistic approach to work-based learning: The capability envelope', in D. Boud and N. Solomon (eds), *Work-Based Learning: A new higher education,* Buckingham: Society for Research into Higher Education and Open University Press: 86–102

Straby, R. (2002), *Life Works by Design,* Ottawa, ON: Elora

Teichler, U. (2004), The changing debate on internationalisation of higher education, *Higher Education,* 48: 5–26

Thompson, F., Hannam, K. and Petrie, K. (2012), Producing ceramic art works through tourism research, *Annals of Tourism Research,* 39(1): 336–360

Thoreson, C. and Mahoney, M. (1974), *Behavioral Self-Control,* New York: Holt, Rinehart & Winston

Tierney, F. (2010), Toward an eccentric (design) pedagogy, *Design Principles and Practices: An International Journal,* 4(1): 435–441

Tinto, V. (2003), 'Learning better together: The impact of learning communities on student success in higher education', In *Promoting Student Success in College, Higher Education,* New York: Syracuse University: Higher Education Monograph Series, 1–8

Tripp, D. (1993), *Critical Incidents in Teaching: Developing professional judgement,* London and New York: Routledge

UKCES (UK Commission for Employment and Skills) (2010), *Ambition 2020: World-class skills and jobs for the UK,* Wath-upon-Dearne, England: UKCES. Available at http://www.ukces.org.uk/publications/ambition2020 (accessed 10 December 2012)

VanVoorhis, C. R. W. (2002), Stat jingles: To sing or not to sing, *Teaching of Psychology,* 29(3): 249–250

Vaux, D. (2012), Research methods: Know when your numbers are significant, *Nature,* 492: 180–181

Verran, J. (1992a), A student centred learning project: The production of leaflets for 'live' clients, *Journal of Biological Education,* 26: 135–138

Verran, J. (1992b), A learning project: Microbiology videos produced for school students by polytechnic students, *Biotechnology Education,* 3: 113–115

Verran, J. (1993), Poster design: By microbiology students, *Journal of Biological Education,* 27: 291–294

Verran, J. (2010), Encouraging creativity and employability skills in undergraduate microbiologists, *Trends in Microbiology,* 18: 56–58

Verran, J. (2013a), 'The Bad Bugs Bookclub', in L. Bowater and K. Yeoman (eds), *Science Communication: A practical guide for scientists*, Oxford: Wiley-Blackwell: 206–208

Verran, J. (2013b), The Bad Bugs Bookclub: Science, literacy and engagement, *Journal of Microbiology and Biology Education*, 14(1)

Vickerman, P. and Blundell, M. (2010), Hearing the voices of disabled students in higher education, *Disability and Society*, 25(1): 21–32

Vleuten, C. P. M. (1996), The assessment of professional competence: Developments, research and practical implications, *Advances in Health Sciences Education*, 1(1): 41–67

Vygotsky, L. S. (1978), *Mind in Society*, Cambridge MA: Harvard University Press

Wagner, J. (2007), What a difference a Y makes: Female and male nascent entrepreneurs in Germany, *Small Business Economics*, 28(1), 1–21

Ward, A. E., Robertson, M. and Holden, R. (2008), *Yorkshire Region Entrepreneurial Intentions Survey 2007/8*, York: University of York

Walters, D. (2010), *Further Education to Higher Education Study: Transitions in music*, paper presented at the 'Supporting students' academic writing in the transition to higher education' symposium at the Writing Development in Higher Education Conference, Royal College of Physicians, London, 28–30 June 2010. Available at http://www.writenow.ac.uk/news-events/wdhe-conference-2010/conference-presentations/tuesday-29–june-2010/#Paper0047 (accessed 6 December 2012)

Weinstein, K. (1995), *Action Learning: A journey of discovery and development*, London: HarperCollins

Wellington, B. and Austin, P. (1996), Orientations to reflective practice, *Educational Research*, 38(3): 307–316

Wellman, B. (2001), Physical place and cyber place: The rise of networked individualism, *International Journal of Urban and Regional Research*, 25(2): 227–52

Wells, F. (2011), 'The importance and power of student voice for promoting informal, formative assessment', in P. Ovens, F. Wells, P. Wallis and C. Hawkins (eds), *Developing Inquiry for Learning: Reflecting collaborative ways to learn to learn in higher education*, London: Routledge

Wenger, E. (1998a), *Communities of Practice: Learning, meaning and identity*, Cambridge: Cambridge University Press

Wenger, E. (1998b), Communities of practice: Learning as a social system, *Systems Thinker*, 9(5)

Wenstone, R. (2012), *A Manifesto for Partnership*. Available at http://www.nusconnect.org.uk/news/article/highereducation/Rachel-Wenstone-launches-a-Manifesto-for-Partnership/ (accessed 18 November 2012)

Whalley, W. B. and Taylor, L. (2008), Using criterion-referenced assessment and 'preflights' to enhance education in practical assignments, *Planet*, 20: 29–36

Whitney, D. and Trosten-Bloom, A. (2010), *The Power of Appreciative Inquiry: A practical guide to positive change* (2nd edn), San Francisco: Berrett-Koehler

Wilcock, A. A. (1998), *An Occupational Perspective of Health*, Slack: Thorofare

Williams, R., Karousou, R. and Mackness, J. (2011), Emergent learning and learning ecologies in Web 2.0, *International Review of Research in Open and Distance Learning*, 12. Available at http://www.irrodl.org/index.php/irrodl/article/view/883 (accessed 16 November 2012)

Wiznia, D., Korom, R., Marzuk, P., Safdieh, J. and Grafstein, B. (2012), PBL 2.0: Enhancing problem-based learning through increased student participation; *Med Educ Online*, 17: 17375. Available at http://dx.doi.org/10.3402/meo.v17i0.17375 (accessed 27 November 2012]

Wright, C.R., Dhanarajan, G. and Reju, S.A. (2009), Recurring issues encountered by distance educators in developing and emerging nations, *International Review of Research in Open and Distance Learning*, 10(1): 1–25

Yorke, M. (2004), *Employability in Higher Education: What it is – what it is not*, Higher Education Academy/ESECT

Yorke, M. (2010), Employability: Aligning the message, the medium and academic values, *Journal of Teaching and Learning for Graduate Employability*, 1(1): 2–12. Available at http://jtlge.curtin.edu.au/index.php/jtlge/article/view/7 (accessed 22 November 2012)

Yorke, M. and Knight, P. (2002), *Employability through the Curriculum*. Available at www.open.ac.uk/vqportal/Skills-Plus/home.htm (accessed 11 November 2012)

Yorke, M. and Knight, P. T. (2006), *Embedding Employability into the Curriculum*, York: Higher Education Academy. Available from www.leeds.ac.uk/educol/ncihe (accessed 22 November 2012)

Young Enterprise (2012), http://www.young-enterprise.org.uk/ (accessed 1 March 2013)

Young, M. R., Caudill, E. M. and Murphy, J. W. (2008), Evaluating experiential learning activities, *Journal for Advancement of Marketing Education*, 13: 28–40

Zhao, C. and Kuh, G. D. (2004), Adding value: learning communities and student engagement, *Research in Higher Education*, 45: 115–138

Zillmann, D., Williams, B. R., Bryant, J., Boynton, K. R. and Wolf, M. A. (1980), Acquisition of information from educational-television programs as a function of differently paced humorous inserts, Journal of Educational Psychology, 72(2): 170–180

Zimmerman, B. (2000), Self-efficacy: An essential motive to learn, *Contemporary Educational Psychology*, 25: 82–91

Zimmerman, B. and Schunk, D. (2001), *Self-regulated learning and academic achievement: Educational perspectives*. New York: Lawrence Erlbaum

Endnotes

► Introduction

1   *Pecha Kucha* is a presentation technique in which speakers show, and talk to, a set number of images that advance automatically after a set time. For example a 5-minute talk might comprise 10 images shown for 30 seconds each. The format, devised in 2003 by Astrid Klein and Mark Dytham originally for architects, is now commonly used.

2   The award by the Higher Education Academy of the title of National Teaching Fellow (NTF) is the most prestigious recognition of excellence in higher education teaching in the UK. It is granted to only 55 new recipients each year and is subject to strong competition from across the sector. As a result of the award NTFs are seen as leaders of change, demonstrators of innovation and champions of learning and teaching. They are often internationally recognised and have links to other similarly prestigious national teaching awards in Australia, Canada and New Zealand.

► Part 1

Chapter 1

1   Quoted from the project's initial funding bid.
2   A full and updated list of projects and outputs is available at http://www.broad-vision.info/publications.html.
3   Images from the Science 2 exhibition of images at Rochester Institute of Technology, USA. Information at http://www.rit.edu/news/story.php?id=46322.

Chapter 2

4   For additional images, see www.hsri.mmu.ac.uk/intheloop.
5   http://www.hsri.mmu.ac.uk/badbugsbookclub.
6   Manchester Children's Book Festivals, http://www.mcbf.org.
7   Zombies, Vampires and Werewolves: Matthew Crossley's mathematical simulations, http://www.matthewcrossley.com/sims.
8   Engage – science, communication and public engagement, http://www.sci-eng.mmu.ac.uk/engage.

Chapter 3

9   *Parallels and Connections* – an international ceramics and glass research conference, organised by the Institute for International Research in Glass (IIRG), http://www.nationalglasscentre.com/whats-on/2011/04/05/parallels-and-connections.html.

10 Chris McHugh, AHRC Collaborative Doctoral Award, Community in Clay, Ceramic Arts Research Centre, University of Sunderland.
11 The Biscuit Factory: contemporary art gallery, Newcastle-upon-Tyne, http://www.thebiscuitfactory.com/.

Chapter 4

12 Heloukee: EdTech and Digital Culture blog, http://heloukee.wordpress.com/2012/05/13/learning-through-frustration-elvss12/#comment-238.
13 While the arguments themselves are not new, social technologies allow like-minded educators to connect and make their voices heard easily.

Chapter 6

14 Assessment Plus was a collaborative project funded by the Fund for the Development of Teaching and Learning, phase 4 (FDTL4) that took place from 2002 to 2004 at London Metropolitan University, Liverpool Hope University and Aston University.
15 Ready for University was an NTF project that took place from 2006 to 2008 at Thames Valley University.
16 The Flying Start project was a collaborative NTF project that took place from 2009 to 2011 at Liverpool Hope University, Derby University and a number of 'satellite' partners across the further and higher education sectors.
17 The Write Now Centre is a collaborative Centre of Excellence in Teaching and Learning (CETL) that took place from 2006 to 2011 at London Metropolitan University, Liverpool Hope University and Aston University (http://www.writenow.ac.uk/).

Chapter 7

18 Clinical Placements, University of Southampton, http://www.southampton.ac.uk/new2placements.
19 The Beyond Competence Project: from classroom to clinical learning, http://www.southampton.ac.uk/medu/research/education_research/beyond_competence/index.page.

Chapter 8

20 Disability Assist: part of the Learning Gateway, Plymouth University, http://www1.plymouth.ac.uk/disability/Pages/default.aspx.
21 Seven Steps to Effective Personal Tutoring, Plymouth University, http://www.plymouth.ac.uk/files/extranet/docs/CAR/7%20steps%20to%20Personal%20Tutoring.pdf.

▶ Part 2

Chapter 9

1   Designs on Learning: Designs on Research – a dynamic learning and teaching project that unites students and staff across a number of universities in the exploration, dissemination and celebration of student research work. http://designsonlearning. blogspot.co.uk.
2   Writing-PAD (Writing Purposefully in Art and Design): research into the teaching and learning of writing in the Higher Education (HE) Art and Design (A&D) community http://www.writing-pad.ac.uk.

Chapter 10

3   The OU Learning Design Initiative (OULDI) is funded under the JISC Curriculum Design programme, http://ouldi.open.ac.uk.
4   These models have been combined to form the 7Cs of learning design framework. See Conole (2013b) for the latest thinking on this.
5   Cloudworks, a place to share, find and discuss learning and teaching ideas and experiences: http://cloudworks.ac.uk.
6   Learning Design Workshop: 7 Cs of Learning design, University of Leicester: http://www2.le.ac.uk/departments/beyond-distance-research-alliance/carpe-diem-folder.
7   See http://www.rjid.com/open/pedagogy/html/pedagogy_profile_1_2.html.
8   *Speed Project-Sharing Practice for Embedding E-design and Delivery*: http://speedprojectblog.wordpress.com/author/bdra/.

Chapter 11

9   Searching *Science* Magazine for recent articles with the search term 'problem-based' brings up an average of about three articles a year.
10 In 2012 *Science* Magazine published at least 54 articles or opinion pieces that make significant references to interdisciplinary research.
11 The programme was originally called I-Science (short for the name of the programme, 'Interdisciplinary Science', or for the Institute of Physics projects that partly supported it, 'Integrated Sciences'); more recently the name has been changed for clarity to 'natural sciences'; the programme is delivered by the (virtual) Centre for Interdisciplinary Science.
12 As well as by external bodies for which we do not have data.

Chapter 12

13 The term ludic, defined in the 1940s, as 'showing spontaneous and undirected playfulness', originates from the French *ludique*, from the Latin *ludere*, 'to play', and from *ludus*, 'sport'.

Chapter 16

14   A critical thinking manifesto for Higher Education, available at http://www.xtranormal.com/watch/13547741/a-critical-thinking-manifesto-for-higher-education.

Chapter 17

15   Boud and Molloy, 2012; Falchikov, 2005; Nicol and Macfarlane-Dick, 2006.
16   ASKe was the Assessment Standards Knowledge Exchange Centre for Excellence in Teaching and Learning based at Oxford Brookes University Business School, http://www.brookes.ac.uk/aske/. The work of the CETL continues at the Pedagogy Research Centre led by Professor Margaret Price – http://business.brookes.ac.uk/research/areas/pedagogy/.
17   AfL was the Assessment for Learning CETL based at Northumbria University.
18   ASEL was led by the University of Bradford, http://www.jisc.ac.uk/whatwedo/programmes/usersandinnovation/asel.aspx.
19   Sounds Good was based at Leeds Metropolitan University, http://www.jisc.ac.uk/whatwedo/programmes/usersandinnovation/soundsgood.aspx.
20   The PASS project on Programme Assessment Strategies has made all its case studies and resources freely available at http://www.pass.brad.ac.uk/.
21   Materials from TESTA – Transforming the Experience of Students through Assessment – are available at the TESTA website at http://www.testa.ac.uk.
22   PASS Position Paper, http://www.pass.brad.ac.uk/position-paper.pdf.
23   This study is described at http://www.centreforconfidence.co.uk/information.php?p=cGlkPTE1NQ (accessed 3 March 2013).

Chapter 20

24   'Internationalisation' is taken here to be the ongoing responses, across *all levels* of higher education, to the various external changes broadly captured as 'globalisation'. Some responses are economic, some structural, and some – the focus of this essay – concern changes to the student experience, specifically internationalising the curriculum (IOC), to help students make their way in the global milieu.

► Part 3

Chapter 23

1   Higher Education Academy, Design and evaluation of the contexts of participation web resource, http://www.heacademy.ac.uk/resources/detail/subjects/health/Design-and-evaluation.

Chapter 24

2 Will Curtis, Jane McDonnell and Sam Shields, *Assessment Reassessed* (2011–12).
3 Will Curtis, Jane Bates, Sue Lewis, Jane McDonnell and David Menendez, *Employability in Education Studies* (2012–13).
4 Assessment Reassessed, http://escalate.ac.uk/8141.
5 Employability in Education Studies, http://www.heacademy.ac.uk/resources/detail/teaching-development-grants/collaborative-round-4/employability-in-education.

Chapter 25

6 RAISE: Researching, Advancing and Inspiring Student Engagement, http://raise-network.ning.com/.

Chapter 34

1 As described by the Effective Lifelong Learning Inventory (ELLI). (Crick, Broadfoot and Claxton, 2004).

Conclusion

1 'What constitutes teacher excellence in higher education?', Literature Review of 'Excellence in teaching and learning', http://www.heacademy.ac.uk/projects/detail/TE_Lit_Review_Excellence_in_T_and_L.
2 Recognising teaching excellence (ReTE) change programme 2012–13, http://www.heacademy.ac.uk/resources/detail/change/RETE_12-13/RETE_info.
3 UK Professional Standards Framework (UKPSF), http://www.heacademy.ac.uk/UKPSF.

Index

academic writing 49
access 60
action research 43
activity profile 76
adaptive activities 80
adult learning 204
African universities 149, 192
art, design and media 29, 69, 72
art/science collaboration 11
assessment 49, 97, 98, 120, 127, 191, 234
Assessment Plus project 49
assimilative activities 79
autonomy 43

behavioural competencies 221
Beyond Competence project 55
blending teaching and research 29
blogs and blogging 228
blurring boundaries 36
Book Project 32
Broad Vision 11

capstone course 107
career adaptability 221
CETL (Centre for Excellence in Teaching and Learning) 84, 120, 254
challenge 191
change agents, teachers as 191
change, institutional 142
changing minds 36
collaborative enquiry and learning 69, 116, 174, 204, 240
communities of practice 11, 142
Community in Clay project 35
competences, behavioural 224
complexity theory 11
contextual learning 135

continuous feedback 127
course design features and mapping 76
creative writing 212
creativity 21, 97, 131, 156, 240
critical action learning 204
critical thinking 114, 118
cross-disciplinary learning and teaching 21, 33, 35, 36, 69, 103
crossing boundaries 58
cultural sensitivity 113, 151
curriculum building, for internationalisation 142
curriculum mapping 138, 234

design 29
digital creativity 89
digital dialogues 247
digital identity 36
disability 60
dissertation 69
distance learning 149
dual-mode universities 149

Education Studies 174
e-learning 76
electronic assessment 138
emergent learning 11
employability 18, 36, 131, 174, 191, 221, 228, 234, 240, 247
enabling learning 167
engagement 36, 109, 156, 198, 240
English as a lingua franca 247
English Language Learning for Employability project 247
enterprise 254
entrepreneurship 254
equal access 149
experience 185

experiential learning 127
extra-curricular learning 12

feedback 97, 120, 125
    formative 126,132
feed-forward 97
Flying Start project t 51
formative assessment 43, 127

games-based learning 89, 116
glass and ceramics 29
global citizenship 144
globalisation 247
graduateness 180
group study, cohesion 133
growth 156

health and social care 198
healthcare placements 54
higher education 149
humour 109
identification 156

Impact Review Sheet 213
inclusion, educational 60
inclusion, social 63
initial teacher education 212
Inquiry into Learning 43
interdisciplinarity 11, 84
international networks 41
international students
    experience of higher education 156
    language issues 35, 146, 156, 247
internationalisation 142, 156, 163
intrapreneurship 254

knowledge exchange 11

leadership and management 204
learned helplessness 103
learning
    by doing 127
    design 76, 77, 139, 206;
        technology-supported 138

English 247
enquiries 43
learning to learn 43
outcomes 80, 87, 93, 97, 112, 121,
    136, 146, 150, 206, 223
partners 45
together 174
safe spaces for 208
learning/experience journal 189
liquidity/fluidity of knowledge 11
live projects 127
ludic engagement 89

marketisation of higher education 115
    internationalisation and 157
mathematics, physical sciences and
    related subjects 84, 104, 109
medical, dental and health
    disciplines 54, 135, 198
microbiology 21
MOOCs (Massive Open Online Courses)
    77
music teaching and learning 185

natural sciences 84
new learning ecosystems 36
new media literacies 36
new technologies in learning 76
non-attendance 133

occupational perspective 167
occupational therapy 167
online networks 39
open education 36
organising reflection 204
outreach 29
ownership 156, 191, 198, 213, 225,
    232, 254

participation, contexts of 171
participatory culture 36
partnership and ownership 36, 174,
    177, 183
patchwork texts 43

pedagogy profile 80
peer assessment 43
peer learning 101, 204
peer learning, international students
    158, 162
performance 114
personal tutor 60
person-centred 43
placement/internship, experience from
    200, 203
play 114
Postgraduate Certificate in Higher
    Education 212
postgraduates, national and
    international 31
practical skills, assessment of 136
preflights 97
problem-based learning 84, 191
professional development and
    competence 135, 191, 198, 212
professional identity 198
professional portfolio 212, 214
professional teaching practice, music
    185
programme assessment 120
Programme-Focused Assessment 120
public engagement 21
public health 235

RAISE network 182
Ready for University project 51
real-world problems and projects 191
reflective practitioner 172, 185, 212
relationships 240
research-based learning 84
research poster 69
research, practice-based 29
research student forum 31
resilience 241
risk-taking 114

scaffolding 84, 167
science and art 21
science and literature 24

self as threshold concept 221
self-authorship 240
self-belief 185
self-regulation 185
shared learning 18
SOAR (Self, Opportunity, Aspirations,
    Results) 221
social media and networking 36
social work 240
soft skills 89
software engineering 89
SPEED (Sharing Practice for Embedding
    E-design and Delivery), Joint
    Information Systems Committee
    for Higher Education project 81
staff development 54
staff/student partnership 11
statistics, statistical literacy 103, 109,
    110
sticking points 97
stories and storytelling 228
storyboarding 80
student achievement 97
student autonomy 180
student engagement 54, 106, 180
student experience 60
student needs, differences 132
student role models 254
student teacher 212
students as partners 174, 180, 198
students as researchers 37, 174
students helping other students 12, 52

teacher values, sharing online 161
teaching fellows 84, 86
Teaching International Students project
    (Higher Education Academy) 157
teaching styles, adjusting to 56
teamwork 89
technical knowledge 89
technology, access to 150
technology-supported learning 36, 135
theory/practice divide 69
third space 247

threshold concept 103
transferability 89, 140, 221
transformative education 163, 167, 212
transition to independent learning 54
transition to university study 49
transitions 36
troublesome knowledge 97, 98, 104,
    169

undergraduate research 70
undergraduate symposia 69, 103
unlearning 114
USEM employability model 229, 235

volunteering 201
VUCA (volatile, uncertain, complex and
    ambiguous) world 114

websites 201
wellbeing 240
work-based learning and assessment
    54, 135, 204, 234
workplace communication 247
writing 69

zombies and vampires 26